S0-BCS-912

Bach's Lunch

Bach's Lunch

Picnic & Patio Classics

Book One

Bach's Lunch

Picnic and Patio Classics

"Music I heard with you was
more than music,
And bread I broke with you was
more than bread."

Published By
THE JUNIOR COMMITTEE
of
THE CLEVELAND ORCHESTRA
Severance Hall
Cleveland, Ohio 44106

Bach's Lunch

First Printing – 2,500 copies – May, 1971
Second Printing – 5,000 copies – June, 1971
Third Printing – 2,500 copies – November, 1971
Fourth Printing – 10,000 copies – July, 1972
Fifth Printing – 10,000 copies – October, 1974
Sixth Printing – 20,000 copies – June, 1977
Seventh Printing – 10,000 copies – June, 1982

Table of Contents

"Music I heard with you was
more than music,
And bread I broke with you was
more than bread."

We would like to thank all who contributed their favorite recipes and worked so willingly on this project. We regret that it was impossible to include all of the recipes we received, and we ask your indulgence for the editorial liberties that were taken. Compiling ***Bach's Lunch*** *has been our pleasure; we hope using it will be yours.*

Co-Chairmen:	Mrs. John E. Culver
	Mrs. George D. Kirkham
Editor:	Mrs. Damaris D. Klaus
Director of Marketing:	Mrs. R. Bennett Eppes

Special thanks to the following people who gave an extra measure of time and talent:

Mrs. Sam Butnik
Mrs. Arthur M. Bylin
Mrs. Alan R. Daus
Mrs. John A. Dettlebach
Mrs. Ellwood M. Fisher
Mrs. Theodore A. Gullia, Jr.
Mrs. Thomas E. Healy
Mrs. Robert P. Mack
Mrs. Charles K. Murray
Mrs. Jon H. Outcalt
Mrs. H. William Ruf
Mrs. Michael Sherwin
Mrs. Wayne R. Sievert
Mrs. Ben S. Stefanski II
Mrs. Michael E. A. Ward

The committee grants laurels to Miss Judy Van Denberg for her hours of creative help on the book.

All recipes submitted to ***Bach's Lunch*** *have been tested by the committee.*

Preludes

Sangria

1 whole orange
1 lemon, thinly sliced
juice of 1 lemon
2 fifths Burgundy or Pinot Noir
½ cup sugar
1 quart club soda

Cut the outer rind of the orange in a spiral. Squeeze the juice. Combine juices, orange spiral and lemon slices. Add wine and sugar. Stir and chill four hours. Just before serving add soda.

20 servings — The Committee

Bill's Fatal Punch

1 bottle brandy (inexpensive brandy is fine, or sweet white wine)
1 bottle gin (or vodka)
1 bottle champagne (or sparkling wine, or club soda)
3 to 4 cans lemonade, limeade, or grapefruit concentrate
lemon juice
mint leaves
cherries
3 trays ice cubes
club soda or ginger ale

In a large bowl, mix together the first three ingredients. Add remaining ingredients (the substitutes also work very nicely). Add soda and ice just before serving. More juice, ice, and soda can be added to taste. We have found there is no hangover afterward!

30 servings — Mrs. Douglas B. Rose

ANTIPASTO SALAD

½ head cauliflower, in flowerets
2 carrots, sliced
2 stalks celery, sliced
1 green pepper, sliced
1 red pepper, sliced
1 large can ripe olives
6 small white onions
¼ lb. fresh green beans
¾ cup water
¾ cup wine vinegar
¼ cup salad oil
1 tsp. olive oil
2 T. sugar
1 clove garlic
1 tsp. oregano
salt and pepper

Combine everything and simmer, covered, for five minutes. Cool and refrigerate forty-eight hours before serving.

THE COMMITTEE

CROUTON SNACK MIX

½ cup butter or margarine
½ to 1 tsp. curry powder
2 cups herb-seasoned stuffing croutons
1 cup Cheerios

Melt butter in shallow pan in a preheated 375° oven. Stir in curry powder. Then toss with croutons and cereal until thoroughly coated. Return to oven for about five minutes until heated through. Serve hot or cold. One cup broken pretzel sticks and one cup mixed nuts may be added if desired.

MRS. ELLWOOD M. FISHER

Artichokes Allegretto

1 artichoke per person
3 T. salad oil
1 T. vinegar
salt and freshly ground pepper
dry mustard to taste
minced pimiento
capers (optional)

Wash and trim artichokes. Boil in salted water for thirty to forty-five minutes depending on size (they should not begin to fall apart), run cold water over artichokes and place in refrigerator for two hours or more to cool (may be prepared a day ahead). Prepare dressing by combining rest of ingredients. Transport dressing and artichokes separately to picnic. Dressing can then be poured into individual shallow dishes, or into a large dish for communal dipping.

Louis Lane

Cucumber Radish Delights

1 cup mayonnaise
½ cup sour cream
¼ cup carrot, grated
3 T. radish, minced
1 T. parsley, minced
salt and pepper to taste
1 large cucumber

Combine ingredients except cucumber. Peel cucumber and slice in half-inch slices. Serve as a dip for the cucumber or spread slices with about half a teaspoon of radish mixture.

Mrs. David Zauder

Sea Island Cheese Straws

¾ cup butter
1½ cups sharp cheese, grated
¼ cup Parmesan cheese
dash cayenne pepper
½ tsp. salt
1 scant tsp. paprika
1 to 1½ cups flour

Cream butter and cheeses together. Sift dry ingredients and work thoroughly into cheese mixture. Chill. On a floured board roll until thin into an oblong shape. Cut into strips about ¼ inch wide and 5 inches long. Place on a cookie sheet, not too close together. Put in a cold oven, turn to 300° and bake for ten or fifteen minutes. They will not brown. Watch closely to make sure they don't burn.

Mrs. Dudley S. Blossom, Jr.

Cheese Trees

The above cheese mixture may also be put through a cookie press and made into any fanciful shape. Place on an ungreased baking sheet and bake at 350° for fifteen to twenty minutes.

Mrs. Merrill B. Wilcox

COCKTAIL CHEESE DOLLARS

1 roll or jar processed cheese, bacon flavored or nippy
½ cup butter or margarine
1⅓ cups flour, sifted
⅛ tsp. salt
¼ tsp. paprika

Soften cheese and butter and cream together. Beat in flour, salt and paprika. On a lightly floured board knead ball of dough and form into a roll about two inches in diameter. Wrap in waxed paper and refrigerate for one hour. Cut into thin slices. Bake at 350° for ten minutes or until light brown. Serve hot or cool, alone or with a dip. Dough can be kept refrigerated several days before using.

Yield: 2 to 3 dozen MRS. WAYNE R. SIEVERT

ENGLISH MONKEY

1 cup bread crumbs
1 cup milk
2 T. butter
½ cup cheese, grated
1 egg, beaten
crackers

Soak bread crumbs in milk for one-half hour. Melt butter in skillet over low heat, add cheese and stir until melted. Add bread crumbs and egg. Cook until consistency of scrambled eggs. Serve on crackers. This recipe has been popular for over one hundred years and most people always have these ingredients on hand in case of emergency.

4 servings MRS. WALLACE J. MULLIGAN

Curried Olive Dip

½ cup ripe olives, chopped
1 – 3 oz. pkg. cream cheese, softened
½ cup mayonnaise
¼ cup sour cream
1 T. lemon juice
1 tsp. curry powder
½ tsp. salt

Mix all ingredients and serve as a fresh vegetable or shrimp dip.

Yield: 1 ½ cups — Mrs. Ellwood M. Fisher

Cream Cheese and Olive Spread

1 – 3 oz. pkg. cream cheese, softened
2 eggs, hard-cooked and diced
1 small bottle stuffed green olives (about 30), diced
1 T. (or more) mayonnaise
1 tsp. onion, grated

Combine ingredients. Serve as a spread for crackers.

Mrs. Nathan W. Oakes, Jr.

Idiot's Delight

1 – 8 oz. pkg. cream cheese
¼ bottle Pickapeppa sauce or Worcestershire sauce

Unwrap cheese and place on a plate. Pour sauce over and serve with English water biscuits.

6 servings — Mrs. Arthur Modell

ANCHOVY DIP

1 – 8 oz. pkg. cream cheese
1 T. anchovy paste
1 T. onion, chopped
2 T. stuffed green olives, chopped
1 tsp. lemon juice
¼ tsp. Worcestershire sauce
1 T. milk

Blend ingredients together and refrigerate. Add more milk if necessary to reach desired consistency for dipping. May be made a day ahead. Serve with raw vegetables or chips.

MRS. WILLIAM COOPER

ANCHOVY STUFFED MUSHROOMS

The above mixture can be used to fill stemless mushroom caps. Sprinkle with chopped chives or parsley and refrigerate until ready to serve.

MRS. CHARLES E. HAMILTON III

P.D.Q.'S

Roll an anchovy filet around a square of Edam cheese.

Wrap a slice of smoked salmon around a piece of raw onion.

Spread sour cream and caviar between cucumber rounds.

Tuna Tahini

3 T. Tahini (ground hulled sesame seed)
½ tsp. salt
juice of 2 fresh lemons
¼ tsp. garlic powder (optional)
1 – 7 oz. can white tuna, drained

Tahini is sesame seed oil paste, sold in airtight cans in specialty food shops. Stir Tahini in can and measure three tablespoons into a bowl. Add salt, lemon juice and garlic. Mix thoroughly. Add flaked tuna. If this is too stiff for dipping, add cold water until desired consistency is reached. Serve with Syrian flat bread or crackers. One can chick peas, drained and mashed; one-half cup eggplant, cooked and mashed; or one avocado, mashed, may be substituted for the tuna.

Mrs. Joseph Nahra

Salmon Ball

1 – 16 oz. can salmon
1 – 8 oz. pkg. cream cheese, softened
1 T. lemon juice
2 tsp. onion, grated
1 tsp. prepared horseradish
¼ tsp. salt
¼ tsp. liquid smoke
½ cup pecans, chopped
3 T. parsley, minced

Drain and flake salmon and combine with cream cheese, lemon juice, onion, horseradish, salt and liquid smoke. Chill several hours. Combine pecans and parsley. Shape salmon mixture into a ball and roll in nut mixture. Chill again. This may be frozen.

Mrs. Thomas F. Van Denberg

Ubiquitous Crab

2 – 3 oz. pkgs. cream cheese, softened
¾ cup mayonnaise
½ lb. sharp Cheddar cheese, grated
1 can crab meat
1 onion, minced
2 eggs, hard-cooked and minced
¼ tsp. dry mustard
½ tsp. paprika
freshly ground pepper

Mix cream cheese with mayonnaise until smooth. Add rest of ingredients and mix well. Refrigerate. Serve as an appetizer with Triscuits, rye thins, sesame thins, or hard tack. This crab mixture may be used in a variety of ways: **1.** Combines well with rice or noodles for casserole. Increase mayonnaise and bake at 350° for forty minutes. **2.** Add chopped celery and/or green pepper for a quick crab salad. **3.** Can be served in a chafing dish as a hot spread. **4.** Makes marvelous crab salad sandwiches. Increase mayonnaise so that it spreads easily.

Mrs. Walter R. Kirkham

Be careful of dishes with creamy sauces and mayonnaise as they spoil quickly if unrefrigerated.

Crab Ring

1 tsp. unflavored gelatin
¼ cup cold water
2 – 8 oz. pkgs. cream cheese, softened
2 T. sherry
¾ tsp. seasoned salt
1 – 2 oz. jar pimiento, drained and minced
1 to 2 pkgs. frozen crab meat, shredded
⅛ tsp. pepper
¼ cup parsley, minced

Soften gelatin in cold water; heat in the top of a double boiler until dissolved. Add cream cheese and beat until smooth. Stir in remaining ingredients, reserving two tablespoons parsley for garnish. Pour into an oiled three-cup ring mold. Refrigerate until set, at least four hours. Garnish with remaining parsley.

8 servings — Mrs. Frank E. Joseph, Jr.

Crab Meat Spread

1 – 6 ½ oz. can crab meat
2 hard-cooked eggs, minced
½ tsp. prepared mustard
½ cup mayonnaise
1 T. lemon juice

Drain crab meat and flake, picking out shell and cartilage. Mix ingredients together and refrigerate. Serve with crackers or party rye bread.

4 to 6 servings — Mrs. H. William Ruf

Shrimp Exotics

9 T. mayonnaise
3 to 4½ tsp. curry powder
3 lbs. large green shrimp, peeled
butter

Blend mayonnaise and curry powder in a large bowl. The amount of curry used depends on individual taste. Add shrimp and toss, making sure that shrimp are well covered. Broil shrimp on charcoal grill, turning once or twice (should be crispy). (For ease in grilling you may want to skewer shrimp.) Remove from heat and serve immediately, or place in a chafing dish that has a small amount of melted butter in the bottom. Swish the shrimp around in the butter and serve with toothpicks.

10 servings PETER K. JOHNSTON

Marinated Grilled Shrimp

½ lb. shrimp
3 T. olive oil
½ tsp. salt
½ tsp. tarragon
parsley, minced
3 T. sherry

Marinate shrimp in remaining ingredients overnight. Skewer and grill over hot coals for five minutes.

4 servings MRS. R. BENNETT EPPES

Shrimp Mold

1 pkg. unflavored gelatin
½ cup cold water
1 can tomato soup or tomato bisque
1 cup mayonnaise
1 - 8 oz. pkg. cream cheese
½ cup green pepper, chopped
1½ cups celery, chopped
½ onion, grated
1½ cups shrimp, cooked

Soften gelatin in water. Heat soup to boiling, add gelatin and stir until dissolved. Cool. Cream mayonnaise and cheese together, add soup. Add remaining ingredients and pour into an oiled four-cup mold. Chill. When ready to serve, unmold and garnish. Serve with crackers or party rye bread. Crab meat may be substituted for the shrimp.

16 to 20 servings

Mrs. Richard Pollack

Shrimp Dip

1 lb. large shrimp, cooked
½ cup mayonnaise
5 drops Tabasco
2 tsp. onion, grated
salt and pepper
2 T. dry sherry
light cream

Mince shrimp with a sharp knife. Add rest of ingredients, except cream. Gradually add enough cream to make mixture desired consistency. Chill. Serve with crackers.

Mrs. Michael C. Beachley

New Orleans Shrimp Remoulade

- 2 cloves garlic, minced
- ⅓ cup prepared horseradish mustard
- 2 T. catsup
- 2 T. paprika
- ¾ tsp. cayenne pepper
- 1 tsp. salt
- ⅓ cup tarragon vinegar
- ½ cup olive oil
- ½ cup green onions with tops, chopped
- 1 lb. shrimp

Combine all ingredients except shrimp. Shake well. Marinate peeled, deveined and boiled shrimp in sauce for several hours in the refrigerator. Serve on lettuce.

6 servings — Mrs. William T. Tucker III

Beef Teriyaki Hors D'oeuvre

- 1½ lbs. flank steak
- ¼ cup chicken bouillon
- ¼ cup sherry
- ¼ cup soy sauce
- 1 T. honey

Slice steak thinly on the diagonal (should get about twenty slices). The steak will slice easily if partially frozen. Prepare marinade by combining rest of ingredients. Marinate meat at least thirty minutes (or meat can be frozen for several days right in the marinade). Thread on skewers. Broil at highest heat or grill until brown.

Mrs. Alan R. Daus

French Country Paté

1 lb. calves' liver
1¼ lbs. country pork sausage
½ lb. cooked ham
½ lb. cooked smoked tongue
1 small onion
1 small clove garlic
1 tsp. salt
½ tsp. freshly ground pepper
pinch of thyme
1 tsp. parsley, minced
1 T. brandy
5 slices bacon
2 or 3 bay leaves

Using the fine blade of a meat grinder, grind together liver, sausage, ham, tongue, onion and garlic. Season with salt, pepper, thyme, parsley and brandy and mix thoroughly, preferably with your hands. Butter a loaf pan and line with bacon slices. Fill pan with meat mixture and lay bay leaves on top. Cover with buttered paper and set loaf pan into a larger pan that is half filled with water. Bake at 350° for one and one-half hours. Paté is done when it shrinks from sides of pan and no moisture bubbles out of it. Remove buttered paper and bay leaves. Cover loaf with a cloth and weight it down with a brick. Chill overnight. Turn meat out of pan onto a platter and garnish with gherkins. Slice. Serve with Dijon mustard and French bread.

10 servings

John E. Culver
Theodore G. Thoburn

Crofter's Paté

½ lb. liverwurst
1 – 8 oz. pkg. cream cheese
2 T. butter
1 T. green pepper, minced
1 T. onion, minced
¼ cup dry red wine

Sauté green pepper and onion in butter until tender. Combine with rest of ingredients and beat with electric mixer until smooth. Spoon into a two-cup mold. Chill overnight. Unmold and serve with crackers.

Mrs. John H. Burlingame

Steak Tartare

1 lb. lean beef (put through grinder twice)
1½ tsp. salt
2 to 3 tsp. dry mustard
1 clove garlic, minced
1 onion, grated
1 T. Worcestershire sauce
½ cup parsley, minced
1 egg yolk
paprika
capers

Combine first eight ingredients. Mound on a platter, sprinkle with paprika and garnish with capers. Serve with party rye bread and have a pepper grinder handy.

John E. Culver

Asparagus Soup

2½ lbs. asparagus
8 cups chicken stock
8½ T. butter
½ cup flour
3 T. green onions, chopped
2 egg yolks, beaten
1 cup heavy cream

Peel asparagus; cut off tips and keep them separate from stalks. Cut stalks into half-inch lengths. Bring stock to a boil (stock can be made with 8 cups water, 3 T. chicken stock base, and 1¼ tsp. salt). Put tips into this broth and simmer until tender. Remove tips, mince, and reserve. Make a roux of 6 T. butter and flour, add to stock and simmer, stirring until thickened. Melt the additional 2½ T. butter and sauté asparagus stalks and onions for three minutes. Add to the stock and simmer until tender. Place in blender and spin until smooth. The soup can be made ahead until this point. When ready to serve, add egg yolks, cream and reserved asparagus tips. Heat, being careful not to boil. Pour into two one quart Thermos jugs to carry to the picnic.

8 servings Mrs. Peter Van Dijk

Spinach Soup

1 pkg. frozen spinach
milk

Cook spinach until tender. Drain well. Put in blender, turn on and add warm milk gradually until consistency pleases you.

2 to 4 servings Mrs. R. Bennett Eppes

Quick Corn Chowder

1 lb. bacon
½ bag frozen chopped onions
1 pkg. frozen whole potatoes
2 cups light cream
4 T. butter
onion salt and pepper to taste
3 cans creamed corn
3 cans corn niblets, undrained

Fry bacon, drain and crumble. Sauté onions in a little bacon fat until transparent. Parboil potatoes in a small amount of water; reserve water. Dice potatoes and add with water to rest of ingredients and heat. Do not boil.

12 servings — Mrs. Henry G. Brownell

Hearty Soup

1 can consomme
1 can pea soup
1 can tomato soup
1 can crab meat

Combine undiluted ingredients and heat slowly. Be sure to check crab meat first for shell and cartilage.

6 to 8 servings — Mrs. William H. West

Go Anywhere Tomato Bouillon

1 – 46 oz. can tomato juice
1 can beef bouillon
1 cup water
½ tsp. marjoram
½ tsp. thyme (optional)
½ tsp. basil
½ tsp. savory
½ tsp. tarragon
10 peppercorns
1 bay leaf, crushed
2 T. lemon juice
½ onion, sliced
5 celery tops
1 bunch parsley

Combine above ingredients in a large saucepan. Simmer thirty minutes, stirring occasionally. Strain. Add more water if necessary. Serve hot in mugs or chilled over crushed ice.

8 servings — Mrs. Walter R. Kirkham

Cranberry Bouillon

2 cans beef bouillon
2 cups cranberry juice

Heat and serve garnished with cubes of cream cheese, slivered almonds, or thin slices of lemon.

6 servings — Mrs. Harold Burkhart

Jellied Mushroom Soup

1 lb. mushrooms, chopped
3½ cups chicken stock
2 T. sherry
salt and pepper
1 to 2 T. lemon juice
1 envelope unflavored gelatin
¼ cup cold water
sour cream
watercress or parsley

Simmer mushrooms in chicken stock for three minutes. Strain through food mill or spin in blender for fifteen seconds. Measure; if necessary add additional stock to make 3¾ cups. Stir in sherry, salt, pepper and lemon juice. Soften gelatin in cold water. Bring soup to a boil and add gelatin, stirring until dissolved. Ladle into mugs and chill thoroughly. Serve garnished with sour cream and a sprig of watercress or parsley.

6 servings — Mrs. Roger Cole

Blossom Consomme

Tuck clean cans of cold consomme, unopened, into your ice chest. Take along a carton of sour cream and some caviar. Spoon jellied consomme into paper cups, top with sour cream and caviar for a special first course. Garnish with lemon wedges.

The Committee

Icy Lemon Soup

1 can cream of chicken soup
1 cup light cream or milk
1 T. water
2 tsp. curry powder (or more to taste)
7 T. lemon juice
lemon slices

Put soup and cream into the blender. Mix curry powder in water and pour into blender. Cover and spin at high speed for one minute. Chill for several hours. At the last possible minute before serving, stir lemon juice into the soup. Serve very cold garnished with thin slices of lemon.

2 servings Mrs. Michael E. A. Ward

Simple Creme Senegalese

⅛ tsp. curry powder
1 can condensed cream of chicken soup
1 soup can milk

Blend curry powder into soup, gradually stir in milk. Chill at least four hours in chilled stemmed glasses, or pour into a Thermos to take on a picnic.

4 servings Mrs. John E. Culver

Picnic Potage (Vichyssoise)

6 leeks or green onions
6 T. butter
4 medium to large potatoes, peeled
6 cups very strong chicken stock
1½ cups heavy cream
½ cup sour cream
salt and white pepper
chopped chives

Thinly slice white part of leeks or onions and gently sauté in butter until limp and golden. Cut potatoes into chunks and sauté with leeks for two or three minutes. Bring stock to a boil and add potato mixture. Bring to a boil again and simmer, covered, until the potatoes are soft. Rub through a sieve or spin in blender until smooth. Chill. Remove any fat that appears. Beat with cream and sour cream (in blender if possible) until frothy. Season to taste with salt and pepper. Sprinkle each serving with chives. Serve well chilled, either in brightly colored mugs, or in crystal cups nestled in crushed ice. Tastes best if made a day ahead.

8 servings — Mrs. Richard T. Lewis

The day before you go on a picnic, freeze water in waxed milk cartons. Use in place of ice cubes in cooler to keep food cold.

Cold Avocado Soup

2 cups leeks, coarsely chopped
1 cup onion, chopped
¼ cup sweet butter
2 to 3 tsp. curry powder
3 cups potatoes, diced
4 cups chicken broth
2 ripe avocados
2 cups heavy cream
Tabasco
salt and pepper

Rinse leeks and pat dry. Cook with onions in butter until golden. Add the curry powder (can use 2 tsp. curry powder, plus ½ tsp. turmeric, 1 tsp. coriander, and ⅛ tsp. ginger) and stir well. Add potatoes and cook over low heat, stirring constantly, about five minutes. Add chicken broth and bring to a boil. Simmer, skimming as necessary, until potatoes are tender. Cool. Peel and dice avocados and add to soup. Pour into a blender and spin. Stir in cream, Tabasco, salt and pepper. Chill. Pour into a Thermos to take on a picnic.

Mrs. Peter Van Dijk

To clean and sweeten a Thermos, put in one tablespoon baking soda and fill with hot water. Let stand overnight; rinse.

GAZPACHO

½ small onion, sliced
½ green pepper, sliced
3 ripe tomatoes, peeled and quartered
1 small cucumber, peeled and sliced
1 clove garlic
1 tsp. salt
¼ tsp. pepper
2 T. olive oil
3 T. wine vinegar
1 cup tomato juice
toasted croutons
green pepper, diced
cucumber, diced
onion, chopped
parsley, minced

Place first ten ingredients in blender. Cover and spin until puréed. Chill. For a picnic, pour into a Thermos bottle and serve with small bowls of assorted garnishes.

4 servings MRS. EDWIN D. ANDERSON, JR.

MENU SUGGESTIONS

Sangria
Gazpacho
Empanadas
Easy Corn Relish
Lace Cookies

Scandinavian Fruit Soup

3 lbs. assorted fresh fruits (peaches, plums, berries, pears, apricots, cherries, etc.)
3 cups water
3 T. lemon juice
sugar
cinnamon
1 T. cornstarch
sour cream

Remove pits from the fruit but do not peel. Slice larger fruits. Put fruit in a saucepan with water and lemon juice. Cover and simmer until fruit is soft. Purēe in a blender. Add sugar and cinnamon to taste. Pour the purēe back into the saucepan. Combine cornstarch with a little cold water and add to soup. Simmer gently until soup thickens. Chill. Serve cold, topped with a dab of sour cream.

6 servings Mrs. Michael E. A. Ward

P.D.Q.'s

Core unpeeled apples and stuff with treats: dates, marshmallows, Brazil nuts, orange sections, etc.

Wrap sticks of honeydew melon with Prosciutto.

Stuff large red Emperor grapes with Bleu cheese.

Main Themes

Rolled Sandwiches

1 loaf unsliced white or whole wheat bread, chilled
butter

Trim crusts from the bread and cut into very thin slices. Spread lightly with butter if desired. Use any or all of the following fillings. Spread a filling on the bread, roll tightly, and fasten securely with toothpicks. Refrigerate, covered with a damp tea towel, until ready to pack in an insulated picnic hamper.

Curried Crab Meat Spread

6 oz. crab meat
1 to 2 T. celery, minced
1 tsp. curry powder
mayonnaise

Mix the above ingredients together with just enough mayonnaise to bind.

Ham and Watercress Spread

½ cup ham, minced
½ cup watercress, minced
mayonnaise

Mix the above ingredients together with just enough mayonnaise to bind. (Minced cucumber could be used instead of watercress.)

Asparagus

Follow the same procedure of rolling the bread around fresh asparagus spears (cooked and cooled), or canned white asparagus spears.

6 servings — Mrs. Robert Small

Tailgate Sandwiches

Syrian flat bread
shredded lettuce
assorted fillings

CORNED BEEF FILLING: combine one can of corned beef, chopped, with pickle relish, mustard and mayonnaise to taste.

EGG SALAD FILLING: combine chopped hard-cooked eggs with grated Swiss cheese and mayonnaise to taste.

DEVILED HAM FILLING: combine one can of deviled ham with three chopped hard-cooked eggs, pickle relish, grated onion, mustard and mayonnaise to taste.

SALAMI FILLING: combine tomato paste and grated Mozzarella cheese to taste, and spread on salami slices.

TUNA FILLING: combine one can of tuna with a little grated cheese and enough mayonnaise to bind.

Cut the bread in half on the diameter to form pockets. Stuff pockets with corned beef, egg salad or deviled ham filling and shredded lettuce. Or stuff with salami or tuna filling, wrap securely in heavy aluminum foil, and heat over a charcoal fire.

Mrs. David S. Beebe

For a quick fire starter: remove the top and bottom from a three-pound coffee can. Punch air holes in lower edge of can with a beer can opener. Place on grill and stuff with crumpled sheets of newspaper. Place coals on top of newspaper. Light paper and in a very short time you will have a blazing charcoal fire.

Rich Man's Poor Boy

2 small loaves French bread
1 clove garlic
pitted ripe olives, halved
1 medium red onion, thinly sliced
1 medium tomato, thinly sliced
artichoke hearts, halved
salt and pepper
rolled anchovies with caper in center
Italian dressing
Bibb or leaf lettuce

Cut bread in half lengthwise and toast the cut sides lightly in the oven. When cool, rub generously with a cut garlic clove (or sprinkle with garlic powder). Spread the bottom slice of bread with the next four ingredients, in order. Season to taste. Add the anchovies (using three to five per sandwich), then drizzle one to two tablespoons of dressing over the sandwich, being careful that it does not run down the side of the bread. Add lettuce and the top half of the bread. Wrap carefully in foil and place the two loaves under a heavy weight for thirty minutes. You may add sliced lamb or chicken but it is not necessary. Do not add salami or bologna. Cut each loaf in half and serve with red wine.

4 servings — Mrs. John M. Cogan

Serve red wine at cool room temperature, white wines chilled.

South Hadley Salad

⅔ cup salad oil
⅓ cup vinegar
½ tsp. sugar
½ tsp. dry mustard
¼ tsp. onion powder
1 tsp. dried salad herbs (tarragon, basil, thyme and marjoram)
½ tsp. celery salt
¼ tsp. MSG
1 tsp. dill seed
¾ tsp. salt
freshly ground pepper
1 avocado, peeled and sliced
1 head iceberg lettuce
2 cups raw spinach
¼ lb. ham, julienne
¼ lb. chicken, julienne
¼ lb. Swiss cheese, julienne
¼ lb. American cheese, julienne
2 tomatoes, cut in wedges
3 hard-cooked eggs, quartered
1 medium onion, sliced in rings
8 radishes

Prepare dressing by combining first eleven ingredients. Marinate avocado in dressing for one hour in refrigerator. Meanwhile, tear lettuce and spinach leaves into a large bowl. Top with arrangement of ham, chicken and cheeses. Remove avocado from dressing, place around outside edge of greens with tomatoes, eggs and onion rings. Garnish with radish roses. Pass dressing.

4 servings

The Mount Holyoke Club

PALM BEACH SALAD

1 head lettuce
1 can ripe olives, pitted
1 jar green stuffed olives
1 cup cooked ham, julienne
1 cup Swiss cheese, julienne
1 cup green pepper, thinly sliced
1 onion, sliced
1 cucumber, sliced
½ cup Parmesan cheese, grated
½ cup salad oil
juice of 3 limes

Combine salad ingredients; toss with Parmesan cheese, oil and lime juice when ready to serve.

6 servings

MRS. JOHN E. CULVER

TOO-EASY TUNABURGERS

tuna fish salad: your favorite recipe for 4
1 cup Swiss cheese, cubed
4 sandwich buns

Add Swiss cheese to the tuna salad. Fill buns. Place bun on a square of heavy duty aluminum foil and wrap securely. Heat on the grill, in the fireplace, or in the oven (at 325° for about thirty minutes) until cheese melts. Serve with relishes and potato chips.

THE COMMITTEE

Baked Seafood Salad

1 large green pepper, chopped
1 small onion, chopped
1 cup mayonnaise
1 cup celery, minced
½ tsp. salt
dash of Worcestershire sauce
1 lb. fresh crab meat, shredded
1 cup shrimp, lobster, or crawfish
1 cup bread crumbs, mixed with
2 T. melted butter
1 can cream of mushroom soup (optional)

Mix all ingredients except crumb mixture. Pour into buttered casserole. Top with bread crumbs. Bake at 350° for about thirty to forty-five minutes, or until top is brown, and serve. May be prepared ahead of time and refrigerated. Soup can be added if you want a softer consistency.

4 servings — Mrs. Thomas Zung

"If music be the food of love, play on."

William Shakespeare
Twelfth Night

Cold Shrimp Quiche

- 2 T. green onions, minced
- 3 T. butter
- ¼ lb. cooked fresh shrimp, chopped
- salt and pepper
- 2 T. white wine or vermouth
- 3 eggs
- 1 cup heavy cream
- 1 T. tomato paste
- 1 partially baked 9-inch pie shell
- ¼ cup swiss cheese, grated

Cook onions in butter until soft. Add shrimp, salt and pepper. Cook three minutes, stirring constantly. Add wine and bring to a boil; remove from heat. Beat eggs in a bowl with the cream and tomato paste. Season and add shrimp mixture. Pour into pastry shell and sprinkle cheese on top. Bake at 375° for one-half hour or until puffed. Serve at room temperature.

6 servings — Mrs. Robert Small

MENU SUGGESTION

Bill's Fatal Punch
Cold Shrimp Quiche
Cole-Ferrell Salad
Maori Kisses

Cold Salmon Loaf

1 large can red salmon
4 T. butter, melted
4 eggs, lightly beaten
½ cup bread crumbs
salt & pepper
1 cucumber, peeled and diced
mayonnaise
dill

Remove skin and bones from salmon. Add butter to fish and rub to a smooth paste. Beat eggs and bread crumbs together, add to fish paste. Season with salt and pepper and stir thoroughly. Mold in a loaf pan; cover with foil and steam for one hour in a small amount of water in the bottom of a covered roaster or a pan on top of stove. Chill. Prepare cucumber sauce by combining last three ingredients in proportions to taste. When loaf is cool, slice thinly and serve with sauce.

6 to 8 servings Mrs. Henry P. Briggs, Jr.

Add seasonings to salad dressing and marinades well in advance to give them time to let flavors blend, but don't add seasonings to hot dishes until the last hour because they cook out.

Sinfully Delicious Stuffed Fish

8 filets (2 lbs.) flounder, sole, snapper, perch or pompano
1 can Cheddar cheese soup
½ cup crab meat, flaked
½ cup shrimp, chopped
3 T. mushrooms, chopped
3 T. green onion, chopped
¼ tsp. salt
¼ tsp. tarragon, crushed
½ clove garlic, minced
butter
¼ cup water
2 T. green onion, chopped
tarragon

Arrange four fish filets in a buttered baking dish. Combine ¼ cup soup with next seven ingredients and spread on filets. Cover with remaining fish and dot with butter. Bake, covered, at 375° for thirty minutes or until fish flakes. Meanwhile, prepare sauce by mixing the remaining soup with water, onions, and tarragon. Heat and pour over fish when served.

4 servings

Miss Betty Cope
General Manager WVIZ-TV

Grilled Lobster

12 lobster tails
1 cup dry white wine
½ cup salad oil
¼ cup fresh lemon juice
1 tsp. salt
Tabasco
1 clove garlic, pressed
Parmesan cheese, grated

Marinate lobster tails in rest of ingredients (except cheese) in the refrigerator for an hour. Slit the undershell down the center and spread sections apart, cracking the back shell slightly if necessary. Broil over hot coals, shell side down, ten to fifteen minutes. Brush the meat side with the marinade and grill for five minutes longer. Sprinkle with Parmesan cheese and serve. Garnish with lemon or lime wedges.

6 servings — Mrs. Clarence J. Doser

To save leftover wine for cooking, add a few drops of olive oil to the partially filled bottle to keep air away from the wine. If cork will not fit back in the bottle, soften by soaking it in boiling water a few minutes.

Lemon Barbecued Fish Steaks

- 3 lbs. fish steaks (halibut, salmon, swordfish, etc.)
- ¾ cup lemon juice
- ¾ cup chicken stock
- 2 T. horseradish
- 1 T. lemon rind, grated
- 1½ tsp. salt
- ½ tsp. each basil, oregano, pepper

Combine marinade ingredients and pour over fish. Marinate several hours or overnight. Drain and reserve marinade. Broil fish five to ten minutes on each side (depending on thickness), basting often with marinade.

8 servings — Mrs. Alan R. Daus

Try marinating fish or meat by placing in a large, strong plastic bag. Close securely. It is easy to turn over the entire bag. Carry in bag to picnic.

Chicken Salad Deluxe

- 2 cups cooked chicken, diced
- 1 cup artichoke hearts, quartered
- 1 tsp. onion, grated or 1 T. chives, minced
- ¾ tsp. salt
- freshly ground pepper
- 1 T. lemon juice
- 2 T. salad oil
- ¾ cup mayonnaise
- lettuce
- ¼ cup toasted almonds, slivered
- watercress

Combine first seven ingredients and marinate in refrigerator at least one hour. When ready to serve, toss with mayonnaise, mound on lettuce leaves, sprinkle with almonds and garnish with watercress.

6 servings — Mrs. Edward B. Brandon

Variations for chicken salad: add pineapple cubes, mandarin oranges, green grapes, apple cubes, Cheddar cheese cubes, whole nuts.

Chutney Chicken Salad

1 cup raisins
1 cup salted peanuts
1 cup mango chutney
1 cup flaked coconut
2 to 3 lbs. chicken, cubed
2 bananas, sliced
lemon juice
salt and pepper
1½ cups mayonnaise
lettuce cups

Plump raisins in warm water for fifteen minutes. Drain and combine with rest of ingredients and toss lightly. Serve immediately on lettuce. Accompany with hot curried fruit and melba toast.

8 servings — Mrs. Damaris D. Klaus

What is a picnic?

A chance to combine a wonderful meal with listening to beautiful music at Blossom.

A chance for families to be together away from everyday routines.

An excuse for two to slip away and be alone in some romantic spot.

Macadamia Chicken Salad

1 tsp. dry tarragon
2 T. white wine
½ cup mayonnaise
½ cup sour cream
2 cups chicken, cooked and diced
⅔ cup Macadamia nuts
salt and pepper
capers
2 hard-cooked eggs, sliced

Soak tarragon in white wine until soft and combine with mayonnaise and sour cream. Toss with chicken and nuts and season. Garnish with capers and egg slices.

4 to 6 servings THE COMMITTEE

What is a picnic?

A chance to share delicious food in a memorable setting with those you love.

A time to eat something quick and simple because there are more exciting things to do: watching a football game, swimming, hiking, skiing.

A chance to sit in front of a winter's fire and forget about the wind howling outside.

Tongue 'n Chick Salad

2 cups white meat of chicken, diced
2 cups deviled cooked tongue, julienne
1 cup cooked artichoke hearts, quartered
½ cup celery, minced
1 cup mayonnaise
¼ cup horseradish mayonnaise
½ tsp. celery seed, pulverized
¼ cup sour cream
1 tsp. prepared mustard
Bibb lettuce
tomato wedges
1 tsp. chopped chives
capers

Place chicken, tongue, artichokes and celery in a bowl. Combine mayonnaise, celery seed, sour cream and mustard. Toss with salad. Serve on a bed of Bibb lettuce, garnish with tomato wedges and sprinkle with chives and capers. Serve with melba toast or rolls.

6 servings

Robert S. Pile
Hough Caterers

Chicken in Aspic

5-lb. roasting chicken
2 large carrots, halved
2 stalks celery, sliced
1 large onion
4 whole cloves
6 peppercorns
1 bay leaf
1 T. salt
2 envelopes unflavored gelatin
2 egg whites, lightly beaten
2 tsp. lemon juice
3 pimiento-stuffed olives, sliced
pimiento, 8 three-inch strips
salad greens
2 tomatoes, sliced
½ lb. fresh mushroom caps

Place chicken in kettle with 5 cups water and next 7 ingredients. Simmer one hour. Turn chicken and cook one hour longer, or until tender. Lift chicken out of stock, let cool. Strain stock and skim off fat. Measure stock; reduce to 4 cups. Soften gelatin in ½ cup cold water. Add to stock with egg whites, bring to a boil, stirring constantly; let stand five minutes. Strain. Add lemon juice. Cool until consistency of unbeaten egg white. Pour ½ cup gelatin mixture into an oiled two quart mold. Add olive slices, arranging decoratively. Brush side of mold with more gelatin mixture. Refrigerate until set, about thirty minutes. Meanwhile, cut breast of chicken into thin, even slices. Remove rest of meat from bones, and cut into one inch pieces. Dip sliced breast meat into gelatin to coat lightly. Arrange with pimiento strips around inside of mold, overlapping slices as needed. Add cut-up chicken to remaining gelatin mixture; turn into center of mold. Refrigerate until firm, at least four hours. Unmold on platter and garnish with greens, tomato slices and mushrooms. Serve with Curry Dressing.

(See following recipe.)

Curry Dressing

1 cup mayonnaise
½ cup sour cream
1 T. lemon juice
2 tsp. curry powder

Combine ingredients and refrigerate until needed.

8 to 10 servings Mrs. R. Henry Norweb, Jr.

Brandied Cornish Hens

2 Rock Cornish game hens
⅓ cup parsley, minced
½ tsp. tarragon
½ tsp. salt
½ cup butter, softened
½ cup currant jelly
½ cup brandy

Remove giblets from hens, rinse in cold water and pat dry. Mix herbs, salt and ¼ cup butter. Put half of the butter mixture in each hen and skewer closed. Rub hens with remaining butter and place in a shallow roasting pan. Roast at 375° for thirty minutes. Heat jelly and brandy together until jelly melts. Pour over hens and roast thirty minutes longer, basting every five to ten minutes with brandy mixture. Remove from pan, cool and chill. Wrap well to take on picnic. This is delicious but messy, so take along some damp towels in plastic bags.

2 servings Mrs. Damaris D. Klaus

EASTERN SHORE DEVILED CHICKEN LEGS

8 chicken drumsticks
dry mustard
fine bread crumbs
salt and pepper
11 T. butter
2 egg yolks
1 tsp. sugar
2 T. vinegar
1 tsp. prepared mustard

Remove skin from drumsticks and spread with a thin paste of dry mustard and cold water. Roll in bread crumbs, season, and place ½ T. of butter on each. Broil for thirty minutes or until golden brown, turning frequently. Meanwhile, prepare mustard sauce: add 2 T. cold water to egg yolks with 6 T. butter, salt, pepper, sugar and vinegar. Cook slowly in the top of a double boiler, beating constantly. When foamy, add 1 T. dry mustard and prepared mustard. Cook slowly for ten minutes, stirring constantly; add 1 T. butter. Serve with broiled drumsticks.

4 servings — MRS. J. MERRILL CULVER

OKEFENOKEE BARBECUE SAUCE

½ cup butter
1 cup vinegar
½ cup water
1 tsp. mustard
1 small onion, chopped
¼ bottle Worcestershire sauce
½ cup chili sauce
½ cup catsup
juice of 1 lemon
1 clove garlic
1 tsp. brown sugar
2 lemon slices

Combine and simmer for five minutes.

MRS. DUDLEY S. BLOSSOM, JR.

White House Barbecued Chicken

2 small chickens, halved
½ cup butter, melted
juice of 2 lemons
1 tsp. garlic salt
1 T. paprika
1 T. oregano
salt and pepper to taste

Combine butter and seasonings. Marinate chicken for three to four hours in sauce. Grill, basting often with remainder of sauce. Or bake at 325° for forty-five minutes, basting often.

4 servings — The White House

Oriental Barbecued Chicken

2 chickens, cut in serving pieces
⅓ cup salad oil
⅓ dry vermouth
⅓ cup soy sauce

Pre-bake chicken for one-half hour. Then grill over hot coals about twenty minutes, basting frequently with sauce made by combining oil, vermouth and soy sauce.

6 servings — John H. Burlingame

Oven-Fried Chicken

2 lbs. chicken pieces
⅓ cup butter or margarine, melted
2 cups potato chips, crushed
¼ tsp. garlic salt
dash pepper

Dip chicken pieces in butter and roll in mixture of potato chips and seasonings.

Place pieces on ungreased cookie sheet. Sprinkle with any remaining butter and crumbs. Bake at 375° for about one hour or until done. Do not turn. Serve immediately, or chill and serve cold.

4 servings

Miss Janet Beighle
The Plain Dealer

Vary by using crushed Rice Krispies or cornflakes in place of potato chips.

Mrs. H. William Ruf

Another variation may be made by combining crushed packaged herb-seasoned stuffing mix, grated Parmesan cheese and chopped parsley as a substitute for potato chips.

Mrs. Bruce F. Rothman

A third variation for oven-fried chicken may be made by frying one minced onion in butter. Coat chicken pieces in this, then roll in a mixture of bread crumbs, minced parsley, chopped nuts and grated Parmesan cheese.

Mrs. Kenneth Haas

CHICKEN EDEN

1 frying chicken, cut up
salt
dried parsley
4 T. margarine
1 – 6 oz. can frozen orange juice, thawed
½ cup pecans, chopped
½ cup orange curacao liqueur

Place chicken pieces, skin side down, in a baking dish. Sprinkle with salt and parsley. Dot with margarine. Cover and bake at 350° for one hour. Just before serving, remove cover and add orange juice. Sprinkle pecans over chicken. Place under broiler for ten minutes. Heat liqueur and pour over chicken immediately before serving. You may flame it. Serve with wheat pilaf made from a prepared mix, adding a bit of chopped onion.

4 servings DAVID L. BLAUSHILD

For delicious golden-brown chicken, baste several times during roasting with a mixture of one-quarter cup honey and three-quarters cup orange juice.

Baked Chicken Hula

4 breasts of chicken, split
1 pkg. onion soup mix
1 cup Russian dressing
¾ cup water
¾ cup pineapple jam
1 T. soy sauce
3 T. lemon juice
rice
watercress

Place chicken, skin side down, in a baking dish. Combine sauce ingredients and pour half of the sauce over the chicken. Bake for one hour at 325°. Turn chicken and pour remaining sauce over it. Bake thirty minutes more. Serve over rice on a heated platter and garnish with watercress.

8 servings — Mrs. Bernard L. Goldman

Joel Grey's Pepper Duck

1 duck per two persons
freshly ground pepper
salt

Cover oven-ready duck with heavy coat of coarse, freshly ground pepper. Tablespoons of pepper!! The pepper will become less pungent and more "nutty" during cooking. Add salt. Roast at 325° for three hours, pricking skin frequently. It will be very crisp and fat free. Quarter with poultry shears and serve with rice and red currant jelly.

Joel Grey

Empanadas
(Spanish Meat Pastries)

1½ cups onions, minced
½ cup shortening
1 lb. ground beef
¼ cup seedless raisins
¼ cup pine nuts
½ cup sweet red pepper, minced
4 tsp. salt, and pepper
¼ tsp. oregano
6 hard-cooked eggs, minced
5 cups flour
¾ cup butter or margarine
1 cup water
24 stuffed green olives
1 egg, lightly beaten
1 tsp. sugar

Sauté onions in shortening until golden. Add meat and cook, stirring frequently, until lightly browned. Add raisins, pine nuts, red pepper, 1½ tsp. salt, pepper, and oregano. Blend thoroughly. Cool. Add hard-cooked eggs. Chill for at least one hour. Sift together flour and remaining salt. Cut in butter until mixture resembles coarse meal. Add water, a little at a time, stirring lightly with a fork, using just enough water to hold ingredients together. Shape into a ball. Chill for thirty minutes. Roll dough ⅛ inch thick on a lightly floured board. Cut into 3½ inch circles. On half of each round place an olive and a rounded tablespoonful of the meat mixture. Fold dough over meat and moisten edges; seal securely by pinching with lightly floured fingers. (May be frozen at this point.) Place on ungreased baking sheet. Combine lightly beaten egg and sugar. Brush over pastries. Bake at 450° for twenty minutes.

Yield: 2 dozen

Mrs. Emilio Llinas

WINEBURGERS

4 stuffed olives
1 lb. ground beef
2 T. salad oil
1 medium onion, minced
2 cloves garlic, crushed
1 medium carrot, minced
⅞ cup dry red wine
⅝ cup beef stock
1 tsp. tomato paste
3 T. parsley, minced
2 T. arrowroot
salt and pepper
garlic salt
1 loaf French bread
2 T. butter

Freeze olives in water in ball-shaped ice cube tray. (You keep the burger juicy by placing these in the meat.) Prepare sauce by frying 2 oz. beef in oil until brown. Add onion and garlic; fry for a minute and add carrot and cook four minutes. Add wine, stock, tomato paste and parsley. Simmer until carrot is tender. Mix arrowroot with a little red wine, pour into the sauce and stir until thickened. Season to taste. Season remaining ground beef with garlic salt and pepper. Divide into four sections. Mold the meat quickly around an olive-ice ball and flatten. Fry for two to four minutes on each side. Slice the bread diagonally into eight half-inch thick slices and butter on both sides. Fry lightly, browning each side. Place a wineburger on one slice of bread, top with another slice, cover with sauce and dust with chopped parsley. Serve immediately, accompanied by a dry red claret. "The hamburger is such a basic that it lends itself to creative variation. This is the wildest variant I've seen." (This recipe originally created for Carlos Montoya.)

4 servings

GRAHAM KERR
The Galloping Gourmet

Burgundy Burgers

2 lbs. ground beef
2 green onions, sliced
1½ tsp. salt, and pepper
¼ cup Burgundy
1 egg
1 cup fresh bread crumbs
2 green onions, sliced and sautéed in ½ cup butter or margarine
¼ cup Burgundy

Combine first six ingredients. Shape into eight patties. cook on the grill or under the broiler until done. Baste with a sauce made by combining remaining onions, butter and Burgundy.

8 servings Mrs. Michael E. A. Ward

Cheesyburgers

2 lbs. ground beef
4 tsp. onion, grated
4 tsp. prepared mustard
1½ cups Cheddar cheese, grated
salt and freshly ground pepper

Blend ingredients, and form into four patties. Wrap individually to carry to picnic. Grill over hot coals and serve.

4 servings The Committee

After cooking hamburgers in your backyard and you still have those great hot coals, put on some chicken or steak to serve cold next day.

Roquefort Burgers

1 small onion, minced
2 T. salad oil
1 clove garlic, crushed
1 lb. ground beef
1 egg
1 tsp. parsley, chopped
salt and pepper
2 T. Roquefort cheese, crumbled
1 T. butter, softened
1 T. brandy

In a saucepan, sauté onion in oil until transparent. Add garlic and and cook mixture over low heat until garlic begins to brown. Combine with ground beef, egg, parsley, and salt and pepper to taste. Shape mixture into two large patties and make a depression in center of each. Blend together cheese, butter, and brandy. Fill cavities of the burgers with cheese mixture and press the meat to seal in the filling. Broil until done. If you wish to grill these hamburgers outside, add bread crumbs to the meat mixture to give added firmness. Serve with Pancho Sauce.

2 servings — Mrs. John F. Turben

To prepare a large number of hamburger patties quickly, roll the meat to an even thickness with a rolling pin, then cut out the patties with the rim of a large glass.

Corn Burgers

1 lb. ground beef
2 T. onion, chopped
2 T. green pepper, chopped
salad oil
salt and pepper
1 bottle chili sauce
3 T. pickle relish
½ tsp. dry mustard
1 can corn
sandwich buns

Brown ground beef with onion and pepper in oil. Season. Add rest of the ingredients and let simmer until heated. You may also add some shredded cheese. Serve on sandwich buns or English muffins.

6 to 8 servings Mrs. Nathan Oakes

Sloppy Joes

3 lbs. ground beef
1 green pepper, chopped
3 small onions, chopped
¾ cup chili sauce
½ cup catsup
½ cup sweet pickle relish
10 to 12 sandwich buns

Lightly brown meat. Add pepper and onions and cook until limp. Add chili sauce, catsup, and relish. Simmer for ten minutes, stirring often. Serve immediately on buns.

10 to 12 servings Mrs. H. William Ruf

Meat Loaf Wellington

⅔ cup butter
2 cups flour
1 egg
⅓ cup sour cream
6 chicken livers
¼ lb. mushrooms, chopped
1 medium onion, chopped
2 T. butter
1 lb. ground veal
1 lb. ground beef
2 tsp. salt
2 cloves garlic, minced
1 tsp. lemon peel, grated
¼ tsp. pepper
¼ tsp. nutmeg
3 eggs, lightly beaten
⅓ cup sour cream
¼ cup Parmesan cheese, grated
1 egg white, lightly beaten
sour cream

Prepare pastry: cut ⅔ cup butter into flour. Stir in egg and ⅓ cup sour cream. Chill. Sauté chicken livers and reserve. Prepare meat loaf: sauté mushrooms and onions in 2 T. butter. Combine with remaining ingredients except egg white and sour cream. Pat half of the mixture into a loaf pan, place chicken livers down the middle, and cover with remaining meat to enclose livers. Bake at 375° for thirty-five minutes. Cool. Roll out pastry to a 12″ x 16″ rectangle. Remove meat loaf from pan and wrap with pastry. Place, seam side down, on a greased baking sheet. Brush with egg white and bake at 375° for thirty to forty minutes. Serve hot or cold, garnished with sour cream.

8 to 10 servings — Mrs. Roger Cole

Meat Loaf Surprise

- 2 lbs. ground meat (beef, veal, and pork)
- 1 cup bread crumbs and/or oatmeal
- 1 large can evaporated milk
- 2 eggs
- 1 medium onion, grated, with juice
- 1 tsp. allspice
- 1 T. prepared horseradish
- 1 tsp. sage
- 2 tsp. salt
- ½ tsp. Worcestershire sauce
- 3 eggs, hard-cooked
- 2 T. butter
- ½ cup water

Mix ingredients in electric mixer in order given as far as hard-cooked eggs. The mixer gives it an especially fine texture. Put half in loaf pan. Place three shelled hard-cooked eggs in a row end to end on top of the mixture, then spoon on remaining meat. Dot with butter and pour on just enough water to cover the surface. Bake at 350° for one and one-half hours. Slice thin and serve. This is especially good cold.

8 servings — Mrs. John H. Burlingame

Conductor's Stew
(A Favorite of Louis Lane)

2 cups dried lentils
salt
1 onion, chopped
2 T. salad oil
garlic salt
2½ to 3 cups canned tomatoes, drained and chopped
2 lbs. sausage (Kielbasa, knockwurst, smoked sausage, or frankfurters: choose two or three)
1 bay leaf
freshly ground pepper
1 T. sugar

Wash lentils. Place in deep saucepan and cover with salted water. Bring to a boil, cover, and simmer about twenty minutes or until lentils are tender but not mushy. Drain, reserving the liquid. Sauté onion in oil until soft. Stir in garlic salt and tomatoes, and cook until mixture is rather dry. Remove casings from sausages and cut into one-inch pieces. Put lentil mixture, sausage, and seasonings into a casserole and stir. Add a little of the lentil cooking water. More can be added later if stew becomes too dry. Bake at 350° for thirty minutes. This can also be cooked on top of stove in a Dutch oven. This stew is delicious reheated. If transporting to a picnic, wrap casserole to keep hot. Serve with herbed French bread and tossed salad.

6 servings Mrs. Bruce F. Rothman

Hobo Stew

2 lbs. lean chuck
6 medium potatoes, peeled and diced
6 T. onions, chopped
6 carrots, sliced
½ cup parsley, chopped
2 cans condensed golden mushroom soup
salt and pepper
Tabasco

Cut beef into one-inch cubes. Divide ingredients into six equal portions. Place each portion on a square of heavy duty aluminum foil. Add a dash of Tabasco and a tablespoon of water to each portion. Bring up the corners of the foil and twist at the top to close bundles. Keep in a cool place until ready to cook. Cook for about one hour with the bundles two inches above hot coals. Remove from grill and serve, right in the foil. For adults you may wish to dress this up a bit by adding wine and/or herbs to taste.

6 servings — Mrs. Claude M. Blair

When packing for your picnic don't forget the marshmallows! In the interest of ecology, take along some wire coat hangers to use for roasting marshmallows instead of breaking off young green twigs. Do remember to discard coat hangers in trash can, or better yet, bring them home to use again.

Cassoulet

- 1 lb. small white beans
- 1 onion
- 2 whole cloves
- 1 bay leaf
- 1 sprig parsley
- 3 T. butter
- ½ lb. fresh pork sausage
- 2 garlic sausages (smoked, Polish type)
- 1 onion, sliced
- 1 clove garlic, minced
- 1 lb. ground beef
- salt and pepper
- 1 cup dry white wine
- 1 can tomato sauce
- ½ tsp. thyme
- 1 cup coarse dry bread crumbs
- 2 T. parsley, minced

Ahead of time, cook beans until tender in two quarts water with next four ingredients. Add 1 to 1½ tsp. salt for the last half hour. Heat 1 T. butter; add sausages and cook a few minutes. Add onion and garlic; cook until soft. Drain excess fat. Crumble beef into pan; cook only until it loses color. Season with about 1 tsp. salt and plenty of freshly ground pepper. Put half the beans, drained (reserve one cup liquid), in a three quart casserole; top with half the meat mixture. Repeat layers. To frying pan add wine, tomato sauce, bean liquid, and thyme. Heat to simmering and pour into casserole. Stir gently. Bake at 350° for one hour. Heat remaining 2 T. butter; stir in crumbs and parsley. Mix and spread over casserole. Bake an additional thirty minutes.

8 servings — Mrs. John E. Culver

Quick Barbecue for a Crowd

1 large sirloin tip roast (about 12 lbs.)
1 quart barbecue sauce
sandwich buns

Bake the roast until medium rare. Remove from oven and let stand one hour. Take back to your butcher and have him slice it very thin on his machine. Reheat in barbecue sauce and serve on buns.

Mrs. Donald Fitzgerald

Sue's London Broil

1 ¾ to 2 lbs. flank steak
1 tsp. salt
½ tsp. pepper
¼ tsp. basil
¼ tsp. rosemary
1 clove garlic, crushed
½ onion, chopped
2 T. wine vinegar
4 T. salad oil

Combine all ingredients in a flat dish. Marinate the steak, turning occasionally, either in the refrigerator or out, for two hours or longer. Broil three inches from the heat for five minutes. Baste with sauce. Turn and broil for five more minutes. It should be served in thin slices cut across the grain.

4 to 6 servings

Mrs. Michael Clegg

Steak au Poivre Rossini

2 lbs. strip steak
4 T. peppercorns, coarsely ground
2 oz. Madeira
truffles

Obtain finest quality steak available and trim away most of the fat. With the palm of the hand press freshly ground pepper into the meat on all four sides. Broil until it reaches the preferred degree of doneness, reserving the juices. Remove to another platter and on the top of the stove heat the juices with the wine and some sliced truffles while scraping the pan to blend all the flavors. If more liquid is needed, add more wine. Remove sauce from the heat and pour over the steak. As it cools, turn the meat to evenly marinate. After the steak is cold, refrigerate. Just before leaving for picnic, slice into finger-sized pieces. Take along sauce for dunking.

2 servings

John F. Schindler
au Pere Jacques

Wine Marinade for Beef

1 cup red wine
1 cup salad oil
1 tsp. salt
freshly ground pepper
1 tsp. marjoram
1 clove garlic, minced

Substitute white wine and tarragon for chicken and fish.

Stuffed Filet of Beef

1 – 3 lb. beef tenderloin
1 small onion, chopped
1 cup fresh mushrooms, sliced
¼ cup butter
1½ cups soft bread crumbs
white wine
salt and pepper

Brown onions and mushrooms in butter. Add bread crumbs and a tablespoon or two of wine to moisten; season with salt and pepper. Split filet open, being careful not to cut through. Spoon stuffing inside, fold together, and secure with string in three or four places. Bake at 450° for forty-five minutes, or on charcoal grill for forty minutes, turning once.

6 servings — Mrs. Darrell Brand

MENU SUGGESTION

Picnic Potage
Stuffed Filet of Beef
Simply Scrumptious Spinach Salad
Lemon Squares

Pancho Sauce

¾ cup catsup
6 T. chili sauce
6 T. mayonnaise
2 T. pineapple juice
2¼ tsp. wine vinegar
2¼ tsp. dry mustard
1½ tsp. Worcestershire sauce
¾ tsp. prepared horseradish
¼ tsp. MSG
¼ tsp. ground ginger
2 or 3 drops Tabasco

Combine above ingredients and mix thoroughly. Serve with Roquefort Burgers.

Mrs. John F. Turben

Lemon Mint Sauce

juice of 3 lemons
2 T. water
⅓ cup salad oil
8 fresh mint leaves, coarsely chopped
1 clove garlic, minced
½ tsp. salt
pepper

Mix ingredients well. Let stand half an hour at room temperature. Serve with grilled steak.

Mrs. Theodore A. Gullia, Jr.

Corned Beef and Beer

1 – 4 lb. corned beef brisket
1½ cans beer
2 T. mixed pickling spices
1 orange, sliced
1 onion, sliced
1 green onion, chopped
1 carrot, sliced
1 stalk celery, chopped

Marinate corned beef in beer for thirty minutes or longer. Place large sheet of heavy duty aluminum foil in a shallow pan. Lift beef from beer and place in center of foil. Pour beer over beef, sprinkle with spices, and arrange orange and vegetables over and around beef. Bring long sides of foil up over beef and seal with tight double folds. Seal ends to prevent liquid from escaping. Bake at 300° for four hours or until tender. Let stand for two hours to cool. Slice thin to make fantastic sandwiches, or slice while still warm to serve for dinner.

Ernest Carteris
Author: "A Cookbook for Lovers"
Consultant: Club Products Company

It is handy to keep a picnic basket ready with all the basic equipment packed. All you then need to add is the food. Package basket in sequence that you will need items. The first things you will need should be at the top.

Molded Corned Beef Salad

1 envelope unflavored gelatin
¼ cup cold water
1¾ cups boiling water
2 beef bouillon cubes
¼ tsp. celery salt
1 can corned beef
1½ cups cooked macaroni
½ green pepper
1 small onion
1½ cups celery, chopped
1½ cups mayonnaise

Dissolve gelatin in cold water. Add boiling water, bouillon cubes, and celery salt. Stir until dissolved and chill until thick. Chop corned beef, macaroni, green pepper, and onion in a food chopper. Combine with gelatin mixture. Add celery and mayonnaise. Pour into an oiled nine inch ring mold and refrigerate, do not freeze. May be made a day ahead.

12 servings — Mrs. Maurice Sharp

To unmold easily, wrap the bottom of the mold with a damp, hot towel.

Barbecued Hamwich

1 cup catsup
¼ cup vinegar
3 T. prepared mustard
½ cup brown sugar
1½ lbs. shaved ham
16 sandwich buns

Heat first four ingredients together. Add ham and simmer twenty minutes. Serve on toasted buns. Wrap in foil and pack in an insulated bag to take on a picnic.

Mrs. Donald A. DePolo

The McIntosh Sandwich

12 slices sandwich bread, lightly toasted
mayonnaise
mustard
12 one oz. slices of baked ham
6 small McIntosh apples, peeled and sliced in rings
24 one oz. slices American cheese

Spread the bread with mayonnaise and mustard and top with a slice of ham. Put a few apple rings on top of the ham, followed by two slices of cheese. Put the open-faced sandwiches on a baking sheet and broil until cheese bubbles. Serve immediately.

6 servings

The Committee

Peanut Barbecued Ham

½ cup peanut butter
¼ cup honey
2 tsp. soy sauce
1 tsp. Kitchen Bouquet
1 onion, grated
1 clove garlic, minced
1 cup chicken broth
¼ tsp. freshly ground pepper
2 center ham slices, 1½ inches thick, fully cooked

Mix together all ingredients except ham slices. Place ham in a flat pan and marinate in half of the sauce in the refrigerator for several hours. Grill over glowing coals for thirty to forty minutes, basting with reserved sauce. Cut into slices and serve.

8 to 10 servings

Ellwood M. Fisher

Spinning Barbecued Ham

1 round fully cooked boneless ham
1 cup extra-hot catsup
⅔ cup orange marmalade
¼ cup onion, minced
¼ cup salad oil
2 T. lemon juice
3 tsp. Shedd's mustard sauce

Remove casing from the ham and score it. Tie it well with cord or string. Center ham lengthwise on a spit and roast for twenty minutes per pound or to 130° on a meat thermometer. Combine ingredients for sauce and brush on ham for the last half hour. Serve remaining sauce with the ham.

Mrs. Jon H. Outcalt

TIMBALE OF HAM WITH MADEIRA SAUCE

3 T. butter
3 T. flour
1 cup milk
2 cups cooked ham
4 eggs
2 egg yolks
½ cup heavy cream
salt and pepper
bread crumbs
2 T. butter
¼ lb. fresh mushrooms, sliced
1 tsp. green onions, chopped
¼ cup Madeira or sherry
1 can brown sauce

Make a cream sauce with 3 T. butter, flour, and milk. Place ham, cream sauce, eggs, and yolks into a blender and spin until very fine. Add cream and season to taste. Butter a two quart mold, coat with bread crumbs and pour in the ham mixture. Place the mold in a shallow pan to which some water has been added. Bake at 350° for about forty minutes. Meanwhile, prepare the sauce. Melt 2 T. butter in a sauce pan, add mushrooms and brown lightly. Add onions, then wine and brown sauce, and bring to a boil. Unmold ham on a platter and serve topped with sauce, or with sauce on the side.

8 servings

RENE VERDON
White House Chef 1961-1966

Two Martini Barbecued Pork Chop Dinner

½ cup orange marmalade
½ cup honey
½ cup soy sauce
½ tsp. powdered ginger
¼ tsp. dry mustard
garlic salt
salt and pepper
4 pork chops, 1 inch thick
4 medium tomatoes
oregano
4 ears of corn with husks
butter

Prepare marinade by combining first seven ingredients. Marinate chops several hours, if possible, turning occasionally. Prepare vegetables: wash tomatoes and lay on squares of heavy duty aluminum foil, sprinkle with oregano and salt and bring corners of foil to top and twist tightly shut. Peel down husks and remove silk from corn, rub with butter and season; replace husks and wrap in foil. Prepare a good bed of coals. Put on chops. Make a generous martini and relax in a comfortable chair on the windward side of barbecue grill with marinade at hand. Check chops often; baste frequently with marinade. (Adjust grill, if necessary, so meat cooks but does not become too brown or dried out.) When martini is gone (½ hour), chops should be browned. Turn them. Mix martini number two and bring out tomatoes and corn. After ten minutes place tomatoes and corn on coals at back of grill. Turn them several times so they cook on all sides. Continue to baste meat. When martini is gone, meat and vegetables should be cooked. Test for doneness: meat should be rich brown and succulent, tomatoes juicy, and corn plump and golden. Carefully remove foil from tomatoes and serve in individual sauce dishes. Husk corn before serving.

4 servings

William F. Le Fevre

Orange Glazed Pork Chops

6 thick pork chops
½ cup orange juice
1 tsp. salt
½ tsp. pepper
½ tsp. dry mustard
¼ cup brown sugar

Trim pork chops if necessary. Place chops in a large shallow baking dish (line with foil for ease in cleaning). Combine remaining ingredients and pour over chops. Bake at 350° for one hour or until done. Baste occasionally during cooking. This recipe can be assembled ahead and allowed to marinate until time for baking.

6 servings — Mrs. Anthony R. Michel

Woody's Patio Pork Chops

½ cup applesauce
2 T. soy sauce
2 T. catsup
½ tsp. lemon rind, grated
6 rib pork chops, 1 inch thick

Combine sauce ingredients. Place pork chops on preheated grill, five inches from coals. Broil ten minutes on each side, then brush with sauce mixture and continue cooking, turning and brushing with sauce until well done, about twenty to thirty minutes longer.

3 to 6 servings — Ellwood M. Fisher

Beer Barbecued Ribs

7 lbs. country-style spare ribs
3 bottles of beer
1 bottle barbecue sauce
½ cup olive oil
½ cup cider vinegar
½ cup dark molasses
garlic
Tabasco
salt and pepper

Simmer ribs in two bottles of beer, covered, for one hour. Combine remaining ingredients with one bottle of beer and simmer for one hour. Drain ribs, baste with sauce, and grill over hot coals until well-glazed.

6 to 8 servings

Mrs. Marilyn Rutter
Union Club manicurist

Pork South Pacific

3 lbs. lean pork
2 – 9 oz. jars kumquats
½ cup soy sauce
1 clove garlic, crushed
¼ tsp. ground ginger
½ cup dry sherry

Cut pork into one-inch cubes. Drain kumquats and reserve. Combine juice with remaining seasonings. Place meat in a bowl, pour marinade over meat, and cover. Refrigerate several hours or overnight. Alternate cubes of pork with kumquats on skewers and broil until well done, basting with marinade if desired.

8 to 12 servings

Mrs. Thomas E. Healy

VEAL AND PORK TERRINE

½ cup Madeira
½ cup brandy
4 cloves garlic (2 of them minced)
½ tsp. Spice Parisienne
1 tsp. sage
1½ lbs. veal cut for scallopine
bacon
1 lb. sausage meat
salt and pepper
1 lb. ground pork and veal

Make a marinade of the Madeira, brandy, two whole cloves garlic, Spice Parisienne, and sage. Marinate veal in this for several hours, then pour off the marinade and reserve. Cover the bottom of a 2½ quart casserole with bacon. Add a layer of sausage meat, a bit of minced garlic, a layer of veal, and salt and pepper to taste. Continue with a layer of ground pork and veal, and repeat until ingredients are used. Pour marinade over the meat, and cover with bacon. Top with minced garlic. Cover casserole, set in a pan of hot water and bake at 375° for two hours. Skim off fat if necessary. Let cool at room temperature. Serve when it is just warm. It should be ready to eat about two hours after you take it from oven.

8 servings MRS. CHARLES K. MURRAY

Dutch ovens or heavy casseroles, wrapped in eight thicknesses of newspaper, retain heat during the trip to the picnic.

Picnic Barbecued Pork Roast

Take a boneless pork roast (or two) and grill over a slow charcoal fire for an hour and a half, basting frequently with your favorite barbecue sauce. Trim fat, slice, and serve on toasted sandwich buns. Or, pre-cook roast in a small amount of water for an hour, on top of the stove, and finish on the grill.

Mrs. David M. Schneider

Hot Dog Casserole

1½ cups corn chips
1 onion, chopped
1 cup Cheddar cheese, grated
1 lb. hot dogs, sliced
1 can baked beans
1 can sauce for tacos

Divide all ingredients but taco sauce in half and layer twice in a casserole. Top with sauce for tacos. Bake at 300° for forty-five minutes.

4 servings

The Committee

Easy Pigs-In-A-Blanket

Wrap warm hot dogs spread with mustard in squares of refrigerated crescent rolls and bake.

The Committee

Butterflied Leg of Lamb

1 – 6 to 7 lb. leg of lamb
1 clove garlic, crushed
¾ cup salad oil
¼ cup red wine vinegar
½ cup onion, chopped
2 tsp. prepared Dijon mustard
2 tsp. salt and freshly ground pepper
½ tsp. oregano
½ tsp. basil
1 bay leaf, crushed

Have your butcher bone and butterfly a leg of lamb. Place fat side down in a shallow pan. Combine other ingredients and pour over lamb. Cover tightly and refrigerate overnight, turning the meat at least once. Remove from refrigerator about one hour before cooking. Preheat broiler. Place meat, fat side up, with marinade in broiler pan. Broil about four inches from the heat ten minutes; turn, baste, and broil for another ten minutes. Transfer meat to oven and roast at 425° about fifteen minutes. Test with a sharp knife; meat should be pink and juicy. Remove from marinade and serve cut into thin slices. If preferred, the browned bits of onion may be removed.

6 servings — Mrs. Harold Ensten

Grilled Lamb Chops

⅓ cup chili sauce
⅓ cup mint sauce
⅓ cup currant jelly
6 to 8 lamb chops

Combine sauces and jelly and heat. Serve over grilled chops.

4 servings — Mrs. H. William Ruf

SHISH KEBOB SCHEHERAZADE

2 lbs. lean lamb, cubed
4 small onions, quartered
8 mushrooms
1 green pepper, cut in squares
1 small eggplant, cubed
tomatoes (optional)
2 T. vinegar
2 T. olive oil
1 tsp. salt
½ tsp. thyme
freshly ground pepper

Combine all ingredients and marinate at least one hour, preferably overnight, in refrigerator. Place on skewers, alternating lamb and vegetables. Broil over hot coals about fifteen minutes, turning frequently. "Shish" is the Arabic word for skewer, and "kebob" is the word for meat. Shish kebob is a style of cooking developed on the battlefield by hungry soldiers gathered around an open fire.

4 servings MRS. JOSEPH NAHRA

MENU SUGGESTION

Tuna Tahini
Shish Kebob Scheherazade
Quick Risotto
Tabbouleh
Surprise Pie

Accompaniments

RATATOUILLE

1 small eggplant, diced, unpeeled
2 medium zucchini, diced, unpeeled
2 green peppers, chopped
2 onions, chopped
½ cup salad oil
¼ tsp. thyme
2 bay leaves
3 cloves garlic, minced
4 tomatoes, quartered
salt and freshly ground pepper
to taste
1 cup ripe olives, pitted
¼ cup olive oil
2 T. parsley, chopped

Sauté eggplant, zucchini, green peppers and onions in salad oil, a few at a time. As the vegetables take on some color transfer them to a four quart casserole. Add the thyme, bay leaves, garlic, tomatoes, salt and pepper. Cook in a slow oven, uncovered so that the liquid will evaporate, for two hours. Refrigerate overnight. When ready to serve, sprinkle the olives, olive oil, and parsley on top.

6 to 8 servings

JACQUES PEPIN
Formerly chef to Charles de Gaulle

Variation: fill pockets of Syrian flat bread with slices of cold filet and ratatouille.

MRS. JOSEPH E. ADAMS

Stuffed Zucchini

6 to 7 medium zucchini
1 small onion, chopped
1 clove garlic, chopped
3 T. butter
½ can seasoned bread crumbs
½ to ¾ cup Parmesan cheese
2 tsp. marjoram
¼ cup parsley, chopped
salt and pepper
2 eggs, beaten

Wash zucchini, cut off ends, and steam until barely tender. Cool. Split lengthwise and scoop out pulp. Mash pulp or spin in blender. Sauté the onion and garlic in butter. Add pulp, crumbs, cheese, herbs and seasonings. Add eggs and cook until mixture thickens. Stuff into zucchini shells and place in a buttered casserole. Bake at 375° until browned, about fifteen to twenty minutes. Serve hot, cooled, or chilled.

6 to 8 servings — Mrs. Robert P. Mack

MENU SUGGESTION

Antipasto Salad
Grilled Lobster
Stuffed Zucchini
Carrot Cake

Marinated Zucchini Salad

1 lb. small zucchini, thinly sliced
1 – 10 oz. pkg. frozen green peas and pearl onions, or green peas and celery
½ cup Italian dressing
2 T. wine vinegar
salad greens

Cover zucchini with boiling salted water. Let stand one minute and drain. Cook peas as directed on package. Combine vegetables with salad dressing and vinegar. Cover and chill at least four hours, stirring gently once or twice. Line a chilled bowl with salad greens or lettuce cups. Spoon in marinated vegetables and serve.

6 servings

Miss Janet Beighle
The Plain Dealer

Peas Pizzicato

2 pks. frozen tiny peas
1 cup sour cream
2 green onions, chopped
6 slices bacon, cooked and crumbled
½ tsp. salt
freshly ground pepper

Thaw peas, drain (do not cook), and toss with rest of ingredients.

8 servings

Mrs. Gerald R. Doser

Dilly Carrots

1 lb. carrots, cut in sticks
dill pickle juice
1 pint sour cream
fresh dill
salt and freshly ground pepper

Boil carrots in pickle juice until barely tender. Let stand overnight in juice. Drain well, add sour cream, fresh dill, salt and pepper. Chill and serve.

Mrs. Luke P. Miller

Pickled Carrots

⅓ cup sugar
1¼ cups white vinegar
1¼ tsp. salt
1½ tsp. celery seed
3 tsp. mustard seed
4 cups carrots, French cut

Combine first five ingredients, and bring to a boil. Add carrots. Simmer until barely tender. Chill in marinade. Drain and serve on a vegetable relish platter

8 servings Mrs. Walter R. Kirkham

MENU SUGGESTION

Artichokes Allegretto
Sue's London Broil
World's Best Onions
Bread on the Grill
Dilly Carrots
Katie's Kentucky Chocolate Cake

Vegetables on the Grill

Place vegetables, butter, and seasonings on a square of heavy duty aluminum foil. Seal securely and grill over hot coals, turning frequently.

FRESH MUSHROOMS
- 1 lb. mushrooms, sliced
- ¼ cup butter or margarine
- salt, pepper and paprika
- 2 T. dry sherry
- ¼ cup parsley, chopped

SQUASH
- 1½ lbs. summer squash or zucchini
- ¼ cup butter or margarine
- 1 tsp. instant minced onion
- salt, pepper and tarragon
- ½ cup green pepper, minced

CARROTS
- 1 lb. fresh carrots, cut in ¼″ slices
- 2 T. butter
- salt, pepper and thyme

4 servings

Mrs. Alan R. Daus

Smoked Sweet Corn on the Cob

- 1 or 2 ears of corn per person
- butter

To prepare the corn for charcoal grilling, pull the husks down just enough to remove all the silk and then put them back in place and tie. Do not remove the husks completely. Soak the corn in water for about half an hour. Put the ears on a hot charcoal grill and roast for about one-half hour, turning occasionally. Serve hot with plenty of butter.

Mrs. James W. Irwin

THE WORLD'S BEST ONIONS

1 medium Spanish onion per person
butter

Do not peel or wash onions. Simply put directly into coals as soon as the fire is started. Make fire larger than usual as they need a lot of heat. Cook at least one hour, turning occasionally. At serving time, peel outer skin, leaving part of the charred inner layer. Cut top crisscross, pinch open and serve as a baked potato with lots of butter.

MRS. GEORGE D. KIRKHAM

POMODORI GRATINATI (BAKED TOMATOES)

4 firm tomatoes
⅓ cup dry bread crumbs
3 T. parsley, minced
1 clove garlic, minced
1¼ tsp. salt
¼ tsp. freshly ground pepper
¼ cup olive oil

Cut tomatoes in half crosswise. Mix together bread crumbs, parsley, garlic, salt, pepper and 2 T. oil. Spread mixture on the cut side of the tomatoes. Arrange in an oiled shallow baking pan; sprinkle with remaining oil. Bake at 400° for fifteen minutes.

4 servings

MRS. KENNETH HAAS

DILLED TOMATOES OR CURRIED TOMATOES

The above recipe may be varied by spreading the cut side of the tomatoes with butter, salt, pepper and either dill seeds or curry powder to taste. Bake or grill over coals.

THE COMMITTEE

Tomatoes Garnis

6 tomatoes, peeled and sliced
6 eggs, hard-cooked and chopped
½ cup celery, chopped
¼ cup green pepper, chopped
¼ cup green onions, chopped
2 T. Shedd's mustard sauce
¼ cup mayonnaise
½ tsp. salt and freshly ground pepper
parsley sprigs

Wrap tomatoes well. Mix remaining ingredients (except parsley) and put into a separate container in your picnic basket. To serve the tomatoes; spoon the egg mixture on top and garnish with parsley. It is a pretty and unusual touch.

6 servings — Mrs. Jon H. Outcalt

Tomatoes Toscanini

8 tomatoes, peeled and sliced
1 onion, minced
basil and minced parsley
oil and vinegar salad dressing

Combine tomatoes, onion and herbs. Season and marinate in dressing in refrigerator for an hour or longer before serving.

8 servings — Louis Lane

MENU SUGGESTION

Cheese Straws
White House Barbecued Chicken
Tomatoes Toscanini
Sweet Corn on the Cob
Apple Pie

Cole-Ferrell Salad

- 1 #2 can dilled green beans
- 2 cups Brussels sprouts, cooked
- 3 stalks celery, diced
- 3 slices Swiss cheese, julienne
- 6 slices bacon, cooked and crumbled
- ½ large avocado, diced
- 2 green onions, minced
- parsley, minced
- ¼ cup mayonnaise
- ⅛ cup Roquefort dressing

Toss ingredients gently in bowl. Chill and serve.

6 servings Mrs. Roger Cole

Curry Bean Salad

- 2 pkgs. frozen Italian green beans or 1½ lbs. fresh green beans
- ½ cup mayonnaise
- 2 T. Parmesan cheese, grated
- 1 T. pimiento, minced
- 1 tsp. salt
- ⅛ to ¼ tsp. curry powder

Cook green beans as directed on package, until barely tender, or prepare fresh beans. Drain well. Combine rest of ingredients. Add beans and toss. Chill. Sprinkle with more Parmesan cheese before serving.

8 servings Mrs. Bruce H. Akers

Green Beans with Country Picnic Dressing

1 lb. fresh green beans (or 3 boxes frozen green beans)
6 T. salad oil
2 T. white vinegar
¼ tsp. coriander
¼ tsp. savory seasoning
⅛ tsp. thyme
⅛ tsp. freshly ground pepper
1 tsp. salt
1 T. Dijon mustard
1 small onion
½ cup mayonnaise
½ cup light cream
3 hard-cooked eggs

Trim and wash fresh green beans. Remove strings, if any. Bring several quarts of salted water to a rolling boil. Add beans a handful at a time; keep water boiling. Reduce heat and cook slowly, uncovered, for eight to ten minutes, or until done al denté. Drain immediately and refresh in cold water to stop the cooking. When cold, drain thoroughly and pat dry on a towel. Cover and refrigerate. To prepare dressing, put ingredients (except eggs) in a blender and spin until onion is chopped. Prepare the garnish; separate the cooked whites and yolks and force through a sieve. Store in separate covered containers. Take the dressing, in a covered jar, to the picnic and pour over beans when ready to serve. Sprinkle with egg whites and yolks. Broccoli, cooked celery or carrot sticks may be used in place of the beans.

6 servings

Rudolph Stanish
Club Products Company

Three Bean Salad

- 1½ cups sugar
- 1 cup vinegar
- ¼ cup salad oil
- 2 tsp. salt
- 2 cans green beans, drained
- 2 cans yellow beans, drained
- 1 can kidney beans, undrained
- 1 cup onion, chopped
- onion rings
- green pepper rings

Combine and heat first four ingredients. Cool. Toss beans and onions with the dressing. Refrigerate overnight or longer. Garnish with sweet onion rings and green pepper rings.

8 servings Mrs. George Goslee

Pasadena Beans

- 2 – 15 oz. cans kidney beans, drained
- ½ cup brown sugar
- ½ cup Burgundy
- ½ onion, grated
- 1 cup sour cream

Marinate first four ingredients overnight in a 1½ quart casserole. Bake at 350° until liquid is absorbed (can leave in oven ½ to 1½ hours). Serve. Pass sour cream in a separate dish.

4 to 6 servings Mrs. Bruce G. Rauch

Baked Beans Beethoven

2 – 15 oz. cans butter beans
½ bottle catsup (regular size)
¼ cup molasses or maple syrup
¼ tsp. dry mustard
½ cup brown sugar
6 to 8 bacon strips

Drain beans and mix with the remaining ingredients except bacon. Put in casserole and top with bacon. Bake uncovered at 350° for one hour. This recipe can be made ahead and frozen, but thaw before cooking.

6 servings Mrs. Stephen M. Gage

Picnic Baked Beans

2 cups canned baked beans (not Boston style)
½ cup chili sauce
6 T. brown sugar
3 T. onion, minced
2 T. green pepper, chopped
½ tsp. salt
3 slices bacon, cut in 1 inch pieces

Combine everything but bacon in a one quart casserole. Arrange bacon pieces on top. Bake at 350° for forty-five minutes. Stir before serving. This is also good cold.

4 servings Mrs. Harry E. Pickering

Celery au Vin, Fines Herbes

1 bunch celery
½ cup chicken broth
½ cup dry white wine
salt and pepper
1 bay leaf
2 whole cloves
1 small onion
½ cup Italian dressing
1 T. white vinegar
1 tsp. parsley, minced
1 tsp. chopped chives
pinch of tarragon

Peel and trim the stalks of celery; do not use the leaves. Cut into three-inch pieces. Pour the broth and wine into a sauce pan. Add salt, pepper, bay leaf, cloves, onion and the celery pieces. Simmer for fifteen to twenty minutes, or until the celery is barely tender. Drain and discard the onion, cloves and bay leaf. Put celery in a serving dish. Combine dressing with vinegar and herbs and pour over the hot celery. Chill well before serving.

8 servings — The Committee

Ants on a Log

celery
peanut butter
raisins

Cut cleaned stalks of celery in four inch pieces. Stuff with peanut butter and place raisins on the peanut butter about one inch apart.

The Girl Scouts

Vegetable Salad Platter

4 medium potatoes, peeled, cooked and diced

1 pkg. frozen peas and carrots, cooked and drained

1 cup mayonnaise

2 T. onion, minced

3 T. lemon juice

1 T. prepared mustard

2 T. sweet pickle relish

1 lemon, sectioned

1 apple, peeled and chopped

½ tsp. garlic powder

salt to taste

3 hard-cooked eggs, yolk and white chopped separately

asparagus, canned

baby carrots, canned

pitted ripe olives, sliced

pimientos, julienne

1 pkg. frozen peas, cooked and drained

Combine potatoes and peas and carrots. Cool. Toss lightly with mayonnaise. Add next eight ingredients and toss again. Shape mixture into a long loaf on a platter. This much can be made a day ahead, but don't garnish until ready to serve. To garnish, cover sides of loaf with asparagus spears and carrots. On top sprinkle sections of egg yolks and egg whites, divided by pimientos and olives. Surround platter with peas. Chill.

8 servings

Mrs. Sam Butnik

Salade Nicoise (A Many Splendored Thing)

½ cup olive or salad oil
3 T. red wine vinegar
½ tsp. salt and freshly ground pepper
1 tsp. Dijon mustard
1 clove garlic, pressed
2 cups green beans, fresh, frozen or canned
3 new potatoes, cooked, peeled and diced (1½ cups)
1 red or green sweet pepper, julienne
3 sweet pickled yellow banana peppers, julienne
8 anchovy filets, drained
1 small red onion, sliced in rings
1 can tuna, drained
12 small tomatoes, halved
1 dozen ripe olives
3 hard-cooked eggs, quartered

Ahead of time, make dressing by shaking together in a jar the first five ingredients. Cook fresh or frozen green beans until barely tender and drain. Drizzle a few drops of dressing over potatoes while warm. Cut anchovies into pieces. At serving time, toss beans, potatoes, peppers, anchovies and onions with about half of the dressing. Add salt and pepper to taste. Heap in a mound on a platter or arrange attractively in a shallow bowl with tuna in the center. Garnish with tomatoes, olives and eggs. Cover with rest of dressing.

6 servings

Thomas Augustus Charles Leonce
Victor Francois du Bois
de Villiers de Broglie

Potato-Tomato Salad

1 medium red onion, thinly sliced
6 medium new red potatoes
4 tomatoes, sliced in wedges
3 or 4 fresh basil leaves or
  1 tsp. dried basil
¼ tsp. oregano
½ cup olive oil
¼ cup vinegar
½ to 1 tsp. salt, and pepper to taste

Soak onion in cold water to cover for one-half hour. Simmer potatoes in salted water until done; peel and quarter. Place in a salad bowl; add tomatoes. Drain onions and add. Toss salad with remaining ingredients when ready to serve.

6 servings Mrs. Theodore A. Gullia, Jr.

Cold Potatoes in Sour Cream

6 large potatoes
1 cup mayonnaise
2 cups sour cream
dash of salt
chopped chives
hard-cooked egg yolk, grated

Peel and boil potatoes, cool to room temperature and slice. Mix together mayonnaise, sour cream and salt. Put a layer of potatoes in a bowl, spread with sour cream mixture and a sprinkle of chives. Repeat until all ingredients are used. Garnish with egg yolk.

10 servings Mrs. Robert Gresham

Ravishingly Rich Potato Salad

12 to 18 medium new red potatoes
2 cups white wine vinegar and oil dressing
½ tsp. Colman's dry English mustard
2 cups home-made mayonnaise (see below)
1½ tsp. salt
½ tsp. freshly ground pepper
2 large cucumbers, peeled, seeded and cubed
6 to 8 green onions, coarsely chopped, including tops

Boil potatoes until barely tender. Cool slightly before peeling. Cut into cubes and marinate at least one hour in the vinegar dressing, then drain. Mix mustard thoroughly with the mayonnaise. Thoroughly mix all ingredients in a large bowl until just coated, not runny. Chill immediately. Garnish the salad with pitted ripe or green olives, anchovies, capers, radish buds, etc.

6 to 8 servings Mrs. Chilton Thomson

Blender Mayonnaise

1 egg
½ tsp. dry mustard
½ tsp. salt
2 T. vinegar
1 cup salad oil

Place egg, mustard, salt and vinegar in blender. Add ¼ cup oil. Cover and turn motor on low speed. Uncover and slowly pour in remaining oil in a steady stream.

POTATO AND HEARTS OF PALM SALAD

12 small new potatoes
oil and vinegar salad dressing
salt and pepper
1 large red onion, thinly sliced
parsley, chopped
1 can hearts of palm, sliced
4 hard-cooked eggs, sliced

Simmer potatoes in salted water until done. Drain and peel. Slice fairly thin and toss with dressing. Season to taste. Cool and chill. Just before packing for the picnic add the onion, parsley and additional dressing. Garnish with hearts of palm and eggs.

4 to 6 servings MRS. CHARLES K. MURRAY

HOT POTATO SALAD

8 large potatoes
1 onion, chopped
2 or 3 hard-cooked eggs, chopped
mayonnaise
vinegar
salt and pepper

Peel potatoes and cook until barely tender. Cube. Add onions and eggs, and toss lightly. Add mayonnaise and vinegar in proportions to taste. Season and serve hot. This salad is also good the second day served cold.

MRS. CHARLES SORKIN

SINKOLA CREAMED POTATOES

1 potato per person plus 1 extra
heavy cream
1 T. butter
½ cup Cheddar cheese, grated

Bake potatoes a day ahead. Cool and refrigerate until about an hour before picnic, then peel and dice. Put into a buttered casserole. Add cream to cover, butter, salt and pepper to taste. Sprinkle with cheese. Bake at 350° for about forty minutes. To take anywhere but the back yard, set in an insulated carrier. Keep warm on back of the grill while cooking meat.

MRS. GEORGE D. KIRKHAM

NOODLES FLORENTINE

½ lb. green noodles
1 clove garlic, minced
½ cup onion, chopped
1¼ cups cottage cheese
¾ tsp. salt, and pepper
Tabasco
1 tsp. Worcestershire sauce
1½ cups sour cream
1½ cups Parmesan cheese, grated

Cook and drain noodles. While hot, add garlic and onion. Then add cottage cheese, seasonings, and sour cream. Blend with fork. Turn into a casserole and bake at 350° for twenty minutes. Sprinkle with Parmesan cheese and bake fifteen minutes longer. This is especially good for a back yard picnic.

8 to 10 servings

MRS. MICHAEL A. CLEGG

Calico Rice Salad

3 cups cooked rice
3 hard-cooked eggs, chopped
½ cup onion, chopped
¼ cup pimiento, chopped
¼ cup green pepper, chopped
¼ cup celery, chopped
¼ cup dill pickle, chopped
½ cup raisins
1 tsp. salt, and pepper
¼ cup French dressing
⅓ cup mayonnaise
2 T. prepared mustard

Combine first ten ingredients. Blend French dressing, mayonnaise and mustard; add to rice mixture and toss. Chill and serve.

5 servings Mrs. Joseph Nahra

Rice and Artichoke Salad

1 pkg. chicken-flavored rice mix
4 green onions, thinly sliced
½ green pepper, chopped
12 pimiento-stuffed olives, sliced
2 – 6 oz. jars marinated artichoke hearts
¾ tsp. curry powder
⅓ cup mayonnaise

Cook rice as directed on package, omitting butter. Cool in a large bowl. Add onions, green pepper and olives. Drain artichoke hearts, reserving marinade, and halve. Combine artichoke marinade with curry powder and mayonnaise. Add artichoke hearts to rice salad and toss with dressing. Chill.

8 servings Mrs. Stuart Buchanan

QUICK RISOTTO

1 small onion, minced
½ cup butter
2 cups chicken broth
1 bay leaf
1 pinch saffron
white pepper
2 cups Minute Rice
Parmesan cheese, grated

Sauté onion in butter until soft. Add chicken broth (or use two cups water and two chicken bouillon cubes) and seasonings. Bring to a boil. Add rice, remove from heat and let stand five minutes, sprinkle with Parmesan cheese and serve. If you want to take this on a picnic, place individual servings on small squares of aluminum foil, sprinkle with cheese, and twist closed. Put packets on the back of the grill to warm while meat cooks. Excellent with shish kaebob.

6 to 8 servings MRS. DAMARIS D. KLAUS

To start a charcoal fire, put charcoal in a papier-mache egg carton, just as you would a dozen eggs. Then close the top and set fire to the carton. When the carton is burned away, you will find your charcoal started.

Macaroni Salad

1 large pkg. (1 lb.) macaroni shells, cooked
4 to 6 hard-cooked eggs, thinly sliced
1 large red onion, thinly sliced
2 cups mayonnaise
1 cup sour cream
10 to 12 strips bacon, cooked and crumbled
salt and freshly ground pepper
dill weed

Combine ingredients and chill.

6 to 8 servings

Mrs. Richard J. Blum

Picnic Macaroni Salad

1 box elbow style macaroni
chopped onion
salami
ham
cheese
mayonnaise

Cook macaroni, drain and chill. Combine with rest of ingredients, in proportions to taste, toss with mayonnaise. Chill and serve.

Mrs. David M. Schneider

Caesar Salad

¾ cup salad oil
1 clove garlic, or garlic powder
1 egg
juice of 1 lemon
salt and freshly ground pepper
2 heads romaine lettuce
6 green onions, including tops, chopped
3 tomatoes, quartered
1 small cucumber, sliced
½ lb. bacon, cooked and crumbled
1 cup croutons
⅓ cup Parmesan cheese, grated

Put garlic in salad oil and let stand (remove garlic clove just before serving). Place unbroken egg in a saucepan with water, bring just to simmer, remove from heat and let stand one minute. Scrape into oil and mix well with a fork. Add lemon juice and seasonings (herbs and a dash of white vinegar may be added at this time if desired). Stir well and refrigerate. Meanwhile, tear romaine into bite-sized pieces and place in a bowl with onions, tomatoes and cucumber. Just before serving toss with dressing, bacon, croutons and Parmesan cheese.

8 servings

Mrs. William G. Hanson

SIMPLY SCRUMPTIOUS SPINACH SALAD

1 clove garlic
½ tsp. lemon rind, grated
½ tsp. salt
¼ tsp. paprika
¼ tsp. pepper
2 T. tarragon vinegar
½ cup olive oil
2 T. sour cream
raw spinach
onion rings
raw mushrooms, sliced in "umbrellas"
tomato wedges
croutons
½ lb. bacon; cooked, drained and crumbled
2 hard-cooked eggs, grated

Combine first six ingredients in a blender and turn on and off. Add oil gradually, spinning continuously. Add sour cream. Chill. Toss with rest of ingredients just before serving.

6 servings MRS. WALTER R. KIRKHAM

Salad prepared ahead of time will stay crisp when the dressing is first in the bowl. Fill the bottom of the bowl with tomato wedges to marinate in the dressing and to lift the leafy greens above the dressing level.

Tabbouleh
(Mint and Parsley Salad)

1 cup finely cracked wheat
1½ cups parsley, chopped (2 or 3 bunches)
½ cup mint leaves, minced
3 tomatoes, peeled and chopped
1 green pepper, chopped
1 cucumber, peeled and chopped (optional)
2 to 3 green onions, chopped
¾ cup olive oil
1 cup fresh lemon juice
salt and pepper

Soften cracked wheat by soaking one hour in cold water. Drain well, pressing out excess water. Toss with rest of ingredients. It is a lot of work to chop all these vegetables, but worth it for an unusual salad. Serve in a bowl lined with lettuce or romaine leaves.

6 servings — Mrs. Joseph Nahra

Parsley stays fresh longer if you wash and refrigerate the damp sprigs in a covered jar.

OUT-OF-THE-WEST SALAD

1 head lettuce
2 cups red apples, chopped, unpeeled
1 cup mild Cheddar cheese, grated
2 T. green onions, sliced
½ cup mayonnaise
1 T. lemon juice
½ tsp. salt
½ cup cheese or garlic croutons

Tear lettuce into bowl. Add apples, cheese and onions. Combine mayonnaise, lemon juice and salt. Toss with lettuce mixture and croutons. Serve chilled.

5 to 6 servings JON E. DENNEY

CALIFORNIA SALAD VINAIGRETTE

2 T. vinegar
6 T. olive oil
1 tsp. salt and pepper to taste
1 tsp. dry mustard
1 cucumber, peeled and diced
1 red onion, diced
1 ripe avocado, diced
lettuce cups

Combine first five ingredients and toss with cucumber, onion and avocado. Chill for two or three hours. Serve in lettuce cups. This may also be served as an appetizer on crackers.

4 to 6 servings MRS. ROBERT F. ZIMMER

Cauliflower Slaw

1 head cauliflower
¼ cup green onions, minced
½ cup celery leaves, minced
1 cup sour cream
½ cup French dressing
2 T. caraway seeds
1 tsp. salt
lettuce cups
sliced tomatoes
chopped chives

Divide the raw cauliflower into flowerets and slice as thin as possible. Combine with next six ingredients. Mound on lettuce. Garnish with tomatoes and sprinkle chives on top.

8 servings — Mrs. Alvin Udelson

Cucumber Salad Supreme

4 huge cucumbers, peeled and thinly sliced
3 green onions, chopped
1 red onion, sliced in slivers
3 cups vinegar
1½ cups sugar
2¼ tsp. salt

Cover cucumbers and onions with vinegar, sugar and salt mixture and let stand in refrigerator two hours to two weeks. May also be served at room temperature.

12 servings — Mrs. David Zauder

Artichoke Salad

2 pkgs. frozen artichoke hearts
2 tomatoes, quartered
1 head lettuce, shredded
4 stalks celery, diced
1 large onion, thinly sliced
salt and pepper
3 T. olive oil (or more to taste)
6 T. lemon juice
1 tsp. oregano

Cook artichokes according to directions on package, cool and quarter. Add rest of vegetables and season. Toss with dressing made from oil, lemon juice and oregano. May be served chilled or at room temperature.

8 servings

Mrs. Stephen M. Gage

Marinated Artichokes and Mushrooms

1 pkg. frozen artichoke hearts
1 cup raw mushrooms, sliced
Italian dressing
cherry tomatoes, halved
lemon, thinly sliced

Cook artichoke hearts according to package directions; drain. Combine with mushrooms. Add dressing and marinate overnight in refrigerator. Add tomatoes. Garnish with lemon slices and serve.

4 servings

Miss Janet Beighle
The Plain Dealer

Ambrosia Salad

1 cup canned mandarin oranges, drained
1 cup canned crushed pineapple, drained
1 cup tiny marshmallows
1 cup flaked coconut
1 cup sour cream

Combine all ingredients in bowl and toss gently. Chill thoroughly and serve.

6 to 8 servings MRS. JOSEPH GIUNTA

Variation: substitute 3 cans fruit cocktail, drained, for oranges and pineapple.

MRS. DAVID M. SCHNEIDER

Grape Salad

1½ lbs. seedless green grapes
1 pint sour cream
fresh raspberries or mandarin oranges

Chill grapes overnight. Mix with sour cream. Cover with blanket of raspberries or oranges. Keep cool until served. If possible edge platter with grape leaves or some other sturdy dark leaf as decoration.

6 servings MISS DOROTHY FULDHEIM
News Analyst

MENU SUGGESTION

Cucumber-Radish Delights
Meat Loaf Surprise
Potato-Tomato Salad
Ambrosia
Wacky Cake

Hot Curried Fruit

1 large can diced pineapple
1 large can pears
1 large can peach halves
12 maraschino cherries
⅓ cup butter
½ cup brown sugar
1½ tsp. curry powder
⅛ tsp. salt
Juice of ½ lemon

Drain fruit thoroughly and reserve juices; pat dry with a towel. Place cut side down in a casserole; top with cherries. Melt butter and add ¼ cup reserved fruit juice, brown sugar, curry powder, salt and lemon juice. Dribble over fruit. Let stand in refrigerator, covered, overnight. Bake, uncovered, at 375° for forty-five to fifty minutes, or until hot and bubbly. Serve with meat course or chicken salad.

8 to 10 servings — Mrs. Irwin Benjamin

Cranberry Compote

1 quart cranberries
2 cups strawberry preserves
1 cup sugar

Put cranberries in water to cover. Bring to a boil and cook, covered, for five minutes. Add strawberries and sugar and cook five minutes longer. Serve cold.

Mrs. Bernard Adelstein

Poppy Seed Salad Dressing

1½ cups sugar
2 tsp. dry mustard
2 tsp. salt
⅔ cup vinegar
3 T. onion juice
2 cups salad oil
3 T. poppy seeds

Mix sugar, mustard, salt and vinegar. Add onion juice and stir well. Add oil very, very slowly, drop by drop, beating constantly at top speed of electric beater. Continue to beat until thick. Add poppy seeds. (If oil is not added slowly it will separate.) Refrigerated dressing will keep for two months. Use with fresh fruit only.

Mrs. Robert Gresham

Variation: substitute celery seeds for poppy seeds.

Mrs. Louis S. Peirce

Pennsylvania Dutch Pickled Eggs

1 pint jar pickled beets
¼ to ½ cup vinegar
1 onion, sliced
8 hard-cooked eggs

Combine beets, vinegar and onion in a bowl. Add peeled eggs and cover. Let stand overnight at least, they will keep for days. The longer they marinate, the better they taste.

8 servings Mrs. Bruce G. Rauch

Sweet and Sour Relish

1 – 16 oz. can sauerkraut, drained
1 – 16 oz. can bean sprouts, drained
2 onions, chopped
5 stalks celery, chopped
1 green pepper, chopped
2 cups sugar
¾ cup vinegar

Combine first five ingredients in bowl. Bring sugar and vinegar to a boil, then cool. Pour dressing over vegetables and refrigerate overnight.

10 to 12 servings Mrs. William Schreiner

Easy Corn Relish

2 pkgs. frozen corn and peas with tomatoes
⅓ cup vinegar
½ cup sliced celery
½ cup green pepper, chopped
2 T. sugar
½ tsp. mixed pickling spice

Combine ingredients and bring to a boil. Reduce heat and simmer, covered, eight minutes. Chill. Place spices in a cheesecloth bag for easy removal.

Mrs. John C. Doser

Bread on the Grill I

1 loaf French or Italian bread
½ cup butter, softened
1½ tsp. lemon juice
½ cup parsley, minced
1 tsp. chives, chopped
Parmesan cheese, grated

Slice bread, being careful not to cut through the bottom crust. Combine butter, lemon juice and herbs. Spread on both sides of bread slices. Sprinkle with cheese. Wrap carefully in aluminum foil and warm at the back of grill for twenty to thirty minutes, turning occasionally.

Bread on the Grill II

1 loaf French or Italian bread
1 cup butter, softened
1 clove garlic, minced
½ tsp. oregano
juice of 1 lemon
½ tsp. Worcestershire sauce
Parmesan cheese, grated

Proceed as above.

8 servings The Committee

MELBA TOAST FIESTA

1 loaf thin-sliced white bread
butter
sesame seeds
Parmesan cheese, grated
HERB BUTTER:
butter
basil
parsley
tarragon
marjoram

Take ⅔ of the loaf of bread and spread each slice with softened butter. Then top half with sesame seeds and half with Parmesan cheese. Make Herb Butter by combining herbs with butter in proportions to taste and spread on rest of bread slices. Toast in a slow oven for fifteen minutes, or until golden brown and crisp. Serve with cocktails, juice, soup or salad.

MISS JEAN KRIZMAN
Stouffer Foods Corporation

PARTY TOAST CRISPS

6 T. butter
3 cloves garlic
1 loaf thin-sliced white bread
Parmesan cheese

Melt butter; add garlic. Heat just until butter bubbles. Let stand for three hours, then discard garlic. Cut circles the size of melba toast rounds from frozen slices of bread, avoiding crusts. Brush rounds with butter and sprinkle generously with Parmesan cheese. Bake at 350° until crisp. Keeps indefinitely in a tightly covered container. May also be cut in various fancy shapes.

MRS. ELLWOOD M. FISHER

Casserole Dill Bread

1 cup creamed cottage cheese
¼ cup warm water
1 pkg. yeast
1 egg, at room temperature
2 T. sugar
2 tsp. dill seed
½ tsp. dill weed
1 T. instant minced onion
1 T. salad oil
1 tsp. salt
¼ tsp. baking soda
2¼ to 2½ cups flour
1 T. butter, softened
onion salt

Heat cottage cheese, stirring frequently, just until lukewarm. Sprinkle yeast over warm water in a large bowl, stirring until dissolved. Stir in cottage cheese, egg, sugar, dill seed, dill weed, onion, oil, salt and baking soda until well combined. Gradually stir in flour. Turn out on lightly floured board and knead about one minute. Return to bowl; cover with towel. Let rise in warm place, one hour, or until double in bulk. Punch down. Place in buttered two quart casserole. Let rise thirty minutes, or until doubled. Bake at 350° for forty to fifty minutes, or until nicely browned. Brush top with butter and sprinkle lightly with onion salt.

Mrs. Damaris D. Klaus

CRANBERRY BREAD

- 2 cups flour
- ½ tsp. salt
- 1½ tsp. baking powder
- 1 cup sugar
- ½ tsp. baking soda
- 1 egg, beaten
- 2 T. butter, melted
- ½ cup orange juice
- ½ cup nuts, finely chopped
- 1½ cups fresh cranberries
- 1 T. lemon rind, grated

Sift together dry ingredients. Stir in remaining ingredients. Pour into a buttered loaf pan and bake at 350° for one hour. Wrap in aluminum foil while lukewarm. Slice, butter and rewrap in foil to take on a picnic. Because the berries are left whole, it really is a picture when served.

MRS. DAVID FREEMAN CONLEY

WINTER PICNIC IN FRONT OF THE FIREPLACE

Spinach Soup

Hobo Stew

Cranberry Bread

Seven Layer Cookies

Orange Marmalade Bread

3 T. butter
1 cup sugar
2 eggs, lightly beaten
3½ cups flour
3 tsp. baking powder
½ tsp. salt
1 cup milk
2 cups orange marmalade
1 cup nuts, chopped

Cream butter and sugar. Add eggs. Add sifted dry ingredients and milk to the egg mixture. Add marmalade and nuts. Stir to blend. Bake in large buttered loaf pan at 350° for about one hour. This bread is moist, unusual in flavor, and keeps well.

Mrs. Horace W. Rich

MENU SUGGESTION

Blossom Consomme

Brandied Rock Cornish Game Hens

Peas Pizzicato

Orange Marmalade Bread

Chocolate Pecan Pie

LEMON NUT BREAD

½ cup shortening
1¼ cups sugar
2 eggs, lightly beaten
1¼ cups flour
1 tsp. baking powder
¼ tsp. salt
½ cup milk
½ cup walnuts, chopped
grated rind of 1 lemon
juice of 1 lemon

Cream shortening and one cup sugar. Add eggs. Sift together dry ingredients and add creamed mixture alternately with milk. Add nuts and lemon rind. Pour into buttered loaf pan and bake at 350° for one hour. Remove from oven and pierce loaf in several places with a small skewer. Combine ¼ cup sugar and lemon juice and pour over hot bread. Let cool on a wire rack; cut into thin slices. This loaf keeps well and is good served warm or cold.

MRS. ARTHUR D. BALDWIN II

Buttering a loaf or cake pan makes the cake taste buttery regardless of the shortening used to make the cake.

Swiss Birchermuesli
(Cereal with Fruit and Nuts)

1 – 18 oz. box quick cooking rolled oats
1 cup non-fat dried skim milk
½ cup brown sugar
1 cup dried apricots
1 cup raisins
1 cup whole nuts
1 cup wheat germ (optional)

Combine ingredients and keep in an airtight jar. Serve dry (for backpack and canoe trips), or let stand overnight in the refrigerator in milk and serve cold, or cook as you would oatmeal and serve warm. Wheat germ is optional because it does not keep well.

Mrs. Arthur Brooks

"The time to hear bird music is between four and six in the morning. Seven o'clock is not too late, but by eight the fine rapture is over, due, I suspect, to the contentment of the inner man that comes with breakfast; a poet should always be hungry or have a lost love."

Donald Culross Peattie

Suites

Friendship Tea

1 cup Tang
½ to 1 cup sugar
¼ to ½ cup instant tea
1 pkg. lemonade mix
½ tsp. cinnamon
¼ tsp. ground cloves

Mix ingredients well and store in a tightly covered jar. Add two teaspoons to a cup of boiling water for tea. Delicious iced in summer or hot in winter. Dressed up in a pretty container, this makes a nice gift for a friend with the sniffles.

Mrs. Luke P. Miller

Hot Fudge Sauce

1 T. butter
1 oz. unsweetened chocolate
⅓ cup boiling water
1 cup sugar
2 T. light corn syrup
½ tsp. vanilla
⅛ tsp. salt

In the top of a double boiler, combine butter and chocolate. Stir over low heat until melted. Add boiling water slowly, stirring constantly. Bring to a boil, add sugar and syrup. Stir until dissolved. Cook for five minutes, then add vanilla and salt. Serve hot over ice cream. The sauce will harden on the cold ice cream. If made ahead of time, add vanilla just before serving.

4 servings

Mrs. Morris Everett, Jr.

ORANGE CHARLOTTE

1½ T. unflavored gelatin
¼ cup cold water
½ cup boiling water
1 cup sugar
¼ cup lemon juice
1 cup orange juice
3 egg whites
1 cup heavy cream
dash of salt

Soften gelatin in cold water. Add boiling water, stir until dissolved. Add sugar, lemon juice and orange juice. Beat egg whites until stiff. Fold into mixture as it begins to set. Whip cream and salt until it holds a firm peak and fold into gelatin mixture. Pour into individual glasses. Chill. Paper cups can be used for a picnic. Garnish with a sugar flower ornament.

6 servings MRS. R. HENRY NORWEB, JR.

EASY RASPBERRY BAVARIAN

1 – 3 oz. pkg. wild raspberry flavored gelatin
¼ cup sugar
1 small carton Cool Whip
1 pkg. frozen raspberries, drained

Dissolve gelatin and sugar in one cup boiling water. Add one cup cold water. Chill until partially set. Blend in Cool Whip. Fold in raspberries. Pour into a mold and chill until ready to serve.

6 servings MRS. JAMES W. IRWIN

Lemon Mousse

1 cup heavy cream
1 envelope unflavored gelatin
2 T. water
⅓ cup lemon juice
4 eggs
1 cup sugar

Whip cream and refrigerate. In a sauce pan, soften gelatin in water. Heat slowly and stir until dissolved. Cool. Add lemon juice. Beat eggs and sugar together until thick and lemon colored. Beat in gelatin mixture. Fold in half of the cream, reserving the rest. Pour into glasses or serving dish and chill. Garnish with remaining whipped cream when set.

6 servings — Mrs. Anthony R. Michel

Rainbow Torte

1 cup flour, sifted
1 tsp. baking soda
1 cup sugar
½ tsp. salt
1 egg
2 cups fruit cocktail, drained (#303 can)
½ cup brown sugar
½ cup nuts
heavy cream

Combine dry ingredients. Add egg and fruit cocktail. Stir by hand. Pour into a buttered eight inch square pan. Sprinkle brown sugar and nuts on top. Bake at 325° for forty-five minutes. Serve topped with whipped cream.

8 servings — Mrs. Ellwood M. Fisher

Melt in your Mouth Blueberry Cake

½ cup margarine
1 cup sugar
¼ tsp. salt
1 tsp. vanilla
2 eggs, separated
1½ cups plus 1 T. flour
1 tsp. baking powder
⅓ cup milk
1½ cups fresh blueberries

Cream margarine and ¾ cup sugar. Add salt and vanilla. Add egg yolks, beat until creamy. Sift 1½ cups flour and baking powder; add alternately with milk to egg yolk mixture. Beat egg whites until stiff, adding remaining ¼ cup sugar. Coat berries with one tablespoon flour, add to batter. Fold in egg whites. Pour into a buttered eight inch square pan. Sprinkle with granulated sugar. Bake at 350° for fifty minutes.

6 to 8 servings Mrs. James E. Sampliner

MENU SUGGESTION

Go Anywhere Tomato Bouillon
Palm Beach Salad
Casserole Dill Bread
Melt in your Mouth Blueberry Cake

Carrot Cake

2 cups sugar
4 eggs
1½ cups salad oil
1 tsp. cinnamon
½ tsp. allspice
3 cups raw carrots, grated
1 tsp. vanilla
2 cups flour, sifted
2 tsp. baking soda
¾ tsp. salt
1 cup walnuts, chopped

Beat sugar, eggs and oil until light and fluffy. Add rest of ingredients in order given and stir. Pour into three eight inch or two nine inch, waxed paper lined pans and bake at 375° for thirty-five minutes. This cake is rich and moist and keeps well.

Frosting

1 – 8 oz. pkg. cream cheese, softened
1 box confectioners sugar
½ cup butter, softened
2 tsp. vanilla

Combine ingredients and spread on cooled cake.

The Committee

Katie's Kentucky Chocolate Cake

2 cups sugar
2 cups flour
½ cup butter or margarine
½ cup shortening
1 cup water
4 T. cocoa
½ cup buttermilk
1 tsp. baking soda
2 eggs
1 tsp. vanilla

Combine sugar and flour in a bowl. Melt butter, shortening, water, and cocoa and bring to a boil. Pour mixture over sugar and flour. Stir well. Add remaining ingredients, and stir until smooth. Pour into two greased and floured layer cake pans. Bake at 325° for twenty-five to thirty minutes. Cool thoroughly before frosting. This rich, fudgy cake is not for weight watchers!

Chocolate Frosting

½ cup butter
⅓ cup milk
4 T. cocoa
1 box confectioners sugar
1 tsp. vanilla
1 cup nuts, chopped

Melt butter, milk, and cocoa and bring to a boil. Add the remaining ingredients and stir well. Frost cake while frosting is still warm.

10 to 12 servings — Mrs. Mary Stevens

Lightning Chocolate Cake

1 egg
1 cup sugar
½ cup cocoa
1½ cups flour
½ cup sour milk
1 tsp. vanilla
1 tsp. baking soda
½ cup hot water
½ tsp. salt

Place all ingredients in a bowl in the order given. Do not mix until last ingredient is added, then beat well. Pour into a buttered eight inch square pan. Bake at 350° for twenty to twenty-five minutes. Cool and frost.

Butter Frosting

4 T. butter, softened
2½ cups confectioners sugar
1 egg, separated

Cream butter and sugar; add egg yolk. Beat egg white until stiff. Fold into sugar mixture. Spread on cooled cake.

8 servings — Mrs. H. William Ruf

WACKY CAKE

3 cups flour
6 T. cocoa (⅜ cup)
2 cups sugar
2 tsp. baking soda
1 tsp. salt
10 T. salad oil (⅝ cup)
2 T. vinegar
2 T. vanilla
2½ cups water
4 oz. unsweetened chocolate
½ cup butter
4 cups tiny marshmallows
3 to 3½ cups confectioners sugar
1 cup nuts
2 tsp. vanilla

Sift first five ingredients into a 9″ x 13″ cake pan. Mix next three ingredients together and add to pan. Pour 2 cups water into pan and stir until well blended. Bake at 350° for twenty-five to thirty minutes. To prepare frosting: combine chocolate, ½ cup water, butter and 2½ cups marshmallows. Stir over low heat until blended. Cool slightly. Add sugar gradually and beat with wooden spoon until smooth. Add remaining marshmallows, nuts and vanilla. Frost cake right in the pan.

LOU ANN WAIT

Southern Caramel Cake

1 cup butter
2 cups sugar
3 eggs
3 cups cake flour, sifted
2 tsp. baking powder
1 cup milk
1 tsp. vanilla

Cream butter and sugar, then stir in eggs, one at a time. Add flour, baking powder, milk and vanilla and beat well. Spoon into two greased and floured nine inch cake pans. Bake at 350° for thirty minutes.

Caramel Frosting

3 cups light brown sugar
1 cup light cream
½ cup butter

Boil all together until thick (226° on a candy thermometer). Remove from heat at once and beat constantly until cooled.

Mrs. Merrill B. Wilcox

Cream Cheese Cake

1¾ cups graham cracker crumbs
3 T. butter, melted
6 – 3 oz. pkgs. cream cheese
1 cup sugar
2 eggs
pinch of salt
2 cups sour cream
1 tsp. vanilla

Mix together graham cracker crumbs and melted butter. Spread crumb mixture on bottom and sides of a spring-form pan. Beat cream cheese, sugar, eggs and salt together until creamy. Fold in sour cream and vanilla. Pour over crumb crust. Bake at 350° for thirty minutes. Chill and serve. Top with canned cherry or blueberry pie filling if you wish.

8 to 10 servings — Mrs. Frank E. Joseph, Jr.

Dessert idea: half fill empty orange shells with gingerbread batter. Place in embers to bake.

Lemon Cheese Cake

- 1 cup gingersnap or Zwieback crumbs
- 2 T. butter, melted
- ¼ cup confectioners sugar
- 1 tsp. cinnamon (optional)
- 3 – 3 oz. pkgs. cream cheese, softened
- ¼ cup lemon juice
- 2 eggs, lightly beaten
- ¾ cup plus 1 T. sugar
- 1 T. lemon rind, grated
- 1 cup sour cream

Make a crumb crust by combining crumbs with butter, confectioners sugar and cinnamon. Press into an eight inch pie pan. Beat cream cheese and lemon juice together. Add eggs and ¾ cup sugar, and beat until fluffy. Pour into crust and bake at 350° for fifteen to twenty minutes. Let cool five minutes. Combine 1 T. sugar with lemon rind and sour cream and spread over the pie. Bake ten minutes longer. Cool and chill.

6 to 8 servings — Mrs. Michael Charry

To squeeze lemon juice easily, soak lemon in hot water before cutting in half, or roll firmly on the hard surface of kitchen counter.

Lemon Velvet Cupcakes

¾ cup cold water
1 pkg. lemon flavored gelatin
4 eggs
1 pkg. Lemon Velvet cake mix
¾ cup salad oil
2 cups confectioners sugar
juice of 2 lemons

Mix together water, gelatin, and eggs and beat well. Beat in cake mix. Add oil and beat again. Pour into prepared cupcake pans. Bake at 350° for fifteen to twenty minutes. Combine sugar and lemon juice. Pierce warm cupcakes with a fork and drizzle icing on top. Cupcakes are easy to pack for a picnic. This can also be baked in a buttered 9″ x 13″ cake pan at 350° for thirty-five minutes. Vary the flavors of gelatin and cake to make orange, cherry, strawberry, pineapple, etc., cupcakes.

Mrs. Earl P. Schneider

To keep cupcake icing from smearing in a picnic basket, cut off the cake tops, spread icing on the cut surface and replace the tops.

BOB HOPE'S FAVORITE LEMON PIE

1 cup plus 2 T. sugar
3 T. cornstarch
1 cup boiling water
4 egg yolks, lightly beaten
2 T. butter
4 T. lemon juice
grated rind of 1 lemon
pinch of salt
9 inch pie shell, baked
3 egg whites
2½ T. sugar

Combine sugar and cornstarch in the top of a double boiler. Add boiling water slowly, stirring constantly, and cook until thickened and smooth. Stir small amount of hot mixture into egg yolks. Add to cornstarch mixture with butter, lemon juice, rind and salt. Cook two or three minutes. Cool and pour into pie shell. Make a meringue by beating egg whites until frothy. Gradually add 2½ T. sugar and continue beating until stiff. Pile lightly on top of pie, completely covering filling. Bake at 275° for fifteen minutes, or until lightly browned.

8 servings

BOB HOPE

THE "I CAN'T MAKE A PIE CRUST" PIE CRUST

3 cups flour
½ tsp. salt
¾ T. sugar
½ tsp. baking soda
1 cup lard
1 egg
2 T. lemon juice
2 T. water

Combine dry ingredients. Cut in lard until pieces are the size of small peas. Beat egg with lemon juice and water. Add slowly to flour mixture. Don't overmix. Divide in half. Roll out crust. Bake in two nine inch pie pans at 450° for fifteen minutes. This recipe is foolproof and delicious. Try it even if you make a great pie crust.

MRS. R. BENNETT EPPES

MENU SUGGESTION

Shrimp Exotics
Picnic Barbecued Pork Roast
Potato and Hearts of Palm Salad
Bob Hope's Favorite Lemon Pie

Seventy-Second Street Crosstown Bus Apple Pie

1 cup dry biscuit mix
4 T. butter
3 T. boiling water
6 apples, cored and sliced
½ cup sugar
2 T. cinnamon
butter
sour cream

In a nine inch pie plate, mix first three ingredients with your fingers. Press evenly around bottom and sides. Fill with apples. Top with sugar and cinnamon. Dot with butter and sour cream. Bake at 425° for thirty minutes. Note that this easy recipe has no bowls to wash!

6 servings FRANK L. PETERSON, JR.

Swedish Apple Pie (A Crustless Pie)

¾ cup sugar
½ cup flour
2 tsp. baking powder
dash of salt
1 cup apples, chopped
1 cup nuts, chopped
1 egg, beaten

Mix together dry ingredients. Add apples, nuts and egg and stir. Spread into a pie plate. Bake at 375° for thirty to forty-five minutes. Test apples for doneness with a toothpick. Serve with whipped cream or ice cream.

6 servings MRS. C. HENRY FOLTZ

Papa Haydn's Surprise Pie

- 16 square saltine crackers, rolled fine
- 16 dates, minced
- ½ cup pecans, chopped
- 1 cup sugar
- ¼ tsp. baking powder
- 3 egg whites
- heavy cream

Combine saltine crumbs, dates, pecans and sugar. Beat egg whites with baking powder until stiff but not dry. Fold egg whites into the saltine mixture and pour into a buttered nine inch pie plate. Bake at 350° for thirty minutes. Refrigerate. When ready to serve, top with whipped cream. This pie freezes well.

8 servings — Mrs. Michael E. A. Ward

Chocolate Pecan Pie

- ⅔ cup butter, melted
- ⅔ cup sugar
- 1 cup light corn syrup
- 4 eggs, lightly beaten
- 1 tsp. vanilla
- 1 – 6 oz. pkg. chocolate chips
- 1 cup pecan pieces
- 9 inch unbaked pie shell

Mix together butter and sugar. Add syrup, then stir in eggs. Add vanilla, chocolate, and pecans. Pour into pie shell. Bake at 375° for fifty to sixty minutes.

6 to 8 servings — Mrs. Stephen M. Gage

Bach's Lunch

Pflaumen Kuchen

- ½ cup butter or margarine
- ½ cup sugar
- 1 egg
- 1½ cups flour
- 1½ lbs. fresh Italian plums (purple)
- ½ cup sugar
- heavy cream

Combine first four ingredients, chill and roll out between layers of waxed paper. Line a buttered nine inch pie pan with the crust. Pit plums and cut into six wedges joined at the bottom. Begin at the outside edge and arrange fruit around the pie crust until filled. Bake at 325° for about one hour until crust is brown. Sprinkle hot pie with sugar to taste. Serve hot or cool, garnished with whipped cream. This kuchen can also be made with chopped nuts and cinnamon added to the sugar topping. When plums are out of season other fresh or canned fruits may be substituted.

6 to 8 servings Mrs. Forest P. Reichert

MENU SUGGESTION

Anchovy Stuffed Mushrooms
Beer Barbecued Ribs
Three Bean Salad
Hot Potato Salad
Pflaumen Kuchen

LEMON SQUARES

½ cup butter
¼ cup confectioners sugar
1 cup flour
2 eggs, well beaten
1 cup sugar
¼ tsp. salt
3 T. fresh lemon juice
½ tsp. baking powder
2 T. flour

Cream butter and confectioners sugar. Add flour. Press into an ungreased nine inch square pan. Bake at 350° for ten minutes. Remove from oven. Meanwhile, prepare topping by combining remaining ingredients. Pour over crust and bake thirty minutes longer. Dust with confectioners sugar and cut into sixteen squares.

Yield: 16 squares MRS. EARL P. SCHNEIDER

EASY SEVEN LAYER COOKIES

½ cup butter
1 cup graham cracker crumbs
1 – 3½ oz. can flaked coconut
1 – 6 oz. pkg. chocolate chips
1 – 6 oz. pkg. butterscotch bits (optional)
1 can condensed milk
1 cup nuts, chopped (may even use peanuts)

Melt butter in a 9″ x 13″ pan. Sprinkle with crumbs, followed by coconut, chocolate and butterscotch bits. Pour milk over all and sprinkle with nuts. Bake at 350° for thirty minutes. Cool and cut into one inch squares. Fun for children to make.

MISS CHRISTEN MILLER

Lace Cookies

½ cup flour
½ cup sugar
¼ T. baking powder
½ cup quick cooking rolled oats
2 T. cream
2 T. light corn syrup
⅓ cup sweet butter, melted
1 tsp. vanilla

Sift together flour, sugar, and baking powder. Add the remaining ingredients and mix well. Using one-quarter of a teaspoon as a measure, drop dough four inches apart on an oiled or Teflon coated cookie sheet. Bake at 375° for six to eight minutes.

Yield: 30 — Mrs. Richard Blum

MENU SUGGESTION

Jellied Mushroom Soup

Cassoulet

Celery au Vin, Fines Herbes

Lemon Mousse

Mom's Mincemeat Cookies

1 cup shortening
1½ cups sugar
3 eggs
3½ cups flour, sifted
½ tsp. salt
1 tsp. soda dissolved in 1 T. hot water
1 pkg. mincemeat
½ cup raisins
1 cup walnuts, chopped

Cream the shortening and sugar. Add eggs, one at a time, beating well after each addition. Add dry ingredients and soda. Crumble mincemeat and add with raisins and nuts. Mix well. Drop mixture by teaspoonsful onto a greased cookie sheet. Bake at 350° for eight minutes.

Yield: 60

Mrs. Jon H. Outcalt

Ideas for Grilled Dessert Kebobs

Skewer several kinds of fruits and dip in a mixture of orange juice and honey. Grill, turning frequently until bubbly. Choose from: pineapple cubes, banana slices, maraschino cherries, pitted cooked prunes, canned apricot halves, candied ginger, orange slices.

Skewer cubes of angel food cake, roll in melted raspberry jam and shredded coconut. Toast over hot coals, turning frequently.

The Committee

Baked Fudge

½ cup margarine
3 oz. unsweetened chocolate
2 cups sugar
3 eggs
1 tsp. vanilla
1½ cups flour, sifted
⅛ tsp. salt
1 cup nuts, chopped

Melt margarine and chocolate together, gradually beat in sugar. Add eggs, one at a time, beating well after each addition. Add vanilla. Sift flour with salt, add to chocolate mixture along with the nuts. Spread in a buttered eight or nine inch square pan. Bake at 350° for thirty minutes. Cool and cut in one inch squares.

Yield: 36 Mrs. Damaris D. Klaus

Sugar Brownies

2 cups graham cracker crumbs (⅓ lb.)
1 can condensed milk
1 – 6 oz. pkg. chocolate chips
sugar

Combine crumbs and milk and stir well. Add chocolate chips. Pour into buttered nine inch square pan. Bake at 350° for fifteen to twenty minutes or until lightly browned on top. Remove from oven, sprinkle with granulated sugar, and cut into squares.

Yield: 16 squares Mrs. John P. Schneider

Brownies "For Thin People Only"

4 eggs
2 cups sugar
1 cup butter
4 oz. unsweetened chocolate
1 cup flour, sifted
1 – 6 oz. pkg. chocolate chips

Beat eggs and sugar together until thick and light. Melt butter and baking chocolate together; add to egg mixture. Mix in flour. Add chocolate chips. Pour into a greased and floured 7″x11″ pan. Bake at 350° for twenty to thirty minutes.

Yield: 24

Mrs. Stephen M. Gage

Peanut Marble Brownies

½ cup peanut butter
4 T. butter or margarine
¾ cup sugar
3 eggs
6 T. flour
1 – 15½ oz. pkg. brownie mix

With electric mixer cream peanut butter with butter and sugar until fluffy. Add two eggs, one at a time, beating well. Add flour and beat at low speed just until blended. Prepare brownie mix with one egg and water as directed on package. Spread one-half of brownie batter in greased and floured eight inch square pan. Spread peanut butter batter evenly on top. Spoon on remaining brownie batter. For marbled effect cut through batters with a spatula. Bake at 350° for forty to forty-five minutes. Cool completely in pan. Cut into squares and wrap in foil.

Mrs. Daniel Ford

PEANUT BUTTER BARS

½ cup butter
½ cup sugar
½ cup brown sugar
1 egg
⅓ cup peanut butter
½ tsp. baking soda
¼ tsp. salt
½ tsp. vanilla
1 cup flour
1 cup rolled oats
1 - 6 oz. pkg. chocolate chips
½ cup confectioners sugar
¼ cup peanut butter
2 to 4 T. milk

Mix together first ten ingredients and spread in pan. Bake at 350° for twenty to twenty-five minutes until lightly browned. Immediately sprinkle chocolate chips on top, allow to melt, and spread evenly over top. Mix last three ingredients and drizzle over chocolate. Cool and cut into small bars.

MRS. BERNARD MARGOLIS

Index

A

B

C

D

E

F

G

H

I

J

K

L

M

N

O

P

Q

R

S

T

U

V

W

REED THOMASON

Bach for More

Fireside Classics

Book Two

Bach for More

Fireside Classics

"A Fire is a delightful thing –
a companion and an inspiration."

Published By
THE JUNIOR COMMITTEE
of
THE CLEVELAND ORCHESTRA
Severance Hall
Cleveland, Ohio 44106

Bach for More

First Printing - 20,000 copies - December, 1975

Second Printing - 20,000 copies - June, 1977

Third Printing - 10,000 copies - June, 1982

Table of Contents

Preludes

Intermezzos

Main Themes

Accompaniments

Suites

BACH FOR MORE – The second of the Bach Series Cookbooks, published for the benefit of The Cleveland Orchestra, could not have been produced without the help and kindness of hundreds of men and women who were willing to share their favorite recipes with us … and you. We are most grateful to all our contributors, and we regret that space does not permit us to present all of the fine recipes we received. To standardize measurements and procedures, editorial adjustments have been made – we trust these will meet with the approval of the contributors.

We sincerely hope that this book will bring great pleasure to you and your guests – apres-ski, apres-paddle, apres-theater or concert, apres-anything!

Bon Appetit!

Chairman: **Mrs. David F. Conley**

Co-Editors: **Mrs. Stuart M. Neye**
Mrs. Damaris D. Klaus

Special thanks to the entire Cookbook Committee and to the Chairmen, who gave an extra measure of time and talent:

Mrs. Louis Bloomfield	*Testing Chairman*
Mrs. William Blunden	*Collection Chairman*
Mrs. Geofrey J. Greenleaf	*Benefit Chairman*
Mrs. Dennis LaBarre	*Testing Chairman*
Mrs. Jonathan Opas	*Publicity Chairman*
Mrs. Stewart Rice	*Sales Chairman*

Mrs. Henry G. Brownell	*Mrs. Alf Jordan*
Mrs. Thomas F. Byrne	*Mrs. William Macon*
Mrs. John E. Culver	*Mrs. Anthony R. Michel*
Mrs. R. Bennett Eppes	*Mrs. Bruce Rauch*
Mrs. Richard Gridley	*Mrs. William H. West*
Mrs. Theodore A. Gullia, Jr.	

*All recipes submitted to **BACH FOR MORE** have been tested, reviewed and edited by the Committee.*

For your enjoyment, we have included wine suggestions where appropriate. We are most grateful to Pat O'Brien for sharing his experience in providing the selections.

Preludes

Cold Weather Tea

40 cups water
4 tsp. whole allspice
1 tsp. whole cloves
2 sticks cinnamon
¾ cup tea leaves (or 36 tea bags)
6 cups of sugar
2 cups of orange juice
1½ cups concentrated lemon juice
2½ cups pineapple juice
rum (optional)

Heat 10 cups water with spices to boiling; remove from heat; add tea leaves, and steep for ten minutes. Combine with remaining ingredients. Serve very hot. Rum may be added to each cup of tea. Freeze in quart containers to use as desired.

50 servings — Mrs. James Houston

Frozen Planter's Punch

1 can frozen Mai Tai Punch, or 6 pkgs. dry Mai Tai mix (mix as directed)
6 oz. rum
4 oz. port
2 oz. brandy

Place all ingredients in blender. Turn on and off. Add one tray of crushed ice. Spin at high speed for two minutes. Serve at a farewell party for your lucky southbound friends!

6 servings — Mrs. Z. K. Kara

Toe Toaster

1 oz. bitters
¾ cup sugar
2 cups claret
2 cups dry sherry
1 cup brandy

Combine ingredients. Serve hot, garnished with several raisins and almonds.

4 to 6 servings — Mrs. Ronald Neuger

Brita's Glogg

8 cups burgundy
1 bottle port
1¾ cups sugar
8 sticks cinnamon
dash cinnamon and nutmeg
15 whole cardamom
15 whole cloves
½ cup raisins
½ cup almonds
2 cups vodka

Combine wines, sugar, spices and raisins and simmer two hours. Strain and refrigerate overnight. Reheat slowly. Add almonds and vodka and serve very hot, garnished with a few almonds and a cinnamon stick.

16 servings — Mrs. Richard Ruhlman

Red Flannel Grog

4 cups apple cider
2 sticks cinnamon, broken
6 whole cloves
2 whole nutmegs
1 cup light rum

Heat first four ingredients until just boiling. Remove from stove, add rum and let sit for a minute. Pour into mugs through a strainer to catch spices. (They may be reused.) Using 151-proof rum will guarantee you'll never notice that it's ten above at the stadium and the Browns are losing!

6 servings *Anne Coleman*

Hot Spicy Cider

8 cups apple cider
3 sticks cinnamon
2 tsp. whole cloves
1 whole nutmeg
1 cup sugar
2 cups orange juice
½ cup lemon juice
½ cup apple brandy (optional)
dash Grand Marnier (optional)

Simmer cider, spices and sugar together fifteen minutes. Add juices and brandy and serve.

6 servings Mrs. T. K. Zung

HICKORY DICKORY DIP

½ cup mayonnaise
½ cup sour cream
1 clove garlic, crushed
2 T. onion, minced
½ tsp. hickory-smoked salt
⅓ lb. (or more) Cheddar cheese, grated
¼ lb. Swiss cheese, grated
¼ cup beer (optional)

Blend ingredients and refrigerate. Return to room temperature before serving. Good as a vegetable dip (use broccoli, carrots, cauliflower, celery, cucumber, green pepper or zucchini which have been crisped in cold water) or with unpeeled apple slices.

MRS. WILLIAM A. BLUNDEN

SHRIMP SALAD SPREAD

2 envelopes unflavored gelatin
1 can tomato soup
1 – 8 oz. pkg. cream cheese
1 lb. small shrimp, cooked
1 cup mayonnaise
1 large onion, chopped
2 stalks celery, chopped
salt and pepper to taste

Soften gelatin in ½ cup cold water. Heat soup, add cream cheese and gelatin; stir until dissolved. Cool. Combine with remaining ingredients and chill. Serve with crackers.

MRS. RALPH J. PERK

Variation: substitute 1 can tuna fish for shrimp.

DEENA MIROW

Chipped Beef Spread

1 – 8 oz. pkg. cream cheese
2 T. milk
2 T. green pepper, grated
2 T. onion, grated
1 – 3 oz. pkg. dried chipped beef, shredded
½ cup sour cream
½ cup walnuts, chopped

Combine cream cheese and milk over low heat. Add the next four ingredients and mix well. Place in a small greased casserole. Top with walnuts and bake at 350° for fifteen minutes. Serve hot with crackers. Leftovers can be served cold.

Mrs. Malcolm B. Vilas III

Bama Pepper Jelly

4 to 6 green peppers, seeded and ground (1 cup)
2 or 3 hot peppers, ground (¼ cup)
1½ cups cider vinegar
6½ cups sugar
1 – 6 oz. bottle liquid pectin

Combine peppers, vinegar and sugar; bring to a rolling boil. Remove from heat and let stand twenty minutes. Reheat and boil for three minutes, stirring constantly. Remove from stove, add pectin and stir five minutes. Pack in hot sterile jars and seal. Serve over a block of cream cheese as an appetizer or serve as a meat accompaniment. Use red and green peppers to make a colorful hostess gift for Christmas.

Yield: 4 pints

Mrs. William C. Judd

Egg Chutney Madras

4 hard-cooked eggs
1 – 3 oz. pkg. cream cheese
1 T. Worcestershire sauce
1 tsp. curry powder
dash cayenne pepper
3 drops hot pepper sauce
2 T. mayonnaise
4 T. chutney, chopped
salt and pepper to taste

Mash eggs and cheese; add remaining ingredients. Chill. Serve as a dip, garnished with chopped hard-cooked egg.

Mrs. Richard T. Brownrigg

Egg Mousse

5 hard-cooked eggs
1 can consomme, chilled
1 tsp. Worcestershire sauce
1 tsp. catsup or anchovy paste
salt and pepper
½ cup heavy cream, whipped

Spin eggs in blender with jellied consomme. Add Worcestershire, catsup and salt and pepper to taste; blend until smooth. Fold cream into egg mixture. Chill in an oiled mold for four hours or longer. Unmold and garnish with chopped jellied consomme, sliced cucumber or caviar.

Mrs. John Maley

Snowbunny

2 cups rye cracker crumbs
¼ cup butter, melted
2 cups sour cream
1 cup sharp Cheddar cheese, grated
½ cup green olives, chopped
¼ cup onions, minced
¼ cup chives, chopped
salt, coarsely ground pepper, celery seed and dry mustard to taste

Blend together cracker crumbs and butter. Line the bottom of a small springform pan with half of the crumb mixture. Combine remaining ingredients and spread on crust. Sprinkle with remaining crumbs and garnish with chopped hard-cooked eggs, parsley and paprika. Refrigerate for several hours. Unmold and serve with crackers or cocktail rye bread.

Mrs. Stuart Neye

Roquefort Cheese Ball

1 clove garlic
3 - 3 oz. pkgs. cream cheese, softened
1 to 2 oz. Roquefort cheese, softened
olive oil
1 T. scallions, chopped
salt and pepper
1 bunch fresh parsley, minced

Rub a bowl lightly with garlic. Add cheeses and blend with a little olive oil until smooth. Add scallions and season to taste. Form into one large ball or several small balls and roll in parsley.

Mrs. Homer Conley

Hot Mushroom Hors D'oeuvres

1 large onion, minced
½ cup plus 1 tsp. butter, melted
¾ lb. fresh mushrooms, minced
1½ – 8 oz. pkgs. cream cheese, softened
½ tsp. Worcestershire sauce
¼ tsp. garlic powder
MSG, salt and pepper
1 loaf thin-sliced white bread

Sauté onion in 1 tsp. butter until golden. Add mushrooms and cook about two minutes; remove from heat. Add cheese, Worcestershire, garlic, MSG and season to taste. Let stand. Remove crusts from bread; spread thickly with mushroom mixture. Cut each slice into four triangles; brush with melted butter. Place on a cookie sheet and bake at 400° or broil until puffy and brown. Serve hot.

Yield: 64

Mrs. Lisa Angle

Caesar's Palace Stuffed Mushrooms

1 lb. large mushrooms
4 T. butter
1 T. lemon juice
½ tsp. seasoned salt
1 T. onion grated
4 T. parsley, minced
2 T. mayonnaise
½ cup almonds, toasted and chopped

Remove stems from mushrooms. Sauté caps lightly in 2 T. butter and lemon juice; drain. Chop stems; sauté in remaining butter; cool and combine with onion, parsley, mayonnaise and almonds. Fill caps and chill.

Yield: 24

Caesar's Palace

SWEDISH MEATBALLS

3 T. onion, minced
5 T. butter or margarine
2 eggs, lightly beaten
½ cup milk
1½ cups water
½ cup bread crumbs
1½ lbs. ground beef
½ lb. ground pork
¼ tsp. allspice
dash cloves
3 T. flour
1 cup light cream
seasoned salt and pepper
dash vermouth
dash Worcestershire sauce

In a large skillet, sauté onion in 1 T. butter until golden. Combine eggs, milk, ½ cup water and crumbs. Add onion, beef, pork, allspice and cloves and season to taste; mix lightly with a fork. Shape into about eighty meatballs. Add 2 T. butter to the skillet; sauté meatballs, a few at a time, until browned on all sides. Add more butter as needed. Remove meatballs as they are browned. To make sauce, pour off all but 2 T. drippings; add flour, stir until smooth; gradually stir in cream, 1 cup water and remaining seasonings. Add meatballs. Heat gently five to ten minutes and serve hot. These may also be shaped into larger meatballs and served as a main course.

Yield: 80 MRS. C. HENRY FOLTZ

Sammy's No Show Ribs

- 1 cup soy sauce
- 1 cup brown sugar
- ½ to 1 T. cinnamon
- 1 clove garlic, minced
- 2 oz. gin
- freshly ground pepper
- 1 rack spareribs

Combine barbecue sauce ingredients, and marinate spareribs in refrigerator for twenty-four hours. Broil over charcoal until tender.

Mrs. John R. Wilson

Avocado Allegretto

- 4 avocados
- 6 T. margarine
- 2½ T. water
- 6 T. catsup
- 2½ T. vinegar
- 2½ tsp. Worcestershire sauce
- dash hot pepper sauce
- 4 tsp. sugar
- ½ tsp. salt

Cut avocados in half; do not peel. Combine rest of ingredients in order given and simmer five minutes. Keep warm. Serve as an appetizer with the hot sauce spooned into the center of the avocado.

8 servings

Damaris D. Klaus

Intermezzos

THE NON-COOK'S GOURMET SOUP

- 1 large can V-8 juice
- ½ lb. bacon, cooked and chopped
- 6 T. Parmesan cheese, freshly grated

Heat juice; do not boil. Place bacon in bottom of each soup bowl and pour in juice. Top with cheese and serve.

6 servings MRS. SEMON E. KNUDSON

CHEDDAR CHEESE SOUP

- 4½ cups milk
- 2½ cups chicken stock
- 1 - 12 oz. can beer
- ½ cup butter or margarine
- ¾ cup flour
- ½ tsp. dry mustard
- cayenne pepper to taste
- ½ lb. sharp Cheddar cheese, grated
- 1 large carrot, minced
- 1 green pepper, minced
- 1 stalk celery, minced
- ½ onion, minced

Combine milk, stock and beer in a heavy kettle; heat. Make a roux of butter, flour, mustard and cayenne, and stir gradually. Add cheese. Sauté carrot, pepper, celery and onion until soft. Add to soup, heat and serve.

Yield: 5 quarts MRS. BRUCE W. ELLIOTT

Soupe A L'oignon Gratinee

5 large onions, thinly sliced
3 T. butter
3 T. flour
4 cups beef consommé or stock
2 cups chicken stock
½ cup dry sherry
1 T. sauce Diable
1½ tsp. Worcestershire sauce
⅛ tsp. pepper
1 bay leaf
¼ cup butter, softened
8 slices French bread (½-inch thick)
1 lb. Parmesan cheese, freshly grated
8 slices Gruyère or Swiss cheese

Sauté onions in butter until lightly browned and tender. Sprinkle flour over onions, stirring to combine. Slowly add next seven ingredients. Cover and simmer twenty minutes. Lightly butter both sides of bread; sprinkle with some Parmesan cheese. Broil until lightly browned on each side. Pour soup into individual crocks; sprinkle with 1 T. Parmesan cheese, add toasted bread, sprinkle with remaining cheese. Top with a slice of Gruyère and bake at 400° for twenty-five minutes.

8 servings — Mrs. Donald Strang, Jr.

Fresh Cream of Mushroom Soup

1 lb. fresh mushrooms, minced
½ cup margarine
½ cup butter
⅓ cup plus 4 T. flour
2 tsp. salt
3 cups milk
2 cups light cream

Simmer mushrooms in margarine for fifteen minutes. Combine butter, ⅓ cup flour and salt; heat. Slowly add milk and cream, stirring constantly, until slightly thickened and smooth; cook for five minutes. Sprinkle 4 T. flour over mushrooms in pan and stir. Add cream mixture. Cook until thickened, stirring constantly. Pour into top of double boiler. Simmer, covered, for one-half hour, stirring occasionally. Add more milk to reach desired consistency, if necessary.

8 servings — Mrs. David H. Cockley

Spinach Soup Aladdin

Sauté 1 onion in butter, add 2 or 3 T. flour. Add 2½ cups hot chicken stock, stir until thickened. Add 1 pkg. frozen spinach, simmer until tender. Spin in blender and cool. Add 1 cup yogurt and season with salt, pepper and nutmeg. Serve cold, garnished with lemon wedges.

4 servings — Dr. and Mrs. John R. Boatright

Swiss Potato Soup

12 slices bacon, coarsely chopped
1 onion, coarsely chopped
2 leeks (or 4 scallions), coarsely chopped
1 lb. cabbage, coarsely chopped
4 potatoes, peeled and diced
6 cups chicken stock
2 cups Gruyere cheese, grated
1 cup light cream
1 T. dill weed
salt and pepper

Sauté bacon in a large kettle for three minutes. Add onion, leeks and cabbage and continue to cook for five minutes. Add the potatoes and chicken stock; bring to a boil, lower heat and simmer uncovered for forty minutes. Pour into blender, a little at a time, and spin until smooth. Pour back into kettle. Add cheese gradually and stir over medium heat until melted. Do not boil. Just before serving, add cream, dill weed and season to taste. Serve with buttered croutons. This is a very hearty soup.

10 to 12 servings

Mrs. John Tucker
Mrs. William L. Frazier

Easy Potage

Cook 3 potatoes, 1 cucumber, 1 onion and 2 bunches watercress in 6 cups of seasoned chicken stock until soft. Spin in blender. Add 1 cup heavy cream. Serve either hot or cold.

6 servings

Mrs. David H. Warshawsky

Lentil Soup

1 – 1 lb. pkg. lentils
2 to 3 quarts beef stock
3 stalks celery, diced
3 large carrots, sliced
3 onions, chopped
marrow bones or beef bones, if possible
salt, white pepper and nutmeg to taste
2 or 3 frankfurters, sliced

Combine all ingredients except frankfurters and cook for two to two and one-half hours. Remove bones and correct seasonings. The soup should be thick. Just before serving, add frankfurters.

6 to 8 servings — Pauline Trigere

Curried Pea Soup

3 cups fresh peas, shelled (or frozen peas)
6 cups strong chicken stock
2½ T. curry powder
¾ cup heavy cream
3 egg yolks, beaten
salt to taste
green apples, sliced

Combine peas with chicken stock and curry. Puree in blender. Heat. Combine cream and egg yolks, add gradually to hot soup, stirring constantly; season. Immediately remove from heat. Chill. To serve, beat well with a fork. Garnish with apple slices. Can also be served hot.

8 servings — Mrs. Harvey Oppmann

HEARTY HAM-BONE SOUP

Simmer a meaty ham bone with 2 lbs. marrow beans in 4 quarts water for two and one-half hours. Cut up 5 stalks celery, 1 potato, 8 carrots, 1 green pepper and 2 onions; add to soup with 1 can tomatoes, oregano and salt and pepper to taste. Simmer forty minutes longer. Remove meat from bone, add to soup and serve.

20 servings MRS. GERALD KUSS

JANIE'S CHILI SOUP

- 2 lbs. ground beef
- 1 large onion, chopped
- 3 to 4 stalks celery, chopped
- ¾ lb. fresh mushrooms, chopped and sautéed
- ½ green pepper, chopped
- 2 – 1 lb. cans tomatoes
- 1 – 15½ oz. can kidney beans, undrained
- 1 large bay leaf
- 1 to 2 T. chili powder
- 2 tsp. salt
- dash cayenne pepper and paprika
- 1 cup macaroni, cooked (optional)

Sauté beef until browned, drain; add onion, celery, mushrooms and pepper; cook until almost tender. Add tomatoes, kidney beans and seasonings; cover and simmer slowly for two hours. If soup gets too thick, add a little water. Remove bay leaf. Macaroni can be added to make a more hearty meal.

6 to 8 servings MRS. THOMAS B. JOHNSON

Snowy Night's Soup

3 onions, chopped
2 T. butter
1 lb. ground beef
1 clove garlic, minced
3 cups beef stock
2 – 28 oz. cans tomatoes
1 cup potatoes, diced
1 cup celery, diced
1 cup green beans, diced
1 cup carrots, diced
1 cup dry red wine
2 T. parsley, chopped
½ tsp. basil
¼ tsp. thyme
salt and pepper to taste

In a large kettle, sauté onions in butter until tender. Stir in beef and garlic and sauté until browned. Add remaining ingredients. Bring to a boil, reduce heat and simmer at least one hour.

6 to 8 servings

Mrs. David F. Clossey

MENU SUGGESTION

Toe Toaster

Snowy Night's Soup

Red, White and Green Holiday Mold

Herbed French Bread

Fudgie Brownies

Chimney Pot Soup

¼ lb. lean salt pork, diced
1 clove garlic, minced
1½ cups tomato juice
1 can condensed black bean soup
1 – 15 oz. can kidney beans, undrained
1 cup carrots, diced
1 cup celery, diced
1 cup cabbage, shredded
1 cup scallions, chopped
6 beef bouillon cubes
1 tsp. basil
1 tsp. MSG
salt and freshly ground pepper
¾ cup spaghetti, broken in 1-inch pieces
¾ lb. Kielbasa sausage
½ to ¾ lb. smoked cocktail sausages

Sauté salt pork with garlic until brown and crisp; drain. Combine with tomato juice, bean soup, vegetables, bouillon cubes, seasonings and 8 cups hot water in a large soup kettle. Bring to a boil and simmer for one hour. Add spaghetti and sausages. Simmer for an additional thirty minutes.

8 servings — John E. Culver

CRAB ROLLS EPICUREAN

- 1 lb. crab meat, drained
- 1 – 8 oz. pkg. cream cheese
- 1 tsp. onion, minced
- 1 tsp. horseradish
- ½ tsp. curry powder
- 2 tsp. lemon juice
- 2 tsp. prepared mustard
- ½ tsp. salt
- ½ cup mayonnaise
- ¼ cup dry white wine
- 6 brioche or French rolls
- ½ cup sliced almonds, toasted
- ½ cup Gruyere cheese, grated (optional)

Mix together first ten ingredients. Remove the top third from roll and hollow out inside. Spoon mixture into shells. Sprinkle with almonds and cheese and bake at 325° for twenty minutes. Place tops on rolls and bake another five minutes.

6 servings MRS. CHARLES SUMMERFIELD

CRAB HOLLANDAISE SANDWICH

- 1 pkg. frozen asparagus spears, cooked
- ¾ lb. crab meat, heated
- 4 English muffins toasted, or toast

Arrange asparagus, then crab meat on muffin. Top with hollandaise sauce (p. 104). bake at 375° until bubbly.

4 servings MRS. DARRELL A. BRAND

Barbecued Beef

5 to 7 lbs. pot roast of beef, cooked
2 – 14 oz. bottles hot catsup
3 – 8 oz. cans tomato sauce
2 T. Worcestershire sauce
2 tsp. hot pepper sauce
1 cup onion, chopped
1 cup green pepper, chopped
1 cup celery, chopped
salt to taste
24 hamburger buns

Shred meat and combine with remaining ingredients. Bake, covered, at 350° for one hour. Fill buns and serve hot.

24 servings

Mrs. Harry Carlson

Mushroom Lovers' Delight

6 slices Italian bread, ¾-inch thick
1 T. butter or margarine, softened
⅞ cup Romano cheese, freshly grated
6 large slices tomato
10 large mushrooms, sliced
seasoned salt and freshly ground pepper
1 cup mayonnaise
2 T. lemon juice
2 T. chives, chopped

Butter bread, toast lightly on one side. Turn, sprinkle with 2 T. cheese; toast. Top with tomato and mushrooms and season. Combine mayonnaise, lemon juice, chives and remaining cheese; spread over mushrooms, covering bread. Broil until top is bubbly.

3 to 6 servings

Irving Nathanson
The Cleveland Orchestra

Hot Browns

½ cup butter
½ cup flour
3 cups milk
1 tsp. salt
2 egg yolks
3 cups cooked chicken or turkey, sliced
6 English muffins, toasted, or toast
½ cup Cheddar cheese, grated
6 slices tomato
6 T. butter
2 T. brown sugar
6 slices bacon, cooked
½ cup mushrooms, sautéed

Prepare cream sauce: melt butter, stir in flour, add milk gradually, season and stir over low heat until smooth. Remove from heat and stir a little of the sauce into unbeaten egg yolks, then combine with rest of sauce and cook, stirring constantly, until thickened. Arrange chicken or turkey on split muffins on a cookie sheet. Spread sauce over chicken, top with grated cheese, arrange a slice of tomato on each, dot with butter and sprinkle with brown sugar. This can be done ahead and refrigerated. Just before serving, broil for about three or four minutes, until lightly browned. Garnish with a strip of bacon and some mushrooms. This recipe originated at the Brown Hotel in Louisville.

6 servings

Mrs. James A. Scott

Meeting Night Special

- 2 T. butter
- 8 thin slices Canadian bacon
- 4 shallots, chopped
- 1 cup Madeira
- 2 English muffins

Melt 1 T. butter and sauté bacon for two or three minutes until lightly browned. Add shallots and cook one more minute. Turn up heat and pour in wine. Let mixture boil fiercely until liquid is reduced by half. Add remaining butter and swirl in the pan. Serve over English muffins or toast, garnished with parsley.

2 servings — Miss Kate Ireland

Famous Sauced Stack-ups

- 3 English muffins, split and toasted
- 6 slices Canadian bacon, ham or turkey
- 1 cup Swiss cheese, grated
- 1 pkg. frozen asparagus spears, cooked
- 1 – 1 oz. pkg. Durkee White Sauce Mix
- 1 T. Durkee Famous Sauce
- ½ tsp. Worcestershire sauce

Place split English muffins on a baking sheet. Top each with a slice of meat, some cheese, four or five asparagus spears, and more cheese. Bake at 425° for fifteen minutes. Meanwhile, prepare medium white sauce according to package directions. Stir in Famous Sauce and Worcestershire sauce. Spoon warm sauce over baked sandwiches.

6 servings — Glidden-Durkee Company

Super Subs

3 cups lean cooked ham, chopped
2 – 3 oz. pkgs. cream cheese
2 tsp. onion, minced
1 T. Dijon mustard
6 sweet midget gherkins, chopped
1 tsp. horseradish
1 T. (rounded) capers
1 tsp. Worcestershire sauce
2 T. parsley, chopped
¼ to ½ tsp. tarragon
¼ cup margarine, softened
dash nutmeg
4 submarine sandwich rolls

Combine all ingredients, except rolls. Fill rolls and wrap in foil. Bake at 350° for ten minutes.

4 servings Frances M. H. Grundy

Helen's Harried Day Quickie

½ cup margarine
¼ cup onion, chopped
¼ cup prepared mustard
1 T. poppy seed
8 hamburger buns, split
½ lb. ham, shaved
¾ lb. Swiss cheese, shaved

Combine first four ingredients and spread on hamburger buns. Add ham and cheese. Wrap in foil and bake at 350° until cheese has melted.

8 servings Mrs. Nathan W. Oakes, Jr.

HAM ROLLS CONTINENTAL

- 6 slices boiled ham, ¼-inch thick
- 6 slices Swiss cheese
- 1 pkg. frozen broccoli spears, cooked
- 1 cup onion rings
- 2 T. margarine
- 2 T. flour
- salt and pepper to taste
- ¼ tsp. basil
- 1 cup milk

Top ham slices with cheese. Place a broccoli spear on each slice and roll. Secure with toothpicks. Arrange in a shallow baking dish. Cook onion rings in margarine until tender; blend in flour and seasonings. Gradually add milk, stir until thickened. Pour over ham. Cover and bake at 350° for twenty-five minutes.

6 servings MRS. JOSEPH NAHRA

SCALLOPED HAM 'N' CHEESE

Layer in thirds: 3 cups cubed French bread, 3 cups cubed ham, ½ lb. cubed Cheddar cheese, a mixture of 3 T. flour and 1 T. dry mustard, and finally 3 T. melted butter. Beat 4 eggs with 3 cups milk and a dash Tabasco and pour on top. Chill four hours; bake at 350° for one hour.

6 servings MRS. J. WILLIAM STANTON

Eleven O'Clock (A.M. or P.M.) Casserole

- 3 pkgs. frozen spinach
- 4 pkgs. Stouffer's frozen Welsh Rarebit
- 2 lbs. bacon, cooked and crumbled
- 2 cans water chestnuts, thinly sliced
- 1 can French fried onions

Partially cook spinach; drain. Thaw rarebit in top of double boiler. Place ⅓ of the rarebit in the bottom of an eight-inch square casserole. Add spinach, bacon and water chestnuts. Top with remaining rarebit. Sprinkle with French fried onions. Bake at 325° for twenty minutes. Serve with toasted English muffins and a platter of fresh fruit.

8 servings — Elizabeth Gullander

Fondue Neufchatel

- 1 clove garlic
- 2 cups white wine
- 3 T. flour
- 1 lb. natural Swiss cheese, grated
- 1 or 2 T. kirsch or vodka
- salt, pepper and nutmeg
- French or Italian bread, cubed

Rub fondue pot with garlic. Heat wine in top of double boiler; do not boil. Mix flour and cheese together and gradually add to wine, stirring constantly. Add kirsch and seasonings to taste. Serve in a fondue pot. Spear cubes of bread on a fondue fork and dip into hot melted cheese.

4 servings — Mrs. Forest P. Reichhert

Swiss Cheese Scramble

1¾ cups milk
2 cups soft bread cubes, crusts removed
8 eggs, lightly beaten
salt and pepper
4 T. butter or margarine
¼ tsp. seasoned salt
½ lb. Swiss cheese, sliced
½ cup fine dry bread crumbs
8 slices bacon, cooked and crumbled

Pour milk over bread cubes. Allow to stand for five minutes; drain and reserve milk. Combine milk with eggs and season to taste. Melt 2 tablespoons butter in skillet, add egg mixture and scramble – just until soft. Add bread cubes and turn into an 8″ square baking dish. Sprinkle with seasoned salt. Arrange cheese over top. Melt remaining butter and combine with bread crumbs; sprinkle over cheese; top with bacon. Bake at 400° for ten to fifteen minutes until cheese bubbles around edge of dish and cheese at center is melted. Serve at once.

8 servings — Mrs. Birtley C. Alcorn

Mr. Flavian Potts' Eggs

4 slices bacon
½ cup butter
½ lb. ham steak, cubed
1 cup mushrooms
½ cup flour
4 cups milk
⅛ tsp. pepper
1 cup evaporated milk
¼ tsp. salt
16 eggs

Sauté bacon, break into pieces and return to pan. Do not pour off the fat. Add ¼ cup butter, ham and mushrooms; cook briefly. Sprinkle with flour and stir well. Gradually add whole milk and cook until thickened and smooth. Season with pepper; set aside. Beat evaporated milk and salt into eggs. Scramble in ¼ cup butter until firm. In a greased casserole, layer half the eggs and cream sauce; repeat. Must refrigerate overnight. Bake at 275° for one hour. Garnish with parsley.

12 servings — Mrs. Nelson F. Graves

Oeufs Lorraine

2 T. butter
4 to 8 slices bacon, cooked
4 eggs
⅓ lb. Gruyere or Emmenthal cheese, grated
2 T. heavy cream
salt and pepper

Melt butter slowly in a skillet. Arrange bacon slices around edge, break eggs in center, sprinkle cheese over egg whites, pour cream around the yolks and season to taste. Cook very slowly until cheese and cream have blended with white of egg.

2 to 4 servings — Cheese World

Eggs Sardu

2 pkgs. frozen creamed spinach
1 pkg. frozen chopped spinach
8 artichoke bottoms
4 egg yolks
6 T. lemon juice
1 cup cold butter
8 eggs

Prepare spinach according to directions, mix together and keep warm. Heat artichoke bottoms and keep warm. Prepare Hollandaise sauce: in a small saucepan, combine egg yolks and lemon juice. Add butter and stir constantly over low heat; remove from stove (or see recipe p. 104). Poach eggs just before serving. To serve: make a bed of spinach on each plate; place two artichoke bottoms in center with a poached egg on each; spoon sauce over all. Garnish with paprika.

4 servings — Mrs. Michael Cargile

Eggs Burgundy Avril

1½ cups onion, minced
2 cups mushrooms, minced
1 cup plus 1 T. butter
½ tsp. pepper
½ tsp. basil
2 cloves garlic, crushed
½ cup parsley, chopped
3 cups vegetable stock
1½ cups burgundy
½ cup soy sauce
2 T. Worcestershire sauce
1 cup whole wheat flour, sifted
12 slices whole wheat bread, toasted
3 large tomatoes, sliced
12 hard-cooked eggs, chopped
4 cups mushrooms, sliced and sautéed

In a saucepan, sauté onions and minced mushrooms in one tablespoon butter until onions are transparent. Season with pepper and herbs. Combine stock, wine, soy and Worcestershire sauces; heat and add to onion mixture. Melt 1 cup butter, add flour gradually; heat, stirring constantly, for five minutes. Pour in wine mixture, stir until thickened; keep warm. To serve, layer toast, tomatoes, eggs, sautéed mushrooms and hot burgundy sauce. Garnish with fresh parsley.

6 to 12 servings

Earth by April Restaurant

Quiche Lorraine

1½ cups flour, sifted
½ tsp. salt
¼ tsp. butter
½ cup lard
¼ tsp. marjoram
½ tsp. chives
1 tsp. parsley
¼ tsp. savory
2 to 4 T. ice water
4 eggs, beaten
2 cups light cream
½ tsp. sugar
salt, pepper, cayenne pepper and nutmeg
2 T. butter, softened
12 slices bacon, cooked and crumbled
1 cup Swiss cheese, grated

Prepare pastry: sift flour with salt, coarsely work butter and lard into flour. Add herbs, blend. Moisten with just enough ice water to hold together. Refrigerate. Combine eggs, cream and sugar, and season to taste. Roll out pastry and line a pie pan. Dot crust with butter, sprinkle with bacon and then cheese; pour in egg mixture. Bake at 350° for fifteen minutes. Reduce temperature to 325° and bake until custard is firm, about thirty minutes longer. Serve hot.

6 servings Mrs. Henry G. Brownell

Seafood Quiche

1 nine-inch pie shell, unbaked
½ lb. Swiss cheese, grated
½ lb. crab meat
¼ lb. small shrimp
2 eggs, beaten
1 cup heavy cream
2 tsp. flour
salt, pepper, cayenne pepper and nutmeg
1 T. butter, melted
1 T. dry sherry

Fill pie shell with cheese, crab meat and shrimp. Combine eggs, cream and flour, and season to taste. Stir in butter and sherry; pour over seafood and bake at 375° degrees for thirty minutes.

6 servings — Mrs. Louis Bloomfield

Coquilles St. Jacques de Bordeaux

2 cups scallops, cooked
1 tomato, peeled and chopped
½ cup onion, chopped
garlic to taste
2 sprigs parsley, chopped
2 T. butter
1 can cream of mushroom soup
1 to 2 T. sherry

Combine scallops and next five ingredients and simmer one minute; add soup and sherry; heat. Place in individual baking shells, top with bread crumbs and Parmesan cheese and broil.

4 to 8 servings — Thomas Augustus Charles Leonce François Du Bois de Villiers de Broglie

Insalata di Riso

4 cups cooked rice, al dente
2 – 7 oz. cans solid white tuna fish, drained
¼ lb. Swiss cheese, cubed
2 hard-cooked eggs, coarsely chopped
Diced raw vegetables, olives, dill pickles and/or capers
1 cup olive oil
¼ cup wine vinegar
salt and pepper

Combine rice with tuna, cheese and eggs. Add vegetables (diced raw carrot, green pepper, green peas), sliced olives, dill pickles and/or capers, for color and flavor, as desired. Blend oil and vinegar and season to taste; pour over the rice and toss gently. Chill. Garnish with mayonnaise, anchovies and hard-cooked eggs.

8 servings Mrs. Aldo Ceccato

Creamed Tuna

2 cups light cream
1 small bay leaf
½ clove garlic
2 whole cloves
¼ cup onion, sliced
1 T. parsley, chopped
3 T. butter, melted
3 T. flour
salt, celery salt and white pepper
2 – 7 oz. cans tuna fish
2 T. pimento, diced

Heat first six ingredients to scalding; strain. In a heavy skillet, blend butter and flour. Add cream mixture slowly, stirring constantly until thickened. Add remaining ingredients and heat. Serve over patty shells.

4 servings Mrs. W. H. Bierman, Jr.

CREPES

1 cup milk
3 eggs, beaten
2 T. butter, melted
½ cup flour, sifted
½ tsp. salt

Combine milk, eggs and butter. Stir in flour and salt and beat until smooth. Grease crèpe pan or small skillet very lightly, pour in a small amount of batter, tip pan back and forth until batter covers the bottom of skillet completely. Cook on one side only; turn out onto a plate. Fill as desired, tuck in ends and roll.

Yield: 8 MRS. HENRY G. BROWNELL

CREAMED CHICKEN CREPES

6 T. butter
1 onion, chopped
1 cup mushrooms, sliced
6 T. flour
1½ cups chicken stock
1½ cups light cream
½ cup green pepper, chopped
¼ cup pimiento, chopped
4 cups chicken, cooked and diced
salt and pepper
1 cup Swiss cheese, grated
½ cup sherry

Melt butter and slowly cook onion and mushrooms. Stir in flour, then chicken stock and cream. Cook slowly until mixture thickens. Add remaining ingredients and heat thoroughly. Fill crèpes and roll.

8 servings MRS. WILLIAM JONES MILLER

Sensational Sausage Crepes

1 lb. bulk pork sausage
¼ cup onion, chopped
¼ cup processed cheese, shredded
1 – 3 oz. pkg. cream cheese
1 – 4 oz. can mushroom stems and pieces, drained
¼ tsp. celery salt
¼ tsp. marjoram
1 cup sour cream
6 to 12 crèpes
¼ cup butter, softened

Sauté sausage and onion until browned; drain. Add cheeses, mushrooms, seasonings and ¾ cup sour cream. Add milk if mixture seems dry. Place 2 T. filling in the center of each crepe; roll. Arrange in a 9″ x 13″ baking dish. Combine butter and ¼ cup sour cream; spread on crepes. Bake, covered at 375° for twenty to thirty minutes. Can be prepared ahead and refrigerated; allow to come to room temperature before baking.

6 servings — Mrs. Darrell A. Brand

Crepes Florentine

Combine 2 egg yolks, 1½ lbs. Ricotta cheese, 1 box frozen chopped spinach, cooked, 1 T. grated Parmesan cheese, salt and nutmeg. Fill crèpes and serve with a bechamel or cream sauce.

4 to 8 servings — Mrs. Henry G. Brownell

Choice Cheese Blintzes

1 cup flour
½ tsp. salt
1½ cups milk
4 eggs
1 tsp. sugar
butter
1 lb. cottage cheese
2 eggs
4 T. sugar
1 tsp. lemon rind, grated
1 tsp. orange rind, grated

Combine first five ingredients and beat well. Pour a scant ¼ cup batter into a small buttered skillet, and tip the pan so batter covers the entire surface. Cook one side only, until lightly browned. Place cooked side down on a paper towel, stacking all the blintzes in this manner until ready for filling. (May be kept a day or two in the refrigerator, or frozen.) Blend remaining ingredients. Place 1 T. cottage cheese filling in the center of browned side of blintz. Tuck in ends and roll. Melt butter in a skillet and brown blitzes on all sides. Serve warm with preserves and/or sour cream.

Yield: 15 to 20 Mrs. Robert A. Barclay

Fluffy French Toast

2 cups light cream
6 eggs
dash cinnamon and nutmeg
1 loaf rich egg bread, unsliced

Beat cream, eggs and spices together. Trim all crust from bread; slice one-inch thick. Arrange close together in a buttered 7″ x 11″ casserole. Top with egg mixture. Cover and refrigerate several hours or overnight. Uncover when ready to bake and pour off any excess liquid. Bake at 400° for forty-five minutes. The toast is done when a toothpick inserted in the center comes out clean. Serve immediately with maple or orange syrup. (below)

6 to 8 servings Mrs. Theodore A. Gullia, Jr.

Orange Syrup

½ cup sugar
¼ tsp. salt
1 T. cornstarch
½ orange juice
1 tsp. orange rind, grated
1 T. lemon juice
2 T. butter

Combine sugar, salt and cornstarch; add ¾ cup hot water gradually. Bring to a boil and cook until thickened, stirring constantly; simmer a few minutes. Add remaining ingredients. Serve warm. Thin with additional orange juice if necessary.

6 to 8 servings Mrs. Theodore A. Gullia, Jr.

Pancakes Delicious

- 3 cups flour, sifted
- 1 T. baking powder
- 3 T. sugar
- 1 tsp. salt
- 2 eggs, separated
- 2¼ cups milk
- 4 T. butter, melted

Sift dry ingredients together. Beat egg yolks and milk; add flour mixture, beating until smooth; stir in butter. Fold in stiffly beaten egg whites. Bake on a hot griddle.

6 servings MRS. RALPH KLOPPENBURG

Cornmeal Buttermilk Pancakes

- 1 cup flour, unsifted
- ½ cup yellow cornmeal
- ¾ tsp. salt
- ¾ tsp. baking soda
- ¾ tsp. baking powder
- 1½ T. sugar
- 2 eggs
- 1½ cups buttermilk
- 1½ T. salad oil

Stir dry ingredients together. Combine eggs, buttermilk and oil and beat well. Stir in dry ingredients. Bake on a hot griddle.

3 to 4 servings GEORGE GOSLEE
The Cleveland Orchestra

GOVERNOR'S FAVORITE COFFEECAKE

¼ cup butter
1 cup sugar
2 eggs, separated
1½ cups flour
2 tsp. baking powder
1 tsp. salt
½ cup sour milk or buttermilk
1 tsp. vanilla
½ cup brown sugar
1 T. flour
1 tsp. cinnamon
pinch nutmeg
¼ to ½ cup pecans, chopped

Cream butter and sugar; beat in egg yolks. Sift flour, baking powder and salt together and add alternately with milk. Fold in stiffly beaten egg whites and vanilla. Combine remaining ingredients. Pour ⅔ of the batter into a greased 7″ x 11″ baking pan. Sprinkle with nut mixture and top with the remaining batter. Bake at 350° for thirty-five to forty-five minutes. Cool. Dust with confectioners sugar and cut into squares.

MRS. JOHN GILLIGAN

Note: one cup milk plus one tablespoon vinegar or lemon juice can be substituted for one cup buttermilk or sour milk.

NOTABLE SOUR CREAM COFFEECAKE

1½ cups sugar
½ cup butter or margarine
2 eggs
1 cup sour cream
2 cups flour
1 tsp. baking powder
1 tsp. baking soda
1 tsp. vanilla extract
½ cup walnuts, finely chopped
1 tsp. cinnamon

Beat 1 cup sugar with butter until light and fluffy. Add next six ingredients and blend; beat three minutes. Combine nuts, ½ cup sugar and cinnamon. Spread ½ of the batter in a greased tube or bundt pan; sprinkle with ½ of the nut mixture. Spread evenly with remaining batter and sprinkle with remaining nuts. Bake at 350° for sixty to sixty-five minutes until cake pulls away from side of pan. Serve warm. May be varied by adding sliced pear or apple to the filling.

BARBARA BRATEL
The Cleveland Press

MENU SUGGESTION

Hot Fruit Compote

Mr. Flavian Potts' Eggs

Notable Sour Cream Coffeecake

SUSIE'S CINNAMON ROLLS

1 cup shortening
2 tsp. salt
2½ cups plus 1 tsp. sugar
1 pkg. dry yeast
1 cup milk
2 eggs
6 to 7 cups flour, sifted
4 T. cinnamon
½ cup butter, melted
1 - 15 oz. box raisins

Melt shortening in one cup boiling water, add salt and ½ cup sugar. Cool slightly. Dissolve one teaspoon sugar and yeast in ½ cup lukewarm water. Stir into shortening mixture with milk and eggs. Combine with flour and stir to make a dough. Cover with towel and let stand in a warm place until doubled in bulk (about two hours). Combine 2 cups sugar and cinnamon. Roll out one-quarter of the dough until thin; trim edges to form a rectangle. Spread with melted butter, sprinkle with cinnamon-sugar and raisins. Roll tightly, beginning at the long side of the rectangle. Slice ½ to ¾ of an inch thick and place in baking pan. Repeat with remaining dough. Cover and let rise two hours. Bake at 400° for ten to fifteen minutes. Glaze with butter frosting.

Yield: 8 dozen MRS. DAVID F. CONLEY

Bear Creek Sticky Buns

Vary Susie's Cinnamon Rolls by combining 1½ cups brown sugar, ¼ cup butter and ½ cup water in a saucepan and bringing to a rolling boil. Pour into the bottom of two baking pans. Sprinkle with pecans if desired. Place cut side of cinnamon rolls (omit raisins) on the brown sugar mixture. Let rise and bake. Invert on waxed paper covered racks and let stand a minute before removing pans.

Mrs. Bruce Rauch

Danish Kringle

1 cup milk, scalded
2 pkgs. dry yeast
3 T. sugar
3 eggs, separated
4 cups flour
1 tsp. salt
1 cup shortening
marmalade or jam

Cool milk, add yeast and stir until dissolved; add sugar and beaten egg yolks. Mix together flour, salt and shortening until crumbly. Add yeast mixture and blend. Chill overnight. Halve dough; roll into two 12″ x 15″ rectangles. Brush with lightly beaten egg whites; spread generously with marmalade or jam. Fold all edges one inch toward center. Place on a greased cookie sheet. Bake at 375° for fifteen minutes. Glaze while warm with a butter frosting.

Mrs. Lisa Angle

BANANA MUFFINS

½ cup butter
1 cup sugar
2 eggs, beaten
2 large bananas, mashed
2 cups flour
1 tsp. (rounded) baking powder
1 tsp. (rounded) baking soda
4 T. (generous) sour cream
1 orange rind, grated
juice of 1 orange

Cream butter and sugar; add eggs, then bananas. Sift dry ingredients together and add to banana mixture. Fold in sour cream, orange rind and juice. Pour into greased muffin cups. Bake at 350° for twenty to twenty-five minutes.

Yield: 18 MRS. PETER W. DANFORD

MRS. PULSFORD'S BLUEBERRY MUFFINS

½ cup butter
1¼ cups sugar
2 eggs
2 cups flour
2 tsp. baking powder
½ tsp. salt
½ cup milk
2 cups blueberries

Cream butter and sugar until fluffy. Add eggs, one at a time, and beat well. Sift dry ingredients together and add alternately with milk. Stir in blueberries. Pour into greased muffin cups. Sprinkle with a mixture of cinnamon and sugar. Bake at 375° for thirty minutes.

Yield: 15 or 16 MRS. NATHAN W. OAKES, JR.

Main Themes

Clams Tetrazzini

6 T. butter
¼ cup flour
3 - 8 oz. cans minced clams
light cream (about 2 cups)
½ tsp. salt
¼ tsp. thyme
¼ tsp. nutmeg
2 or 3 drops hot pepper sauce
2 T. dry sherry
1 egg yolk, beaten
1½ cups mushrooms, sliced
1 - 16 oz. pkg. cooked linguini, al dente
1 - 5 oz. pkg. Parmesan cheese, grated
¼ cup Italian flavored bread crumbs
2 T. parsley, chopped

Heat 4 T. butter in a saucepan; stir in flour until well blended. Drain clams; reserve juice. Combine clam juice and enough cream to make 2¾ cups. Add to butter and stir constantly until mixture thickens; simmer for one minute. Remove from heat; add next five ingredients, then add egg yolk and stir. Heat remaining 2 T. butter and sauté mushrooms until soft. Add mushrooms and minced clams to sauce. Place one-half of the linguini in a large baking dish; pour over one-half of the sauce; sprinkle with one-half of the cheese and bread crumbs. Repeat. Garnish with parsley and bake at 400° for twenty minutes. May be made early in the day and refrigerated until baking time.

6 to 8 servings — Mrs. Richard H. Pollack

Filets of Sole Valenciennes

1 tsp. salt
⅛ tsp. black pepper, freshly ground
⅛ tsp. mace
⅛ tsp. thyme
2 lbs. sole filets
½ cup dry vermouth
2 T. lemon juice
2 T. butter, melted
2 T. fresh chives, chopped
2 T. onion, chopped
24 small mushroom caps

Combine salt, pepper, mace and thyme and sprinkle on both sides of the filets; place in a buttered flame-proof casserole. Combine vermouth, lemon juice and butter and pour over the fish. Sprinkle with chives and onion; arrange mushrooms on top. Cover and very slowly bring to a boil on top of the stove. Immediately uncover and put casserole in oven. Bake at 325° for fifteen minutes, basting frequently with the wine mixture. Leave fish in baking dish, garnish with parsley and lemon wedges, and serve with rice.

4 to 6 servings

Kenneth Haas
Assistant General Manager
The Cleveland Orchestra

Fish Filets with an Italian Touch

- 4 small onions, sliced
- 1 clove garlic, minced
- 2 T. olive oil
- 1 – 6 oz. can tomato paste
- 2 bay leaves, crumbled
- ⅛ tsp. cinnamon
- salt and pepper to taste
- 1 cup water
- 2 lbs. fresh or frozen fish filets, thawed

Sauté onions and garlic in oil until soft. Add remaining ingredients except fish and simmer sauce slowly until it is thick and smooth, about twenty-five minutes. Layer filets in a shallow casserole and pour the sauce over them. Bake at 350° for twenty-five to thirty minutes or until fish is white and flaky. Garnish with buttered crumbs if desired. Serve with parsley potatoes.

4 to 5 servings Mrs. Geofrey Greenleaf

Hot Fish Mousse

Skin, bone and cube 1½ lbs. fresh fish (sole, pike, salmon); combine with ⅛ tsp. cayenne pepper and 1 cup milk. Spin, one cup at a time, in a blender; fold in 3 beaten egg whites. Whip 2 cups heavy cream and chill both cream and fish mixture and refrigerate for five minutes. Repeat this process until all of the cream has been used. Season with about 1 tsp. salt and pile into a buttered mold. Place the mold in a pan of water. Bake at 350° for twenty to twenty-five minutes. Unmold and serve hot with Hollandaise sauce.

6 servings Mrs. John Hay Whitney

Crab-Artichoke Medley

6 T. flour
6 T. butter or margarine, melted
2 cups milk
1 cup chicken stock
½ to 1 cup Cheddar cheese, grated
1½ tsp. Worcestershire sauce
2 T. sherry or white wine
1 – 3 oz. can mushrooms
parsley, chopped
pimiento, chopped
2 cups rice, cooked
1 pkg. frozen artichoke hearts, cooked and drained
4 hard-cooked eggs, sliced
1 to 1½ lbs. crab meat
1 – 8 oz. can water chestnuts
2 T. Parmesan cheese, grated
2 T. cornflake crumbs

Mix flour with butter in a saucepan and gradually stir in milk. Cook until thickened, stirring constantly. Slowly blend in stock. Add Cheddar cheese and Worcestershire sauce; cook until cheese melts. Add sherry, mushrooms, parsley and pimiento; remove from heat. Place rice in bottom of a buttered casserole. Alternate layers of artichoke hearts, eggs, crab meat and water chestnuts. Top with sauce; sprinkle with Parmesan cheese and cornflake crumbs. bake, uncovered, at 350° for thirty minutes. Garnish with parsley or mixed herbs.

4 to 6 servings — Mrs. Howard D. Kohn

Palm Springs Shrimp Rockefeller

½ cup butter
1 T. Worcestershire sauce
½ tsp. hot pepper sauce
1 clove garlic, crushed
½ lb. fresh spinach, minced
6 small onions, minced
½ head lettuce, minced
1½ stalks celery, minced
½ cup parsley, chopped
½ cup fresh bread crumbs
2 lbs. shrimp, cooked
3 T. flour
3 T. butter
1¼ cups milk
¼ tsp. Worcestershire sauce
3 T. Parmesan cheese, grated
salt and pepper to taste
¼ cup sherry

Combine ½ cup butter, Worcestershire and hot pepper sauces, garlic and vegetables. Simmer ten minutes; stir in bread crumbs and place in a two-quart casserole. Add shrimp and top with white sauce made by heating remaining ingredients together until thickened. Serve over rice.

6 servings Mrs. William C. Judd

Following the Lieder (Chicken-Shrimp Casserole)

- 8 chicken breasts, skinned and boned
- margarine
- 1 or 2 one-lb. cans tomato wedges
- 1 can beef bouillon
- ½ cup dry sherry
- 1½ lbs. shrimp, slightly undercooked

Cut chicken into cubes; sauté in margarine until no longer pink inside, remove chicken. To remaining pan drippings, add part of the juice from tomatoes (sauce should not be too runny), bouillon and sherry; heat. Stir in tomato wedges, chicken and shrimp, and marinate in refrigerator until just before serving. Lift out chicken and shrimp and allow sauce to simmer. Return chicken and shrimp to sauce and heat for ten minutes. Serve over rice.

8 to 10 servings — Judith Raskin

Chicken Dijon

- ¼ cup Dijon mustard
- 2 T. onion or shallots, minced
- ¼ tsp. tarragon
- ⅛ tsp. hot pepper sauce
- 5 T. butter or margarine, melted
- 1 – 2½ lb. frying chicken, cut up
- ¾ cup bread crumbs

Blend mustard, onion, tarragon, pepper sauce and 1 T. butter. Coat chicken pieces, dip in bread crumbs, arrange in a baking dish and drizzle remaining butter over chicken. Bake at 375° for about one hour or until done.

2 to 4 servings — Frank L. Peterson, Jr.

ERMA'S ANNUAL HOT MEAL

- 6 medium thighs (chicken, of course!)
- 4 whole breasts
- 1 pkg. frozen broccoli flowerets, thawed
- 1 cup mayonnaise
- 2 cans cream of chicken soup
- 1 tsp. curry powder
- ½ tsp. lemon juice
- ½ cup butter, melted
- ¾ pkg. herb stuffing mix

Bake chicken at 350° for thirty to forty-five minutes. Strip meat from bones and place in a well-greased 9″ x 13″ casserole; arrange broccoli over chicken. Combine mayonnaise, soup, curry and lemon juice and pour over broccoli. Add butter to stuffing mix and sprinkle on top. Bake at 350° for thirty minutes.

Serves: depends on how many people like broccoli ERMA BOMBECK

BRANDIED CRANBERRIES

- 1 lb. fresh cranberries
- 2 cups sugar
- 4 to 5 T. brandy

Arrange cranberries in a single layer in a large shallow baking pan. Sprinkle sugar to top. Cover tightly with foil and bake at 350° for one hour. Cool and sprinkle with brandy and a little more sugar.

MRS. STEPHEN GAGE

Chicken Continental

6 whole chicken breasts, boned and split

6 chicken legs and thighs, disjointed

salt and pepper

½ cup lemon juice

2 cups sour cream

2 cloves garlic, crushed

2 tsp. celery salt

2 tsp. paprika

2 cups walnuts, ground (or bread crumbs)

1 cup butter, melted

½ cup white wine

Season chicken with salt and pepper to taste. Add ¼ cup lemon juice and let stand one to two hours. Combine sour cream, remaining lemon juice, garlic, celery salt and paprika. Coat chicken with sour cream mixture and refrigerate twenty-four hours. Before baking, roll chicken in nuts; place in a greased baking pan. Spoon half the butter over chicken. Bake at 350° for forty-five minutes. Baste with remaining butter to which wine has been added and bake ten to fifteen minutes longer.

8 servings — Sylvia Balslew

BEER BATTER CHICKEN

salt and pepper
1 tsp. paprika
½ tsp. garlic powder
1 cup flour
½ cup stale beer
1 - 2 lb. frying chicken, boned and cut into serving pieces
salad oil

Place salt, pepper, paprika, garlic and ½ cup flour in a small bowl; stir in beer. Add more beer if necessary to reach desired consistency. Dip dry chicken pieces into remaining flour and then into batter. Let the batter run off so that it is not too thick. Fry chicken in oil until nearly done; drain. Place on a cookie sheet and bake at 350° for ten minutes to finish cooking and browning. This chicken can also be topped with a slice of Provolone cheese and tomato sauce and heated under the broiler until bubbly.

3 servings

MRS. Z. K. KARA

MENU SUGGESTION

Hot Mushroom Hors d' Oeuvres

Beer Batter Chicken

Potato Pudding with Peas

Baked Cheese Stuffed Tomatoes

Apple Crisp

The John Wayne (Barbecued Chicken Breasts)

2 cups bourbon
1 cup Southern Comfort
3 or 4 stalks celery, coarsely chopped
½ cup carrots, coarsely chopped
1 cup mushrooms, chopped
½ cup onions, coarsely chopped
½ lb. (1¼ cups) ripe tomatoes, peeled and chopped
1 cup brown sugar
1 cup barbecue sauce
¼ cup Worcestershire sauce
8 chicken breasts, boned

To prepare barbecue sauce: combine all ingredients except chicken in an electric blender and spin. Pour over chicken and marinate for twenty-four hours. Grill, basting frequently. Serve with plenty of sauce.

4 to 8 servings — The Last Moving Picture Company

Clubhouse Chicken

Combine ½ cup olive oil, ¼ cup lemon juice and ¾ cup dry white wine; add 2 tsp. oregano, 2 tsp. chopped parsley and 2 cloves garlic, minced. Pour over 6 whole boned chicken breasts. Season to taste. Bake at 350° for one and one-half hours, basting frequently.

6 servings — Mrs. David F. Conley

CHICKEN BALI HAI

- 6 whole chicken breasts, boned and skinned
- 6 thin slices baked ham
- 3 ripe bananas
- 3 T. butter, melted
- ⅔ cup bread crumbs
- 2 cups orange juice
- 1 T. orange rind, grated
- 1 T. sugar
- 1 tsp. curry powder

Stuff chicken breasts with a slice of ham and half a banana. Secure with toothpicks. Place in a casserole, brush with butter and sprinkle with bread crumbs. Bake, uncovered, at 400° for fifteen minutes. Meanwhile combine remaining ingredients, simmer five minutes and season. Pour over breasts, cover and bake at 350° for thirty minutes longer.

6 servings MRS. WILLIAM H. WEST

HOT CHICKEN SALAD

- 1¼ cups mayonnaise, not salad dressing
- ⅛ cup onion, minced
- ¾ cup cheese, shredded
- 3 cups chicken, cooked and diced
- 1½ cups celery, sliced
- 1½ cups pineapple chunks, drained
- ¾ cup almonds, toasted and chopped

Combine mayonnaise, onion and cheese and toss with remaining ingredients. Garnish with crushed potato chips and bake at 400° for ten minutes.

4 servings MRS. JAY P. AUWERTER

Cranberry Ice

Boil 3 cups fresh cranberries in 1¼ cups water for ten minutes. Add 1½ cups sugar and ¼ cup lemon juice, stir until sugar has dissolved; put through a food mill or spin in a blender. Cool. Pour into parfait glasses and freeze. Serve with the main course – especially good with roast fowl, and may become a welcome edition to your holiday dinners.

8 servings Mrs. John Marshall

Chicken Casserole Orientale

- 1 large onion, diced
- 3 cups celery, thinly sliced
- ½ cup mushrooms, sliced
- 6 T. butter
- 4 T. flour or 2 T. cornstarch
- 1 can water chestnuts, sliced
- 1 small jar pimientos
- 3 cups cooked chicken or turkey, diced
- ½ can Chinese noodles
- ¾ cup slivered almonds, toasted

Cook onion and celery in ½ cup water until barely tender. Add enough water to vegetable stock to make two cups. Stir some cool stock into the flour, return to pot, bring to a boil and stir until thickened. Sauté mushrooms in butter for three minutes. Add chestnuts, pimientos and chicken to celery sauce. Pour into a three-quart casserole and top with Chinese noodles and almonds. Bake, uncovered, at 350° for forty-five minutes. 1½ pounds cooked shrimp may be substituted for meat.

8 servings Mrs. Robert Riesz

CHICKEN VIVALDI

½ cup onion, minced
1 T. olive oil
1 – 6 oz. can tomato paste
1 cup water
¾ cup white wine
salt and pepper to taste
½ tsp. sugar
½ tsp. oregano
1 bay leaf
3 chicken breasts, boned, skinned, split
2 eggs, lightly beaten
1 cup unseasoned bread crumbs
½ cup salad oil
6 slices Prosciutto, thinly sliced
6 slices Mozzarella cheese

Sauté onion in olive oil until tender. Combine with next seven ingredients and simmer thirty minutes, stirring occasionally. Dip breasts in eggs, then bread crumbs, and season. Sauté in oil until evenly browned. Arrange chicken in a single layer in a baking dish, top with slices of Prosciutto and cheese; cover and bake fifteen minutes longer. Serve topped with hot tomato sauce.

3 to 6 servings

MRS. LESLIE JACOBS

MME. RENOIR POULET SAUTÉ

1 large fryer, cut into serving pieces
¼ cup olive oil
3 T. butter
1 clove garlic, minced
2 small onions, minced
2 tomatoes, peeled and chopped
2 sprigs parsley
1 sprig thyme (about ½ tsp. dried)
1 bay leaf
salt and pepper to taste
¾ cup hot water
12 small mushrooms
chicken liver, diced
12 ripe olives
¼ cognac or brandy

Sauté chicken in olive oil in a heavy casserole until brown. Drain oil from casserole and add next nine ingredients. Cover pot and simmer for thirty minutes (or longer if you like chicken falling off the bone). Add mushrooms, chicken liver and olives. Cook, uncovered, for fifteen minutes. At the last minute warm cognac and pour over chicken. Ignite. Serve garnished with parsley.

4 servings MRS. R. W. HARDY

Fondue Bourguignonne

½ lb. beef steak per person, trimmed and cubed
salad oil (preferably peanut oil)

Place individual servings of raw meat on lettuce leaves. Preheat oil to 375°. To serve, carefully pour hot oil into fondue pot and keep hot. With a long-handled fondue fork, guests spear the uncooked steak and cook, individually, in the hot oil. A dinner fork is used for eating the steak, and dipping in a variety of contrasting sauces. Other meats (chicken breast, chicken liver, veal kidney, Kielbasa, firm meatballs) or seafoods (cubed salmon, shrimp) may also be used.

Blender Bearnaise Sauce

2 egg yolks
1 T. lemon juice
1 tsp. tarragon vinegar
1 tsp. tarragon
¾ cup butter, melted

Place first four ingredients in blender and turn on and off. With blender at highest speed, very gradually add hot butter in a steady stream. Serve immediately.

Wine Butter

1 cup red wine
1 tsp. onion, minced
½ tsp. lemon juice
½ tsp. meat extract
dash hot pepper sauce
2 tsp. parsley, minced
¾ cup butter, softened

Simmer wine with onion until reduced to about ¼ cup. Stir in remaining seasonings. Cool. Blend into butter and serve at room temperature.

Deviled Roquefort Butter

½ lb. Roquefort cheese, softened
½ cup butter, softened
1 T. prepared mustard
1 clove garlic, crushed
3 drops bitters

Whip all ingredients together until fluffy. Cover and refrigerate several hours. Return to room temperature and whip again before serving.

Molto Mustard Sauce a la Grant Park

1 cup brown sugar
⅓ cup dry mustard
1 T. (heaping) flour
½ cup vinegar
1 beef bouillon cube
2 eggs, well-beaten

In a saucepan combine brown sugar, mustard and flour; add vinegar, ½ cup water and bouillon cube; add eggs. Cook over low heat until thickened. Serve either warm or cold. Also excellent with baked ham or as a sandwich spread.

Mrs. Roy Stucka

Horseradish Sauce

1 cup sour cream
2 to 3 T. prepared horseradish, drained
1 tsp. vinegar
1 T. chives, chopped and/or
1 tsp. onion, grated
salt and pepper

Combine and chill.

Mrs. Alf Jordan

Cossack Sauce

2 T. chili sauce
1 T. onion, minced
1 tsp. prepared horseradish
½ cup sour cream

Combine ingredients and serve with meats.

Mrs. W. Daniel Driscoll

Fresh Blender Mayonnaise

1 whole egg or 2 egg yolks
2 T. vinegar
½ tsp. dry mustard
1 tsp. salt
1 cup salad oil

Place egg, vinegar, seasonings and ¼ cup oil in blender; turn on and off. Turn to high speed and add remaining oil in a slow steady stream.

Mild Curry Sauce

½ onion, chopped
1 clove garlic, minced
2 pieces candied ginger, slivered
1 T. butter
½ T. curry powder
½ tsp. brown sugar
1½ T. flour
¼ tsp. salt
1 cup chicken stock

Sauté onion, garlic, ginger and butter in a saucepan until onion is transparent. Stir in curry and sugar, and then flour and salt. Gradually add chicken stock and cook, stirring until sauce is thickened, about ten minutes. Strain and serve hot or cold. One chopped tomato or apple can be added to this sauce.

Mrs. Z. K. Kara

Hotsy-Totsy Tomato Sauce

2 T. flour
2 T. butter, melted
½ tsp. garlic salt
⅓ cup catsup
⅓ cup sherry
1 T. wine vinegar
2 T. beef bouillon
1 tsp. brown sugar
1 tsp. mustard
1 T. onion juice
dash cloves, salt and pepper

Stir flour into butter; when thickened, add remaining ingredients and simmer five minutes, stirring constantly. Serve warm or at room temperature.

Mrs. William A. Blunden

Czarda Sauce

3 T. onion, minced
3 T. butter
2 T. flour
1 T. Hungarian paprika
1½ cups tomatoes, coarsely chopped
salt
2 T. sour cream

Simmer onion in 2 T. butter until tender. stir in flour and paprika, add tomatoes and season. Cook until thickened and smooth. Spin in blender or strain. Swirl in remaining butter and sour cream and serve hot.

BAKED SIRLOIN STEAK

1 – 4 to 5 lb. sirloin steak,
1½ to 2 inches thick
1 clove garlic, sliced
⅓ cup olive oil
1¼ tsp. rosemary
salt and pepper
½ cup red wine
1 T. butter

Wipe steak and rub both sides with garlic. Heat oil in a heavy skillet until very hot; sear steak three to five minutes on each side. Place in a shallow baking pan; add rosemary and garlic, and season to taste. Bake at 350° for twenty-five to thirty minutes, until medium rare. Place steak on a serving platter. Skim fat from baking pan; add wine and butter to pan juices and bring to a boil, stir to loosen brown particles. Pour wine sauce over meat.

4 servings MRS. RICHARD T. BROWNRIGG

FILET FLAMBEAU

1 clove garlic
1 T. sweet butter
4 beef tenderloin filets, 1-inch thick
¼ to ½ cup good cognac

Warm frying pan; rub garlic clove around bottom of pan; discard. (If stronger garlic flavor is desired, allow to remain in pan.) Melt butter, add beef and sauté until cooked as desired. Just before serving, pour cognac over filets in pan and ignite carefully. Allow flame to die out. Serve, spooning juices from pan onto filets. The cognac used for this purpose must be of good quality because inexpensive cognac, when heated and flamed, does not have a good flavor.

4 servings GEOFF STEIN

Beef Filet Avocado

2½ to 3 lbs. beef filet
2 cloves garlic
salt and pepper
¼ cup butter or margarine, melted
1 ripe avocado
1 T. lemon juice
½ cup salad oil (approximately)

Trim fat from meat. Crush garlic with a little salt and blend with butter. Place meat in baking dish, spread with garlic butter and season to taste. Bake at 425° for ten minutes, reduce heat to 325° and continue cooking until done to taste. Cut into thick slices. To prepare sauce: peel avocado, mash and push through a sieve; add salt, pepper and lemon juice; stir in oil until sauce is consistency of mayonnaise. Strain again or spin in a blender. Do not prepare ahead as avocado will discolor. Spoon over meat or serve separately.

5 or 6 servings — Mrs. Mark Schulze

Skewered Ginger Peaches

Peel two fresh peaches and halve. Dip in melted butter and roll in a mixture of 1 cup brown sugar and 2 T. chopped candied ginger. Thread on skewers and broil under moderate heat for eight to ten minutes. Serve with barbecued meats or with ice cream as a dessert.

4 servings — Mrs. Mark Schulze

Flank Steak on the Hibachi

- 1 flank steak
- soy sauce
- freshly ground pepper
- 1 tsp. thyme
- 1¼ cups shallots or scallions, chopped
- 1¼ cups red wine
- ½ cup butter
- 2 T. parsley, minced

Brush flank steak with soy sauce; sprinkle with pepper and thyme. Let stand for at least one hour. Combine shallots and wine in a saucepan, bring just to the boiling point; add butter and parsley; keep warm. Brush steak again with soy sauce and grill over a brisk fire on the hibachi, three to four minutes on each side for rare steaks. Carve on the diagonal, into thin slices. Spoon sauce over steak and serve.

2 or 3 servings — Mrs. Thomas T. K. Zung

Deluxe London Broil

- 3 T. (heaping) tomato paste
- ¼ cup wine vinegar
- 1 tsp. garlic salt
- 1 bay leaf
- 1¾ to 2 lbs. flank steak

Combine tomato paste, vinegar, one cup water, garlic and bay leaf. Score flank steak on both sides and marinate overnight, turning occasionally. Grill steak for about ten minutes, turning and basting frequently with marinade. Slice across the grain; serve with Cossack Sauce (p. 69).

4 to 6 servings — Mrs. W. Daniel Driscoll

Elegant Beef with Artichokes

2 lbs. top sirloin, cubed
salt and pepper
⅓ cup flour
2 T. salad oil
2 – 8 oz. cans tomato sauce
1 clove garlic, crushed
1 cup dry red wine
2 beef bouillon cubes
½ tsp. dill weed
1 can artichoke hearts, drained
1 – 1 lb. can small white onions, drained
1 – 4 oz. can mushrooms, drained

Dredge meat with seasoned flour and brown in oil; set meat aside. Add tomato sauce, garlic, wine, bouillon cubes and dill to skillet and mix well. Return meat to pan and simmer for ninety minutes. Add vegetables and heat for thirty minutes longer. Serve with rice.

6 servings Mrs. H. Brockman Anderson

MENU SUGGESTION

Fresh Cream of Mushroom Soup

Elegant Beef with Artichokes

Mandarin Spinach Salad

Pears de Cacao

Spiced Nuts

Hungarian Beef Gulyas

4 slices bacon, diced
3 lbs. beef round, cubed
1 large onion, chopped (1 cup)
2 cloves garlic, crushed
1½ paprika
1 can beef bouillon
salt to taste
½ tsp. caraway seed
1 lb. small white onions, peeled
4 T. flour
1 - 12 or 16 oz. pkg. egg noodles, cooked
sour cream

Sauté bacon until crisp, reserve. Sauté beef cubes, half at a time, in the remaining bacon fat; remove as they are browned. Sauté chopped onion until golden; stir in garlic and paprika; cook, stirring constantly, for two minutes. Return beef to pan, stir in bouillon, salt and caraway seed. Heat to boiling; lower heat, cover and simmer for one and one-half hours. Add bacon and white onions and simmer forty-five to sixty minutes longer, or until tender. Beat flour and 6 T. water into a smooth paste, add to gulyas; cook, stirring constantly, until sauce thickens and bubbles. Arrange noodles on a preheated deep platter. Pour gulyas over noodles. If you wish, garnish with sautéed slices of green pepper and chopped parsley. Pass sour cream at the table.

8 servings

Alan De Petro
WKBF - TV

Sauerbraten

- 4 to 5 lbs. rolled rump roast
- 2 cups wine vinegar
- 2 onions, sliced
- 1 lemon, sliced
- 10 whole cloves
- 4 bay leaves
- 6 peppercorns
- 1 tsp. mixed pickling spices (optional)
- 2 T. salt
- 3 T. sugar
- 3 T. flour
- 3 T. salad oil
- ⅓ cup butter, melted
- 8 to 10 gingersnaps, crushed

Place meat in a deep bowl. Combine next eight ingredients plus 2 T. sugar and 2 cups water; pour over meat. Cover and refrigerate for two or three days, turning frequently. Lift meat from marinade; pat dry and rub with 2 T. flour. Heat oil in a Dutch oven, add meat and brown. Strain marinade and pour 2 cups over meat, cover and bring to a boil. Reduce heat and cook for three hours. In a saucepan combine butter, 1 T. flour and 1 T. sugar; heat and stir until rich brown in color. Add remaining marinade; stir until thickened. Pour over meat. Simmer one hour or until tender. Remove and slice meat. Add gingersnaps to gravy, stir; pour gravy over meat. Serve with broad noodles and red cabbage.

6 servings — Mrs. Calvin F. Hurd, Jr.

Baked Spaghetti Sicilian Style

2 onions, chopped
2 cloves garlic, minced
½ cup salad oil
2 – 2 lb. cans tomato puree
1 – 12 oz. can tomato paste
1 lb. hot Italian bulk sausage
2 tsp. brown sugar
2 tsp. oregano
2 tsp. parsley, minced
salt and pepper
crushed red pepper or cayenne pepper
1 lb. ground beef
1 large cauliflower, partially cooked
1 lb. cooked spaghetti, al dente
butter
Parmesan cheese, grated

Sauté onions and garlic in oil until golden; add tomato puree, tomato paste, and 4 cups water; blend and cook over low heat, uncovered. In a separate pan sauté sausage, drain and add to sauce mixture with sugar, and season to taste. Sauté beef, stirring until crumbled and browned, drain and add to sauce. Simmer, covered, for two and one-half hours. Sauté cauliflower in butter until lightly browned. Arrange half of the spaghetti and cauliflower and ¼ of the sauce in layers in a buttered 9″ x 13″ baking dish. Dot with butter and sprinkle with cheese. Repeat. Bake, uncovered, at 375° for thirty minutes. Cool fifteen minutes and cut into four-inch squares. Heat remaining half of the sauce and pass separately.

8 to 12 servings — Mrs. John A. Murphy, Jr.

Lasagna Nita

1 lb. lean ground beef
1 onion, chopped
4 cups tomato sauce (homemade best)
1 tsp. sugar
salt and freshly ground pepper
1 tsp. oregano
1 cup creamed cottage cheese
1 – 8 oz. pkg. cream cheese, softened
¼ cup sour cream
⅓ cup scallions, sliced
¼ cup green pepper, chopped
1 – 8 oz. pkg. lasagna noodles, cooked and drained
½ cup Parmesan cheese, grated

Sauté meat and onion until meat is lightly browned and crumbled and onion tender; stir in tomato sauce, sugar, salt, pepper and oregano; heat. Combine cheeses, sour cream, scallions, and green pepper. Arrange half of the noodles in a 7″ x 11″ baking dish, spread on part of the meat sauce and all of the cheese mixture. Add remaining noodles and sauce. Sprinkle with Parmesan cheese. Bake at 350° for thirty to forty minutes.

6 to 8 minutes

Mr. and Mrs. Elliot L. Richardson

Tennessee Lasagna

1 onion, coarsely chopped
2 cloves garlic, minced
2 T. salad oil
1 small bunch celery, coarsely cut
1 green pepper, cut in broad strips
2 lbs. ground beef (including 1 lb. hot Italian sausage if desired)
salt and pepper to taste
1 tsp. chili powder
¼ tsp. cumin seed
dash Worcestershire sauce
pinch oregano
6 to 8 mushrooms, thinly sliced
crushed red pepper
4 cups tomatoes
1 – 8 oz. can tomato sauce
1 – 1 lb. pkg. elbow macaroni, cooked
butter
1 lb. sharp Cheddar cheese, cubed
Parmesan or Cheddar cheese, grated

Sauté onion and garlic in oil; add celery and green pepper; cook until soft. Remove from pan. Add meat to oil, break up and brown well; add seasonings, mushrooms and celery mixture. Sprinkle with red pepper. Add tomatoes and tomato sauce and cook slowly for one hour. Layer macaroni in a casserole, dot with butter, add cheese cubes and sauce. Repeat, ending with sauce. Top with grated cheese. Bake at 350° for thirty minutes until cheese is melted and dish is thoroughly heated.

10 to 12 servings DINAH SHORE

Hamburger Maison

2 lbs. ground beef
1 onion, chopped
1 egg
1 clove garlic, minced
1 T. tomato paste
2 T. parsley, chopped
2 tsp. prepared mustard
1 T. soy sauce
salt and pepper
8 to 12 tomato slices
16 to 24 asparagus spears

Combine all ingredients except tomato and asparagus and let stand for one hour in refrigerator. Form into patties, making two per person. Sauté for one minute on each side. Place one slice of tomato and two asparagus spears on top of each patty. Season to taste, dot with butter and wrap each patty in foil. Bake at 375° for thirty minutes.

4 to 6 servings

Antal Dorati

Bachburgers

For each person, form two thin beef patties. Make a sandwich of patties by filling with 3 T. Roquefort or grated Bleu cheese. Seal edges and wrap with bacon. Season to taste with garlic salt and freshly ground pepper. Grill or broil to taste. Serve on hot buttered English muffins with Worcestershire sauce.

David F. Conley

WELL-TEMPERED "CLASSEROLE"

2 lbs. ground beef
½ cup onion, chopped
1 can cream of mushroom soup
1 cup milk
1 tsp. thyme
juice of 1 lemon
1 tsp. chives, chopped
¾ cup stuffed green olives, chopped or sliced
1 – 8 oz. pkg. medium noodles, cooked
½ lb. Cheddar cheese, grated
1 can Chinese noodles
¼ lb. slivered almonds

Sauté beef and onion until browned, add next six ingredients. Layer noodles and beef mixture in a large casserole and top with cheese. Bake, covered, at 375° for thirty minutes. Garnish with Chinese noodles and almonds and serve.

8 to 10 servings ARTHUR J. STOKES, JR.

MENU SUGGESTION

Non-Cook's Gourmet Soup
Well-Tempered "Classerole"
Spinach Salad
Orange Curaçao
Party Crescents

San Diego Super Taco

1 head lettuce, finely shredded
1 green pepper, minced
1 onion, minced
2 tomatoes, minced
1 – 15 oz. can tomato sauce
1 – 10 oz. can enchilada sauce (hot or mild)
1 tsp. sugar
salt and pepper
2 lbs. ground beef
2 cups kidney beans, drained (#303 can)
1 T. butter
1 – 11 oz. pkg. Fritos
4 cups Cheddar cheese, grated

Combine vegetables and chill well. Combine sauces, sugar and season to taste; simmer. Sauté beef, crumble and drain; add to sauce. Simmer beans in butter. Place Fritos in a large deep casserole and heat at 300° until crispy. Remove from oven; layer rest of ingredients in this order: ½ the cheese, beans, ½ the meat sauce, vegetables, remaining sauce and remaining cheese. Bake for twenty minutes. Serve at once.

6 to 8 servings

Thyra Maitre

Western Casserole

1 lb. lean ground beef
2 T. salad oil
½ cup onion, chopped
¼ cup green pepper, chopped
1 cup brown rice, uncooked
2½ cups canned tomatoes
1 cup ripe olives, coarsely chopped
2 to 3 tsp. chili powder
½ tsp. Worcestershire sauce
salt and pepper to taste

Sauté beef in oil until browned; remove from pan. To the same oil, add onion, green pepper and rice; cook, stirring until browned. Add tomatoes, one cup water, olives, meat and seasonings and bring to a boil. Pour into a two-quart casserole, cover and bake at 350° for forty-five to sixty minutes.

2 to 4 servings BARBARA WALTERS

Rio Grande Pie

Sauté 1 lb. ground beef and 1 chopped onion in butter; add 1 can tomato sauce, 1 T. sugar, 2 tsp. chili powder, salt and 1 cup whole kernel corn. Prepare your favorite corn bread. Pour hot meat mixture into a casserole, top with corn bread batter and bake at 425° for twenty minutes.

6 servings MRS. R. FRANKLIN OUTCALT

Chuckwagon Bean Casserole

½ lb. bacon
3 lbs. ground beef
3 cups onion, chopped
1 cup celery, chopped
2 beef bouillon cubes
1 or 2 cloves garlic, minced
1½ cups catsup
3 T. mustard
salt and pepper
2 – 29 oz. cans molasses-style baked beans

Sauté bacon until crisp, set aside. In the same pan sauté beef, onion and celery until browned, drain. Dissolve bouillon cubes in ½ cup boiling water; stir with remaining ingredients into meat mixture. Crumble bacon and add. Bake at 350° in individual covered ramekins for forty-five minutes or in a large casserole for seventy-five minutes, or until hot and bubbly.

12 servings Mrs. Alan R. Daus

Fantastic Veal

½ lb. fresh mushrooms
4 T. butter
4 veal cutlets or veal steaks
flour
1 cup dry white wine

Sauté mushrooms in butter in a large skillet. Dredge cutlets with flour and pound thin. Sauté with mushrooms; add wine, cover and simmer for twenty minutes. Serve with noodles. Veal can be prepared ahead of time and then warmed in a casserole at 300° for thirty minutes before serving.

2 to 4 servings Mrs. Howard E. Rowen, Jr.

Vitello Tonnato

1 – 7 oz. can tuna fish, drained
½ cup cold beef bouillon
½ cup mayonnaise
2 tsp. wine vinegar
1 – 3¼ oz. jar capers, drained
1 small sour pickle
salt to taste
slices of well-seasoned cold veal, ⅛-inch thick (or turkey or chicken)

Combine all ingredients except veal and puree in a blender. Arrange sliced meat on a serving platter and cover with the sauce. Refrigerate for two hours, and serve cold, garnished with a few capers.

6 servings Mrs. Aldo Ceccato

Variation: puree 1 can drained tuna fish, ¼ cup lemon or lime juice, ½ cup minced fresh parsley and several anchovies in a blender. Combine with 2 cups mayonnaise, 1 T. minced fresh dill and ½ cup capers. Serve over slices of cold veal or veal loaf, prepared as follows. Stir 2 lightly beaten eggs into 2 lbs. ground veal, add ½ cup bread crumbs which have been soaked in 1 cup chicken stock, ¼ cup butter and 4 T. minced fresh dill. Season to taste and refrigerate one hour. Divide into thirds. Press one-third into a greased loaf pan, top with anchovies and strips of thickly sliced cooked tongue. Repeat twice. Place pan in one inch of water and bake at 350° for forty minutes. Cool. Wrap in foil and refrigerate overnight. Can be garnished with pimiento strips, watercress, olives and sweet gherkins.

6 servings Mrs. Gary Graffman

VEAL GOULASH

2 large onions, chopped
2 lbs. veal, cubed
2 T. salad oil
2 tsp. (or more) paprika
½ green pepper, minced
2 T. catsup
salt and pepper
¾ sour cream or yogurt

Sauté onions and meat in oil. Sprinkle with plenty of paprika until veal is quite red. Add green pepper, catsup and season to taste. Cover and cook two and one-half hours or until veal is tender, adding water as necessary. Stir in sour cream just before serving.

4 servings MRS. PAUL EPSTEIN

VIVA LA VEAL

1 clove garlic, minced
2 T. butter
2 lbs. veal, cubed
2 T. flour
salt and pepper
2 one-inch strips lemon peel
1 cup heavy cream

Sauté garlic in butter in a heavy skillet. Remove garlic and sauté veal in the butter. Sprinkle flour, and salt and pepper to taste, over the meat; heat. Add lemon peel and one cup boiling water; cover and simmer about one hour or until tender. Remove lemon, stir in cream and heat through.

4 servings MRS. CHARLES M. FAIRCHILD

Veal Scaloppine al Limone

1½ lbs. veal scallops
salt and freshly ground pepper
flour
4 T. butter
3 T. olive oil
¾ cup beef bouillon
6 lemon slices, paper thin
1 T. lemon juice

Season and flour veal, sauté in two tablespoons butter and olive oil until golden. Remove scallops, drain most of the fat; add ½ cup bouillon and boil, scraping browned bits from bottom of pan. Return veal to skillet with lemon slices on top. Cover and simmer for ten minutes or until veal is tender. To serve, arrange veal and lemon slices on a heated platter. Add ¼ cup bouillon to the juices in the skillet and boil briskly until reduced to a syrupy glaze. Add lemon juice and cook, stirring, for one minute. Remove from heat, stir in remaining butter and pour sauce over the scallops.

4 servings — MISHA DICHTER

MENU SUGGESTION

Shrimp Salad Spread

Veal Scaloppine al Limone

Mushrooms Florentine

Toffee Meringue Torte

Ten-Boy Curry

- 1 onion, sliced
- 1 tart apple, diced
- 3 T. margarine
- ½ cup raisins, preferably dark
- 1½ cups beef or chicken bouillon
- 1 tsp. curry powder
- 3½ tsp. flour
- 1 cup light cream
- salt and pepper
- 2 to 3 cups cooked lamb, veal, beef, poultry or seafood, cubed

Sauté onion and apple in margarine. Add raisins and bouillon. Mix curry powder and flour together, then add cream and blend. Pour into apple mixture; stir over low heat until thickened and creamy. Add chunks of meat and season to taste. Serve over rice with ten sweet, salty, sour or crunchy curry accompaniments.

6 servings

Mrs. William H. West

Variation:

Curried Seafood

Omit fruits in above recipe; add ¼ pound mushrooms and substitute ½ pound each scallops, shrimp and lobster for the meat; season with prepared mustard and Worcestershire sauce.

Mrs. Richard D. Birk

Variation:

Rijsttafel a la Madar

Make coconut milk by combining one cup coconut flakes or ½ fresh coconut, grated, and 2 cups scalded milk. Let stand in refrigerator two hours. Use in place of cream in above recipe. Omit fruits but stir in a three-inch length of fresh ginger-root, chopped.

Mrs. William Madar

Curry Accompaniments

Mango chutney
Chopped watermelon rind or sweet pickles
Pickled kumquats
Drained crushed pineapple
Dark or golden raisins plumped in sherry or brandy
Currants plumped in sherry, brandy or port
Grated fresh or candied ginger
Chopped fresh apple in a bit of yogurt or mayonnaise
Sliced bananas or avocados in lime juice
Flaked coconut

Chopped salted peanuts, cashews or almonds
Crumbled bacon
Crumbled potato chips
Shredded ham or dried beef
Bombay duck
French fried onion rings

India relish
Sliced ripe or green olives
Chili sauce with chopped hot chili peppers and onions
'Bama pepper jelly
Chopped sour or dill pickles
Pickled tiny white onions
Cucumber sambal (sliced in vinegar)
Fresh vegetable chutney (chopped onion, green pepper, tomato in lemon juice)

Chopped scallions
Chopped green peppers
Lime wedges
Chopped hard-cooked egg yolks
Chopped hard-cooked egg whites

Devilish Lamb Chops

4 T. butter
4 T. Worcestershire sauce
4 T. lemon juice
4 T. gin
freshly ground pepper
6 thick loin lamb chops
½ cup mint jelly

Combine first five ingredients, pour over lamb chops and marinate for several hours. When ready to serve, remove chops from marinade and broil about eight minutes on each side. Add mint jelly to marinade; heat and serve over chops.

6 servings

Mrs. Harry H. Stone

New Zealand Peachy-Creamy Sauce

8 canned peach halves
1 T. butter
¼ cup brandy
½ cup light cream

Drain peach halves, reserving ¼ cup syrup. Sauté peaches in butter in a heavy skillet until warmed through, remove from pan. Stir reserved syrup into remaining butter; heat. Pour brandy into pan and ignite. Douse flames with cream. Stir thoroughly and spoon over warm peach halves. Serve with roast lamb.

Mrs. Eric Maxwell

Lamb-Eggplant Italiano

2 T. salad oil
1 large eggplant, pared and sliced
1 onion, minced
flour
1½ lbs. lamb, cubed
1 tsp. Italian herbs
1 T. sugar
1 to 2 tsp. salt
¼ tsp. pepper
1 - 16 oz. can Italian style tomatoes
3 to 4 T. bread crumbs
6 slices Mozzarella cheese (or Provolone)

Heat oil in a large skillet; arrange eggplant slices in oil, slightly overlapping if necessary. Drizzle more oil and 2 T. water on top; cover. Steam gently about ten minutes. Remove and drain on paper towels. Sauté onion until tender in the same pan. Arrange eggplant and onion in the bottom of a large casserole. Sauté floured lamb cubes in skillet until brown. Add herbs, sugar, salt, pepper and tomatoes. Simmer for about fifteen minutes, stirring occasionally. Add to eggplant and onion. Top with bread crumbs. Bake, covered, at 350° degrees for one hour or more, until meat is tender. Uncover. Criss-cross cheese slices on top. Bake an additional ten minutes or until cheese has melted.

4 to 6 servings — Mrs. William A. Blunden

Variation: use ground beef in place of lamb.

Bavarian Pork Cordon Bleu

6 pork cutlets, butterfly cut
6 to 12 slices brick cheese
6 slices ham
2 eggs, beaten
unseasoned bread crumbs
salt and pepper
salad or olive oil and butter

Cut the cutlets in half. On one half place one slice of ham and one or two slices of cheese. Cover this with the other half of pork cutlet and secure on four sides with toothpicks. Dip into eggs and then bread crumbs. Season to taste. In a large skillet heat about one inch oil and butter. Cook cutlets on each side until golden brown and crisp. Blot and serve with a lemon wedge and home-fried potatoes.

6 servings — Mrs. Jan Preston Wilkison

Plum Dandy Pork Chops

4 thick loin pork chops
salt, pepper and sage
1 junior baby food jar plums with tapioca
1 tsp. lemon rind, grated
¼ tsp. cinnamon
⅛ tsp. cloves
½ cup port

Season pork chops, dredge with flour and brown in butter. Combine plums, lemon rind, spices and port. Transfer chops to a shallow baking pan, cover with sauce and bake at 325° for one to one and one-half hours, basting occasionally.

4 servings — Mrs. Gerald Gordon

PORK WITH CHERRY SAUCE

1 cup cherry preserves
2 T. light corn syrup
¼ cup red wine vinegar
¼ tsp. each cinnamon, nutmeg, ground cloves
3 T. slivered almonds
3 lbs. pork roast, boned

Combine first four ingredients. Simmer, stirring frequently. Reduce heat, add almonds. Keep warm. Rub meat with salt and pepper. Bake at 325° for two and one-half hours. Baste with sauce during last half hour of cooking. Pass remaining sauce.

6 servings MRS. WILLIAM L. MACON

SWEET AND SOUR PORK

3 lbs. pork shoulder, trimmed and cubed
1 T. salad oil
1 - 12 oz. can pineapple chunks
3 T. brown sugar
3 T. cornstarch
¼ cup vinegar
2 T. soy sauce
¼ tsp. nutmeg
2 green peppers, julienne
1 onion, thinly sliced
3 stalks celery, cut into ½-inch pieces
½ cup blanched almonds

Sauté pork in oil until brown. Season to taste and add enough water to almost cover pork. Simmer for sixty-five minutes. Drain pineapple; reserve ½ cup juice. Combine juice, ¾ cup water, brown sugar, cornstarch, vinegar, soy sauce and nutmeg. Add to pork, stirring until slightly thickened. Add remaining ingredients and simmer for five minutes. Serve immediately with additional soy sauce and fried rice.

6 servings MRS. CALVIN F. HURD, JR.

Tagliatelle Alla "Pastorale" (Ham and Noodle Casserole)

¼ cup butter
¼ lb. mushrooms, thinly sliced
2 cups cooked ham, diced
1 pkg. frozen peas
1½ T. basil
salt and pepper
1 lb. cooked tagliatelle (¼-inch flat noodles) or fettuccini, al dente
1 to 1½ cups Cheddar cheese, grated
1 cup Parmesan cheese, grated

Melt butter in a large skillet and sauté mushrooms. Add ham and heat. Cook peas for three minutes; add to ham mixture with basil and season to taste. Simmer until heated thoroughly. Combine with hot tagliatelle, cheeses and a few tablespoons water in a casserole and serve.

6 to 8 servings — Francesco Mander

MENU SUGGESTION

Avocado Allegretto

Tagliatelle Alla "Pastorale"

Nesselrode Sundae Pie

Accompaniments

Ratatouille

3 or 4 onions, chopped
2 to 4 T. margarine
1 lb. green beans, cut
1 - 28 oz. can tomatoes
4 zucchini, cubed
2 medium or 1 large eggplant, cubed
2 green peppers, minced
1 small hot pepper, minced
3 beef bouillon cubes

Sauté onion in margarine until browned; add beans and ½ can tomatoes and juice; simmer while preparing vegetables. Add rest of tomatoes, vegetables and bouillon cubes. Simmer forty-five to sixty minutes. Can be served hot or cold.

10 to 12 servings — Mrs. J. William Fulbright

Noonie's Zucchini

4 zucchini
⅔ cup mayonnaise
1 to 2 T. Bleu cheese, crumbled
¼ tsp. garlic salt
¼ cup Parmesan cheese, grated

Parboil zucchini and halve. Combine remaining ingredients, spread on zucchini. Broil until browned and bubbly, about five to ten minutes.

4 servings — Sue K. Markus

Bavarian Red Cabbage

1 head red cabbage, shredded
3 T. bacon drippings
1 onion, chopped
salt and freshly ground pepper
1 cup red wine
2 apples, diced
1 T. brown sugar
1 T. vinegar

Sauté cabbage in bacon fat, turning frequently until it begins to get limp. Add onion and lightly brown; cook five minutes. Add seasonings and wine; cook ten minutes longer. Add apples, brown sugar and vinegar; cover and simmer until tender. Serve with pork, pot roast or sauerbraten.

6 to 8 servings — Damaris D. Klaus

Carrots Sylvia

3 bunches small young carrots
½ tsp. salt
1 T. sugar
½ cup butter, melted
½ cup orange marmalade

Peel carrots and cook in water to cover (salt and sugar added) until tender. Drain. Combine butter and orange marmalade in a saucepan; add carrots and simmer until blended. Garnish with parsley and serve.

6 servings — Sylvia Balslew

Elegant Spinach Souffle

2 cups mushrooms, sliced
1 onion, thinly sliced
1 tsp. tarragon
¼ cup butter
1 nine-inch pie shell, partially baked
2 pkgs. Stouffer's Frozen Spinach Souffle, partially thawed

Sauté mushrooms, onion and tarragon in butter. Spread evenly in pie shell. Pile soufflé over mushrooms making a smooth layer, but working soufflé as little as possible. Cover crust with foil to prevent scorching. Bake at 375° for one hour or until soufflé is golden. Garnish with lemon wedges and serve immediately.

6 servings — Mrs. Dennis LaBarre

Spinach-Artichoke Casserole

2 cans artichoke hearts, drained
3 pkgs. frozen leaf spinach, cooked
freshly ground pepper
3 – 3 oz. pkgs. cream cheese, softened
¼ cup margarine
6 T. milk
⅓ cup Parmesan cheese, grated

Arrange artichokes on the bottom of a 1½ quart casserole, cover with spinach and season with pepper. Beat cream cheese, margarine and milk together. Spread over the spinach. Refrigerate about twenty-four hours. Sprinkle Parmesan cheese on top of the sauce and bake at 375° for forty minutes.

6 to 8 servings — Mrs. W. E. MacDonald III

Artichoke Hearts Louisiana

2 cans artichoke hearts, drained
2 cups fresh mushrooms
3 T. butter, melted
juice of 1½ lemons
1 T. dry sherry

Sauté artichoke hearts and mushrooms in butter and lemon juice for ten minutes. Add sherry and cook for an additional five minutes. Excellent with beef.

6 servings — Mrs. Richard Hahn

Baked Cheese-Stuffed Tomatoes

6 to 8 tomatoes
1½ cups Swiss cheese, grated
1 egg beaten
5 T. onion, chopped
½ tsp. marjoram
1 tsp. prepared mustard
1½ tsp. salt
2 T. butter, melted
⅓ cup herb stuffing mix

Cut off top of tomato. Gently scoop out and coarsely chop pulp. Combine ¾ of tomato pulp with remaining ingredients. Spoon mixture into tomato shells and sprinkle with a few stuffing crumbs. Place in a 9″ x 13″ casserole and bake at 350° for twenty-five minutes or until tender.

6 to 8 servings — Mrs. Gordon Taubenheim

Corn Pudding

2 eggs, beaten
1 tsp. salt
⅛ tsp. pepper
1 can shoepeg (white) corn, drained
¾ cup evaporated milk
2 T. sugar
2 T. cornstarch
2 T. butter

Combine all ingredients and mix well. Pour into a buttered one-quart baking dish. Set the dish in a pan of hot water and bake at 350° for about one hour.

4 servings — Mrs. J. Merrill Culver

Mushrooms Florentine

1 lb. fresh mushrooms
2 pkgs. frozen spinach, thawed
1 tsp. salt
¼ cup onion, chopped
¼ cup butter, melted
1 cup Cheddar cheese, grated
garlic salt

Remove stems from mushrooms and sauté stems and caps, browning cap side first. Line a shallow casserole with spinach which has been combined with salt, onion, and melted butter. Sprinkle with half of the cheese. Arrange mushrooms over spinach. Season with garlic salt. Cover with remaining cheese. Bake at 350° for thirty minutes.

6 to 8 servings — Mrs. John E. Culver

Baked Mushrooms

- 2 small onions, chopped
- 3 T. butter, melted
- 2 eggs
- ⅔ cup bread crumbs
- ¾ cup milk
- ¾ cup light cream
- 2 tsp. salt
- ¼ tsp. pepper
- 1 lb. fresh mushrooms, coarsely chopped

Sauté onions in butter until golden. In a 1½ quart casserole, beat eggs; then add crumbs, milk, cream, salt and pepper and mix well. Carefully fold in mushrooms and onions. Bake at 350° for sixty to seventy minutes until golden and set.

6 servings

David Skylar
ComCorp

Variation: use whole mushrooms topped with a mixture of 8 T. cream of chicken soup, ½ cup butter, oregano and chives; bake for twenty minutes.

Mrs. W. Daniel Driscoll

Arkansas Mushrooms

Trim, wash, dry and quarter 1 lb. fresh mushrooms. Sauté in 2 T. butter and 1 tsp. garlic salt until dark brown. Turn heat to low. Squeeze juice of one-half lemon over mushrooms; cover and simmer one minute. Toss and serve with rare beef.

David F. Conley

Annie's Mushroom Pie

6 T. butter
3 lbs. mushrooms, quartered
2 T. lemon juice
salt and pepper
9 T. flour
2 cups clear chicken stock
¼ cup sherry
½ cup light cream
½ cup Cheddar cheese, shredded
pastry for 2 nine-inch pies
1 egg yolk, beaten

Melt 4 T. butter; add mushrooms and lemon juice and season to taste. Cook in a covered skillet for ten minutes, shaking pan frequently. Lift out mushrooms, arrange on the bottom of a greased 9″ x 13″ baking dish. To remaining juice in pan, add 2 T. butter and the flour. Stir in stock, cook until thick and smooth. Add sherry, cream and cheese and pour over mushrooms. Top with pastry rolled to fit. Brush crust with egg yolk; make slits in top. Bake at 400° for thirty to thirty-five minutes. Serve warm. Can be frozen unbaked. The mushroom mixture can also be used to fill a 9″ two-crust pie.

10 to 12 servings — Mrs. John T. Makley

ONION PIE

1 cup cracker crumbs
¼ cup butter, melted
2 to 2½ cups onions, thinly sliced
2 to 3 T. butter
¾ cup light cream or heavy cream
2 eggs, lightly beaten
¾ tsp. salt
pepper, garlic salt and paprika
1 cup Swiss cheese, shredded

Combine crumbs and melted butter and press into a 9″ pie plate. Steam onions in butter slowly until cooked (about fifteen minutes). Place in pie shell. Combine cream and eggs; season to taste, and pour over onions. Sprinkle cheese on top and bake at 350° for forty-five minutes. May be made several hours ahead and refrigerated. Serve as a side dish with any meat.

4 or 5 servings MRS. JEROME R. STRICKLAND

BLENDER HOLLANDAISE SAUCE

3 egg yolks
2 T. lemon juice
pinch salt and cayenne pepper
½ cup butter, melted and hot

Combine egg yolks, lemon juice, salt and cayenne pepper in blender. Turn on and off. Pour in hot butter while spinning. Serve over vegetables.

MRS. DARRELL A. BRAND

Spanakopeta (Athenian Spinach Pie)

½ cup onion, minced
¼ cup butter or margarine
3 pkgs. frozen chopped spinach, thawed and well-drained
3 eggs, beaten
½ lb. feta cheese, crumbled
¼ cup fresh parsley, chopped
2 T. fresh dill, chopped (or 1 T. dill weed)
salt and pepper
¾ cup butter or margarine, melted
½ lb. phyllo or strudel leaves (16 – 12″ x 15″ sheets)

Sauté onion in ¼ cup butter until golden. Add spinach, stir and remove from heat. Combine eggs, cheese, parsley, dill and salt and pepper to taste; add to spinach mixture; mix well. Brush a 9″ x 13″ pan with melted butter. Start laying eight phyllo leaves, one-by-one, brushing the top of each with melted butter. Keep unused pastry leaves covered with a damp towel to prevent drying out. Spread evenly with spinach mixture. Cover with eight more leaves, brushing each with butter; use up any extra butter on top. Cut through top layer of pastry to form diamonds or squares. Bake at 350° for thirty to thirty-five minutes or until top is puffy and golden. Serve warm. This looks like a lot of work, but it is very easy. It is a spectacular and delicious appetizer or side dish with meat, fish or poultry.

12 servings — Mrs. Alan J. Shapiro

Steamed Cranberry Pudding

½ cup molasses
½ cup water
2 tsp. baking soda
2 cups fresh cranberries, ground
1½ cups flour
1 cup confectioners sugar
½ cup butter
½ cup light cream

Combine first five ingredients, place in steamer. Steam one hour more. (If you do not own a steamer, pour batter into a greased one-pound coffee can; covered with doubled wax paper. Place on top of a saucer in a large kettle, half filled with water. Weight top of can so it won't bounce. Cover kettle and keep water boiling.) Remove after cooling slightly and cut in six horizontal slices. Combine sugar, butter and cream in the top of a double boiler. Mix well and serve warm over pudding slices.

6 servings — Mrs. S. Timothy Kilty

Augmented Acorn Squash

Bake 2 whole acorn squash at 350° for thirty minutes. Split and scoop out seeds. Sprinkle with the grated rind of an orange and a lemon. Squeeze fruits; combine juices and 2 T. sherry and pour into center. Bake fifteen minutes longer, basting once.

4 servings — Mrs. Clarence J. Doser

Jacques-au-Lantern Compote

1 perfect small pumpkin
2 cups tart apples, peeled and diced
1 cup raisins
1 cup pecans, chopped
⅓ cup water
⅓ cup sugar
1 tsp. lemon juice
¼ tsp. cinnamon
¼ tsp. nutmeg

Wash and dry pumpkin. Cut off top, leaving a generous slice for lid. Clean out and place on a pie pan. Combine all other ingredients in a saucepan and bring just to a boil. Pour apple mixture into pumpkin and cover with lid. Bake at 350° for forty-five to sixty minutes, until apples are tender. Serve as accompaniment, scooping out some pumpkin with each spoonful of fruit. Delicious hot or cold.

8 servings — Elizabeth Gullander

Sherried Sweet Potatoes

2 – 22 oz. cans sweet potatoes
¾ cup butter
¼ cup milk
¾ cup dry sherry
¼ tsp. nutmeg
¼ tsp. cinnamon
½ cup pecans, chopped, or tiny marshmallows

Heat potatoes, then whip with butter, milk, and sherry. Add seasonings. Turn into casserole; sprinkle with pecans or marshmallows. Bake at 375° for twenty minutes. Delicious with baked ham or turkey.

8 servings — Mrs. William T. Tucker

Potato Pudding

5 large potatoes, peeled
2 large onions
2 eggs
1½ to 2 tsp. salt
¼ to ½ tsp. pepper
2 T. parsley
2 T. salad oil

Coarsely grate potatoes and rinse thoroughly. Grate onions, mix with eggs and add salt, pepper and parsley; blend thoroughly. (Potatoes and onions may be grated separately in a blender.) Pour into a greased six-cup ring mold or shallow casserole. Sprinkle oil on top. Bake at 400° for one hour or until top is golden. If you use a ring mold, cool for five minutes and unmold on a heated platter. Center can be filled with a vegetable; i.e., peas, sautéed mushrooms or glazed carrots. Can also be made au gratin by adding ½ to 1 cup grated Cheddar or Swiss cheese; however, a casserole dish must be used if cheese is added.

5 or 6 servings Mrs. Geofrey Greenleaf

Jackson Potatoes

½ to 1 lb. bacon
6 to 12 potatoes, unpeeled and thickly sliced
2 to 4 onions, thickly sliced

In a large frying pan (on stove or over open fire), cook bacon until just tender. Throw in potatoes and onion. Toss around and cook until done to your taste.

8 to 16 servings Mrs. Alan R. Daus

Snowy Mashed Potato Casserole

12 potatoes, cooked
1 - 8 oz. pkg. cream cheese, softened
1 cup sour cream
1 clove garlic, crushed
salt and white pepper
⅛ cup chives, chopped

Whip potatoes. Add cheese, sour cream and garlic; season to taste and whip until light. Stir in chives. Spoon into a lightly greased ten-cup casserole. Sprinkle with paprika and dot with butter. Bake, uncovered, at 350° for thirty minutes or until lightly browned.

10 servings Mrs. Anthony R. Michel

New Zealand Rice

4 T. butter
1 small onion, chopped
1 cup long-grain rice
1½ cups chicken stock
salt and pepper
¼ cup currants or raisins
¼ cup slivered almonds

Melt 3 T. butter in a flameproof casserole, add onion and cook until golden. Stir in raw rice and cook three minutes. Add stock, season to taste, and bring to a boil. Cover and bake at 375° for twenty minutes or until tender. Add extra stock if necessary. Combine remaining butter, currants and almonds and pour over rice just before serving.

6 servings Mrs. Mark Schulze

NOODLES ENCORE

1 – 8 oz. pkg. medium noodles, cooked
½ lb. Swiss cheese, grated
1 T. onion juice
1 T. Worcestershire sauce
¼ cup butter, melted
½ tsp. salt
¼ tsp. pepper
2 cups sour cream

Add cheese to hot noodles; stir in all other ingredients except sour cream. Cool. Add sour cream and toss lightly. Place in a buttered casserole and bake at 350° for one hour.

6 to 8 servings MRS. MICHAEL R. WEIL

SUNSHINE NOODLES

1 – 8 oz. pkg. egg noodles, cooked
1 – 3 oz. pkg. cream cheese
½ cup butter or margarine, melted
4 eggs
1 cup sour cream
1 – 8 oz. jar apricot preserves
2 T. brown sugar

Place half of the noodles in a two-quart buttered casserole. Blend cream cheese, butter, eggs and sour cream together. Pour half of the cheese mixture over the noodles; spread half of the preserves on top. Repeat. Sprinkle with brown sugar. Cover and bake at 350° for one to one and one-half hours.

10 servings MRS. MERIL MAY, JR.

NOSTALGIC NOODLE RING

3 eggs, beaten
½ tsp. salt
2 T. sugar
¼ cup butter, melted
1 – 12 oz. pkg. broad egg noodles, cooked
½ cup pecan halves
½ cup brown sugar

Combine eggs, salt, sugar and butter. Gently fold in noodles until well mixed. Butter a large ring mold thoroughly and place small lumps of butter around bottom. Press pecan halves, upside down, into buttered bottom of mold (pecans should touch, so that they form a complete circle when mold is inverted). Sprinkle brown sugar over pecans. Pack noodle mixture firmly into mold. May be refrigerated at this point until one hour before serving. Place mold in 1″ of water in a shallow pan. Bake at 350° for one hour. Remove from oven and quickly invert on a serving dish. Fill center with green peas, if desired.

6 to 8 servings EUNICE PODIS

Spinach Salad

1 lb. fresh spinach
½ can bean sprouts
1 can water chestnuts, sliced
red onion rings
3 hard-cooked eggs, chopped
½ cup salad oil
½ cup vinegar
3 T. catsup
¼ cup sugar
1 tsp. salt
5 slices bacon, cooked and crumbled

Tear spinach leaves into bowl, add next four ingredients and chill. Combine next five ingredients, in a covered cruet; shake well. Toss dressing and salad about one-half hour before serving. Garnish with bacon at serving time.

4 to 8 servings — Mrs. Paul H. Prasse

Flaming Spinach Salad Marilyn Horne

Wash and chill 1½ lbs. fresh spinach. Sauté ½ lb. diced bacon in a chafing dish just until it begins to brown. Stir in ½ cup red wine vinegar, 3 T. Worcestershire sauce, juice of 1 lemon and ½ cup sugar; simmer. Reserving bacon pieces, drizzle dressing over spinach leaves and toss. Divide into individual salad bowls. Add ¼ cup brandy to the bacon; ignite and while flaming, pour over the individual salads. Do not season with salt or pepper as this salad has a delicate sweet and sour taste. It was a favorite dish served to Marilyn Horne during her Cleveland Orchestra visit.

4 to 6 servings — Janet S. Dinkel

MANDARIN SPINACH SALAD

- 2 lbs. fresh spinach
- 12 hard-cooked eggs, sliced
- 4 cans mandarin oranges, drained
- 2 red onions, sliced and separated into rings
- 1½ cups salad oil
- ¼ cup vinegar
- ½ cup sugar
- 2 tsp. salt
- 2 tsp. paprika
- 2 tsp dry mustard
- 2 tsp. celery seed
- 2 tsp. onion, grated
- 2 cloves garlic, cut crosswise

Tear spinach; combine with eggs, oranges and onion rings. When ready to serve, toss with dressing made by combining oil, vinegar, sugar and seasonings. (Let garlic stand in dressing for two hours, then remove.)

12 servings

SMITH COLLEGE CLUB OF CLEVELAND

CALIFORNIA SALAD BOWL

Drain liquid from 3 (6 oz.) jars marinated artichoke hearts into a small bowl. Arrange pieces of lettuce, artichoke hearts, 3 tomatoes cut in wedges and cubes of ½ cantaloupe in a salad bowl. Beat ¼ cup mayonnaise, ¼ cup lemon juice, 1 tsp. seasoned salt and 1 tsp. sugar into the artichoke liquid. Toss with salad just before serving.

6 to 8 servings

ALAN DE PETRO
WKBF-TV

Bibb Mezzo Vinaigrette

1 tsp. salt
2 T. tarragon vinegar or lemon juice
3 T. salad oil
3 T. light cream
¼ tsp. white pepper
¼ tsp. dry mustard
2 or 3 heads Bibb lettuce

Combine ingredients except lettuce in a blender and spin for thirty seconds. Store in refrigerator. Bring to room temperature before serving on Bibb lettuce or other greens.

6 servings — Rice Hershey

Layered Vegetable Salad

1 head iceberg lettuce, shredded
1 lb. carrots, sliced
1 green pepper, chopped
1 bunch scallions, sliced
1 or 2 pkgs. frozen tiny green peas, thawed
3 cups mayonnaise
1 tsp. Worcestershire sauce
6 to 8 slices bacon, cooked and crumbled

In a 9″ x 13″ casserole, layer vegetables in order given. Frost with a thick layer of mayonnaise by beginning with a thin layer over the peas and then building up the thickness. The secret is to seal the edges completely to prevent air from reaching the lettuce. Sprinkle Worcestershire on top and swirl with spatula. Garnish with crumbled bacon. Salad can be prepared ahead and refrigerated.

8 servings — Mrs. John F. Herrick

BROCCOLI MOLDED SALAD

- 2 heads fresh broccoli, stems removed, cooked
- 1 envelope unflavored gelatin
- 1 can beef consommé (undiluted)
- ¾ cup mayonnaise
- 3 hard-cooked eggs, chopped
- ½ cup slivered almonds
- 2 tsp. lemon juice
- 1 tsp. salt
- ½ tsp. Worcestershire sauce
- 12 to 16 cherry tomatoes

Place cooked broccoli, heads down, around a four-cup ring mold; set aside. Soften gelatin in ¼ cup consommé. Heat the remaining consommé, add gelatin, and stir until dissolved. Add remaining ingredients except tomatoes and pour over broccoli. Chill until set and unmold onto a platter covered with leaf lettuce. Fill the center of the mold with tomatoes.

6 to 8 servings MRS. GORDON R. TAUBENHEIM

TOMATO ASPIC

- 3 – 3 oz. pkgs. raspberry flavored gelatin
- 3 – 1 lb. cans stewed tomatoes
- 6 drops hot pepper sauce

Dissolve gelatin in 1¼ cups boiling water. Stir in tomatoes, breaking up large pieces with a fork. Add pepper sauce; mix thoroughly. Pour into a lightly oiled three-quart ring mold and chill. Serve with horseradish sauce (p. 68).

16 servings SMITH COLLEGE CLUB OF CLEVELAND

Red, White and Green Holiday Mold

1 – 3 oz. pkg. lime flavored gelatin
1 cup sliced pineapple
2 T. lemon juice
1 – 3 oz. pkg. lemon flavored gelatin
2 – 3 oz. pkgs. cream cheese, softened
⅓ cup mayonnaise
1 – 3 oz. pkg. strawberry flavored gelatin
2 bananas, sliced

To prepare pineapple-lime layer: dissolve lime gelatin in 1 cup hot water; drain pineapple, reserving syrup; add lemon juice to syrup and enough water to make 1 cup; add to dissolved gelatin. Chill until partially set. Cut pineapple slices in thirds; arrange in an "S" design in the bottom of a large loaf pan. Pour small amount of gelatin mixture over pineapple; refrigerate until partially set. Then add rest of gelatin mixture; chill until firm. For lemon-cheese layer: dissolve lemon gelatin in 1 cup hot water; chill until thickened and whip until light and fluffy. Blend cream cheese and mayonnaise; fold into lemon gelatin. Pour mixture over lime layer; chill until firm. Finally, dissolve strawberry gelatin in 2 cups hot water. Arrange banana slices over lemon layer; pour strawberry gelatin over all. Chill until firm.

8 to 10 servings — Mrs. William H. Steinbrink

Fruit Salad Dressing

1 – 3 oz. pkg. cream cheese, softened
16 marshmallows, chopped
1 cup heavy cream

Beat cheese; add marshmallows and cream. Let mixture stand overnight and whip before serving.

Mrs. Richard D. Birk

Russian Raspberry Cream

- 1 pkg. raspberry or strawberry flavored gelatin
- 1 T. lemon juice
- 1 pkg. frozen whole raspberries or strawberries, drained
- 1 cup light cream
- ½ cup sugar
- 1 envelope unflavored gelatin
- 1 cup sour cream
- 1 tsp. vanilla

Dissolve raspberry gelatin in 1 cup hot water. Blend in lemon juice and raspberries and pour into a ring mold. Refrigerate until firm. Heat cream and sugar in a saucepan. Soften unflavored gelatin in ½ cup cold water and add to warm cream mixture. Stir until dissolved. Add sour cream and vanilla. Beat well. Pour slowly over chilled red layer. Refrigerate until firm. Unmold onto a serving platter and garnish as desired.

6 servings

Mrs. Alan J. Shapiro

Spiced Peach Salad

- 1 jar spiced peaches
- 1 – 3 oz. pkg. peach flavored gelatin
- 3 T. brown sugar
- 1 cup sour cream
- 1 bunch seedless grapes

Drain peaches, reserving 1 cup syrup, and cut into small chunks. Dissolve gelatin in 1 cup boiling water and add reserved syrup and peaches. Pour into an oiled 1-quart mold and refrigerate. Stir sugar into sour cream and let stand overnight. Combine with grapes just before serving. Unmold gelatin and top with grape dressing.

6 to 8 servings

Mrs. Willard C. Barry

Father Samanski's Bread

2 T. prepared mustard
1 small onion, minced
1 T. poppy seed
5/8 cup butter, softened
1 loaf Italian bread, unsliced
2 – 8 oz. pkgs. Mozzarella cheese
2 slices bacon, uncooked

Blend mustard, onion, poppy seed and butter. Slice bread almost through and spread with butter mixture. Put a slice of Mozzarella between each bread slice. Arrange bacon slices on top of bread, wrap in foil, and bake at 350° for forty-five to sixty minutes or until cheese is melted. Remove bacon before serving. Eat with fingers!

4 servings — Mrs. Arthur E. Pape

Herbed French Rolls

8 Pepperidge Farm French rolls
1/2 cup butter, softened
1/2 cup Parmesan or Romano cheese, grated
1/2 cup parsley, chopped
1 clove garlic, crushed
1/2 tsp. basil

Slice rolls in 1/2-inch slices, not all the way through. Mix together remaining ingredients and spread between slices. Wrap rolls individually in foil and refrigerate or freeze until needed. Bake at 375° for twenty minutes. Serve individually, wrapped in foil to keep warm.

Yield: 8 — Mrs. A. Bill Kieger

BUTTERMILK BREAD

1 cup buttermilk
3 T. sugar
2½ tsp. salt
⅓ cup butter
1 pkg. dry yeast
5¾ cups unbleached flour
¼ tsp. baking soda

Scald buttermilk (it will curdle) and stir in sugar, salt and butter. Cool to lukewarm. Meanwhile dissolve yeast in 1 cup warm water in a large bowl. Combine milk mixture with yeast. Stir in 3 cups of flour and the baking soda. Beat until smooth. Add approximately 1½ cups more flour and place rest of flour on board. Knead dough until smooth. Place into a greased bowl and let rise in a warm place until doubled in bulk, about one hour. Punch down, let dough rest for fifteen minutes. Shape into two loaves, place in greased loaf pans and let rise until dough comes to top of pan, about one hour. Bake at 375° for thirty minutes or until golden brown.

Yield: 2 loaves HELGA HAZELRIG

Della's Bread

2 T. shortening or butter
2 T. sugar
2 tsp. salt
1 cake compressed yeast
2 cups milk, scalded
6 cups flour

Combine shortening, sugar and salt in a large bowl. Dissolve yeast in 1/4 cup lukewarm water. Pour milk over the sugar mixture and blend well. When mixture is lukewarm, add yeast and beat in three cups flour. Stir in remaining flour. Turn out onto board and knead for four minutes. Return to bowl, cover with a towel and let rise in a warm place until doubled in bulk; punch down and let rise again. Form into loaves and place in greased loaf pans; cover and let rise. Bake at 350° for forty-five to sixty minutes.

Yield: 2 loaves

Mrs. Homer Conley

MENU SUGGESTION

Beef Fondue

Bearnaise Sauce

Horseradish Sauce

Czarda Sauce

Bibb Mezzo Vinaigrette

Della's Bread

Cold Lemon Souffle

Hugo's Wine Bread

- 2 cups biscuit mix
- 1 tsp. sugar
- 1 tsp. instant minced onion
- ½ tsp. oregano
- ¼ cup butter, melted
- ¼ cup sauterne
- 1 egg, beaten
- ½ cup milk
- Parmesan cheese

Combine dry ingredients. Blend in liquids. Turn into a greased eight-inch square pan. Sprinkle Parmesan cheese on top. Bake at 400° for twenty-five minutes.

Mrs. Stuart Neye

Pumpkin Bread

- 3 cups sugar
- 1 cup salad oil
- 2 cups canned pumpkin
- 4 eggs, beaten
- 3⅓ cups flour
- 2 tsp. baking soda
- 1 tsp. salt
- 1 tsp. cinnamon
- 1 tsp. nutmeg
- ½ cup golden raisins
- ½ cup pecans, chopped

Combine sugar, ⅔ cup water, oil, pumpkin and eggs and beat well. Mix in dry ingredients. Add raisins and nuts. Bake in greased loaf pans at 350° for one hour.

Yield: 3 large or 4 small loaves

Sue K. Markus

Carrot Bread

1 cup sugar
¾ cup salad oil
1½ cups flour
1 tsp. baking powder
¼ tsp. salt
1 tsp. baking soda
1 tsp. cinnamon
1 cup carrots, grated
2 eggs
½ cup walnuts, chopped

Combine sugar and oil. Sift together dry ingredients and add to sugar mixture. Stir in carrots. Add eggs, one at a time, beating well after each addition; add nuts. Pour into a greased loaf pan and bake at 375° for one hour. Cool slightly and slice.

8 to 10 servings

Mrs. Louis Bloomfield

Cowboy Cornbread

3 cups cornbread mix
2½ cups milk
3 eggs
¼ lb. bacon, cooked and diced
1½ cups Cheddar cheese, grated
¼ cup pimientos (optional)
1 large onion, diced
¼ cup hot peppers
¼ cup salad oil or bacon drippings
1 cup whole grain corn, drained

Mix ingredients together, pour into a 9″ x 13″ pan and bake at 400° for thirty-five minutes.

Mrs. John Schulze

Suites

Spiced Fruit Medley

1 – 17 oz. can unpeeled apricot halves, drained
1 – 1 lb. can pear halves, drained
1 – 15½ oz. can pineapple chunks, drained
1 large orange, sectioned
⅓ cup brown sugar
½ tsp. cinnamon
¼ tsp. nutmeg
¼ cup butter or margarine
vanilla ice cream (optional)

Combine fruit in a two-quart casserole. Blend brown sugar and spices, sprinkle over fruit and dot with butter. Bake at 350° degrees for twenty minutes. Serve warm in individual bowls. Top with ice cream, if desired.

6 servings

Janet Beighle French
The Plain Dealer

Hot Fruit Compote

¼ cup lemon juice
2 T. brown sugar
½ tsp. cloves
¼ tsp. nutmeg
¼ cup butter or margarine, melted
4 bananas, sliced
1 – 1 lb. can dark sweet cherries, undrained
1 large orange, sectioned
sour cream
brown sugar, sifted

In a saucepan, stir lemon juice, brown sugar, cloves and nutmeg into melted butter; add fruits and heat. Serve hot. Separately pass sour cream and brown sugar to sprinkle on top. Leftovers are good served cold over pound cake or ice cream.

10 servings

Mrs. William T. Tucker

ORANGE CURACAO

6 whole thin-skinned oranges
¼ cup Curaçao or Grand Marnier (orange liqueur)
½ cup coconut, grated (preferably fresh)

Peel, slice and seed oranges. Marinate in Curaçao in refrigerator for at least twelve hours. Rearrange orange slices to form the original orange shape. Pour marinade over and garnish with coconut. These look attractive served in champagne glasses.

6 servings MRS. DENNIS LABARRE

MANGOES MINUET

2 large, ripe mangoes, sliced
1 cup good white table wine

Test mangoes by slicing a small piece a day or two ahead if you are not sure of ripeness. Marinate mangoes in wine in refrigerator. Nice for dinners which need a light ending.

6 servings MRS. E. TERRY WARREN

PEARS DE CACAO

1 – 28 oz. can pear halves
2 oz. creme de cacao
heavy cream, whipped

Combine pears, syrup and creme de cacao; refrigerate for at least three days (or up to three weeks). Serve garnished with whipped cream.

4 servings MRS. WILLIAM H. WEST

Cold Lemon Souffle

1 envelope unflavored gelatin
grated rind of 2 lemons
½ cup lemon juice, unstrained
1 cup sugar
1 cup egg whites (6 jumbo), stiffly beaten
1 cup heavy cream, whipped

In a small saucepan soften gelatin in 2 T. cold water; add lemon rind, juice and sugar; stir over low heat until dissolved. Chill for ten minutes. Fold egg whites into lemon mixture; then fold in whipped cream. Pile into a large soufflé dish, cover and chill overnight. Garnish with lemon or lime rind if desired.

8 servings Mrs. Oliver C. Henkel, Jr.

Rum Cream

1½ tsp. unflavored gelatin
3 egg yolks
½ cup sugar
1 cup heavy cream, whipped
⅓ cup dark rum

Soften gelatin in 3 T. cold water, then dissolve in the top of a double boiler. Beat egg yolks and sugar until thick and lemon-colored, add to gelatin and beat briskly. Fold into whipped cream flavored with rum. Place bowl over cracked ice and stir until it starts to thicken. Chill.

6 servings Freida Schumacher

Berries 'n' Almond Cream

4 almond macaroons, crumbled
4 tsp. frozen orange juice concentrate or Grand Marnier
1 pint French vanilla ice cream, softened
½ cup heavy cream, whipped
2 T. almonds
2 tsp. confectioners sugar

Stir macaroons and orange juice into ice cream; fold in whipped cream. Pour into a three-cup mold. Sprinkle surface with a mixture of almonds and confectioners sugar. Cover and freeze until firm, about four to six hours. Unmold and serve with Hot Berry Sauce.

Hot Berry Sauce

1 pint fresh berries, or 1 pkg. frozen berries
sugar
4 tsp. frozen orange juice concentrate or Grand Marnier

Prepare sauce just before serving. Place fresh or frozen berries in a saucepan with sugar to taste, heat thoroughly; stir in flavoring. Serve hot over ice cream.

6 to 8 servings — Mrs. Harvey B. Willard

Mince Brandy Cream

½ gallon vanilla ice cream, softened
1 – 18 oz. jar mincemeat
¼ cup brandy

Combine ingredients and freeze at least three hours to blend flavors. Serve garnished with crème de menthe or whipped cream.

10 to 12 servings — Mrs. William H. North

Toffee Meringue Torte

3 egg whites
1 tsp. vanilla
1 cup sugar
dash salt
¼ tsp. cream or tartar
2 cups heavy cream, whipped
1 - 6½ oz. Heath bar, crushed
1 - 6½ oz. semi-sweet chocolate bar, crushed

Beat egg whites and slowly add vanilla, sugar, salt and cream of tartar; whip until stiff. Make two nine-inch circles out of brown paper; place half of the meringue mixture on each circle on a cookie sheet. Bake at 275° for one hour. Turn off heat and leave in oven with door closed for at least two hours longer. Cool before filling. Combine whipped cream and candy. Fill and frost like a layer cake. Chill at least eight hours.

6 to 8 servings

Mrs. Richard D. Birk

Variation:

Coffee Pavlova

Substitute 1 tsp. dry instant coffee dissolved in 2 T. hot water for vanilla in the above meringue recipe before baking. Boil 2 – 3 T. milk with 1 tsp. sugar, ½ tsp. instant coffee and a small handful of chopped walnuts for three minutes. Strain and cool. Whip 1 cup heavy cream; reserve a bit for the garnish and fold in glazed nuts. Fill meringue shells and chill overnight. Before serving, garnish with reserved whipped cream and chocolate chips.

Mrs. Robert Boyd

Strawberry Fondue

¼ cup cornstarch
2 T. sugar
2 pkgs. frozen strawberries, thawed and crushed
4 oz. cream cheese, softened
¼ cup brandy (optional)

Blend together cornstarch, sugar and ½ cup water. Combine with strawberries in a saucepan; cook and stir until thick and bubbly. Remove from heat, add cream cheese and stir until melted. Gradually add brandy, if desired. Pour into a fondue pot and keep warm. Serve with fresh fruits (pears, peaches, pineapple), cubed angel food cake and/or marshmallows to dip into the sauce.

6 to 8 servings — Mrs. James Houston

Chocolate Fondue

6 T. light cream
dash salt
1 – 12 oz. pkg. chocolate chips
1 – 6 oz. pkg. milk chocolate chips
1½ cups tiny marshmallows
½ cup sour cream
1 Stouffer's frozen Lemon Pound Cake

Heat cream and salt, stir in chocolate chips, then marshmallows and stir until melted. Remove from heat and add sour cream, stir mixture until smooth. Pour into fondue pot. Keep warm. Defrost pound cake and cut into bite-sized pieces. Spear cake with fondue fork and dip into sauce.

10 to 12 servings — Stouffer Foods

Stravinsky Firebird Crepes

4 oz. sweet cooking chocolate, grated
2 T. almonds, ground
Cointreau (orange liqueur)

Combine chocolate and almonds with enough Cointreau to moisten. Add 3 T. sugar to Crèpe recipe (p. 41) and cook on both sides. Fill and roll crèpes; place side by side on a serving dish. Warm about ½ cup Cointreau, pour over crèpes and ignite. Serve flaming, if desired.

Walter Klien

Skillet Pineapple Upside-Down Cake

½ cup butter
1 to 1½ cups brown sugar
8 pineapple rings
1 scant cup flour, sifted
1½ tsp. baking powder
dash salt
2 eggs, separated
1 cup sugar
¼ tsp. vanilla

In an eleven-inch skillet, melt together butter and brown sugar. Add pineapple rings and cook until bubbly. Sift flour, baking powder and salt into a bowl. Beat egg yolks; add sugar, a little at a time, and vanilla. Stir in ⅜ cup hot water, and combine with dry ingredients. Fold in stiffly beaten egg whites. Pour batter over pineapple rings. Bake in the skillet at 325° for fifty minutes. Cool for ten minutes, invert onto a platter. Serve with whipped cream or light cream.

6 to 8 servings

Mrs. Jack W. Nicklaus

Apple Crisp

- 6 tart apples, peeled and sliced
- 1 cup flour, sifted
- ½ to 1 cup sugar
- 1 tsp. baking powder
- ¾ tsp. salt
- 1 egg
- ⅓ cup salad oil or butter, melted
- ½ tsp. cinnamon

Place apples in a greased eight-inch square baking pan. Mix together with fork until crumbly: flour, sugar, baking powder, salt and unbeaten egg; sprinkle over the apples. Pour oil over all and sprinkle with cinnamon. Bake at 350° for thirty to forty minutes. Serve warm with cream.

8 servings — Damaris D. Klaus

Cranberry Harvest Cake

- 1 orange, pulp and rind, chopped
- ¼ cup raisins
- 1 – 1 lb. can whole cranberry sauce
- 5 T. margarine, melted
- ¼ cup sugar
- 1 pkg. gingerbread mix

Mix orange with raisins and cranberry sauce. Pour margarine into an eight-inch square pan, sprinkle with sugar, cover with cranberry mixture. Prepare gingerbread according to directions on package and pour over cranberry mixture. Bake at 350° for forty-five minutes. Serve with whipped cream or hard sauce.

8 servings — Mrs. A. Bill Kieger

Williamsburg Orange Cake

2½ cups flour
1½ cups sugar
1½ tsp. baking soda
¾ tsp. salt
1½ cups buttermilk
3 eggs
½ cup butter
¼ cup shortening
1½ tsp. vanilla
1 T. orange rind, grated
1 cup golden raisins
½ cup nuts, chopped

Combine dry ingredients; stir in milk, eggs, butter and shortening; beat three minutes. Add remaining ingredients and blend. Pour into two greased and floured nine-inch layer cake pans and bake at 350° for thirty to thirty-five minutes. Cool and frost.

Orange Frosting

4½ cups confectioners sugar
½ cup butter, softened
1 T. orange rind, grated
4 to 5 T. orange juice

Combine ingredients; beat until fluffy.

8 servings — Mrs. William A. Blunden

Almond Cream Cake

2 eggs
1 cup heavy cream, whipped
(stiff peaks)
¾ tsp. almond extract
1½ cups flour
1 cup sugar
2 tsp. baking powder
⅛ tsp. salt
2 T. butter
⅓ cup sugar
1 T. flour
1 T. heavy cream
¼ cup slivered blanched almonds

Beat eggs, one at a time, into whipped cream; add extract. Sift dry ingredients together and stir into cream mixture. Pour into a greased and floured eight-inch springform pan. Bake at 350° for thirty-five minutes, or until lightly browned and a toothpick inserted in the center comes out clean. Combine remaining ingredients in a saucepan and stir over low heat until blended; pour over cake and bake ten minutes longer.

6 servings

Mrs. Stuart Neye

MENU SUGGESTION

Caesar's Palace Stuffed Mushrooms

Baked Sirloin Steak

New Zealand Rice

Tomato Aspic

White Chocolate Coconut Cake

White Chocolate Coconut Cake

¼ lb. white chocolate
1 cup butter
2 cups sugar
4 eggs, separated
1 tsp. vanilla
2½ cups cake flour
1 tsp. baking soda
1 cup buttermilk
1 cup pecans, chopped
1 cup coconut

Combine chocolate and ½ cup boiling water, stir until melted; cool. Cream butter and sugar; add egg yolks one at a time, beating well after each addition. Add chocolate mixture and vanilla. Sift flour and baking soda together, add alternately with buttermilk to above mixture. Fold in stiffly beaten egg whites and then pecans and coconut. Bake in three greased and floured nine-inch layer cake pans at 350° for twenty to twenty-five minutes. Cool and frost. Refrigerate; remove one hour before serving.

White Chocolate Coconut Frosting

2 cups sugar
1 cup butter
1 – 5⅓ oz. can evaporated milk
¼ to ½ lb. white chocolate
1 cup coconut
1 cup pecans, chopped
1 tsp. vanilla

Combine sugar, butter and milk and bring to a full boil. lower heat and add white chocolate, stirring until melted. Add coconut, pecans and vanilla. Cool.

8 servings

Lois Knutsen

COCA-COLA CHOCOLATE CAKE

1 cup butter
3 T. cocoa
1 cup Coca-Cola
½ cup buttermilk
1 tsp. baking soda
1 tsp. vanilla
1½ cups tiny marshmallows
2 cups sugar
2 eggs
2 cups flour

Heat butter, cocoa and Coca-Cola together until boiling; cool slightly. Combine buttermilk, soda, vanilla and marshmallows; add to chocolate mixture. Combine sugar and eggs, stir in flour and add to above. Pour into a greased and floured 9″ x 13″ pan and bake at 350° for fifty-five to sixty minutes. Pierce hot cake with a fork and let frosting run into the holes.

"COKE" FROSTING

1 cup butter
3 T. cocoa
6 T. Coca-Cola
1 box confectioners sugar
½ cup nuts (optional)

Bring first three ingredients to a boil. Add sugar and beat well; add nuts. Spread over hot cake.

10 to 12 servings MRS. WILLIAM H. STEINBRINK

New York State Flat Apple Pie

½ cup butter
½ cup margarine
2 cups flour
11 or 12 New York State Apples (tart)
1 cup sugar
1 T. cinnamon
juice of ½ lemon
½ cup New York State maple syrup
New York State sharp cheese

Cut butter and margarine into the flour with knife or pastry blender until as fine as cornmeal. Add 3 to 4 T. ice water gradually and work in just enough to hold together. Roll out on lightly floured board until one-inch thick and place in refrigerator for twenty minutes. Remove and roll again, this time to one-eighth-inch thickness. Place prepared crust on the bottom of a 10″ x 15″ baking sheet. Peel, core and cut each apple into six sections; arrange evenly on crust. Mix sugar and cinnamon and sprinkle over the apples, then sprinkle with lemon juice. Bake in a preheated 450° oven for twenty minutes; then reduce heat to 350° and bake another thirty minutes. Sprinkle with maple syrup and serve warm with a generous slice of cheese.

10 to 12 servings — Mrs. Nelson A. Rockefeller

IRISH WHISKEY PIE

1 envelope unflavored gelatin
½ cup cold strong coffee
⅔ cup sugar
⅛ tsp. salt
3 eggs, separated
6 T. Irish whiskey
¼ cup coffee liqueur (Kahlua or Tia Maria)
2 cups heavy cream
1 nine-inch graham cracker pie shell

Soften gelatin in coffee; add half the sugar, salt and egg yolks. Heat, stirring until gelatin is dissolved and mixture thickens. Add whiskey and liqueur and chill until thickened, but not firm. Beat egg whites until stiff, gradually adding remaining sugar; fold into gelatin mixture. Whip 1 cup heavy cream and add. Pile into pie shell and chill several hours or overnight. Before serving, whip the remaining cream and sweeten to taste. Spread over the chilled pie and garnish as desired.

8 servings

CRAIG CLAIBORNE
Food Editor, the New York Times

Variations:

BRANDY ALEXANDER PIE

Substitute ½ cup cold water, ¼ cup cognac and ¼ cup crème de cacao for the coffee, Irish whiskey and coffee liqueur in the above recipe and proceed as directed.

IAN HABERMAN

EGGNOG CHIFFON PIE

Vary Irish Whiskey Pie by substituting 1½ cups milk and ¼ cup light rum for the coffee and spirits and adding an additional egg.

MRS. WILLIAM H. WEST

NESSELRODE SUNDAE PIE

1 egg white
¼ tsp. salt
¼ cup sugar
1 cup walnuts or pecans, chopped
1 pint coffee ice cream, softened
1 pint vanilla ice cream, softened
3 T. butter
1 cup brown sugar
½ cup light cream
1 tsp. vanilla
½ cup light or dark raisins

Beat egg white with salt until stiff; gradually beat in sugar. Fold in nuts. Spread evenly on bottom and sides of a buttered 10″ pie pan. Prick with fork. Bake at 400° for ten to twelve minutes. Cool and chill. Spoon in coffee ice cream; freeze. Top with a layer of vanilla ice cream and return to freezer. Stir butter and brown sugar together until melted, remove from heat and slowly add cream. Heat one minute longer, then add vanilla and raisins. Serve warm over frozen pie.

8 servings

MRS. DENNIS LABARRE

Petite Pecan Tarts

½ cup butter
1 – 3 oz. pkg. cream cheese, softened
1 cup flour
1 egg beaten
1 T. butter, softened
¾ cup light brown sugar
1 tsp. vanilla (or brandy)
¾ cup pecans, chopped
24 pecan halves

Combine butter, cream cheese and flour and chill for two hours. Mix together next four ingredients. Roll dough into twenty-four small balls and press into tiny muffin tins. Sprinkle chopped nuts into the shells, add about 1 tsp. of the brown sugar mixture and top with a pecan half. Bake at 350° for twenty-five to thirty minutes.

Yield: 24 Kathryn Klaus

Apricot Turnovers

1 cup flour
1 – 3 oz. pkg. cream cheese
½ cup butter
apricot preserves

Sift flour, cut in cream cheese and butter. Form into a ball and chill two hours. Roll out dough and cut into two-inch rounds. Put a dab of apricot preserves in the center of each. Fold in half and press edges together. Bake at 375° for ten minutes. Sprinkle with confectioners sugar.

Yield: 5 dozen Mrs. John Doser

Party Crescents

1 cake compressed yeast
4 cups flour, sifted
½ tsp. salt
1¼ cups butter
3 eggs, separated
2 tsp. vanilla
1 cup sour cream
confectioners sugar
1 cup sugar
1 cup pecans or walnuts, ground

Crumble yeast into flour and salt. Cut in butter until fine. Add beaten egg yolks, 1 tsp. vanilla and sour cream. Mix well. Divide into seven balls; coat with confectioners sugar. Roll into thin circles; cut each into eight pie-shaped wedges. Prepare filling by folding sugar, nuts and 1 tsp. vanilla into stiffly beaten egg whites. Place 1 tsp. filling on each triangle and roll tightly, starting at the broad end. Shape into crescents and place on an ungreased cookie sheet. Bake at 400° for fifteen to twenty minutes. Sprinkle with sifted confectioners sugar.

Yield: 4 to 5 dozen

Mrs. Garen N. Kelley

Coconut Crisps

1 cup butter or margarine
1 cup brown sugar
1 cup sugar
2 eggs
1½ cups flour
1 tsp. baking soda
1 tsp. salt
3 cups quick-cooking rolled oats
½ cup nuts, chopped
1½ cups coconut
1½ cups raisins

Cream butter, add sugars and beat until light and fluffy; add eggs, beat well. Sift together flour, soda and salt and add to sugar mixture with remaining ingredients; mix well. Drop by teaspoonfuls on a cookie sheet, then flatten with a fork dipped in water. Bake at 375° for about ten minutes.

Yield: 12 dozen — Mrs. Ralph Kloppenburg

Walnut Meringue Kisses

4 egg whites
1 cup sugar
½ tsp. white vinegar
¼ tsp. salt
1 cup walnuts, chopped

Beat egg whites at high speed for two minutes. Add sugar, vinegar and salt and continue beating until mixture forms stiff peaks. Fold in walnuts and drop by teaspoonfuls onto a cookie sheet. Bake on center oven rack at 275° for fifty minutes.

Yield: 20 to 24 — Mrs. Victor J. Scaravilli

Molasses Snaps

¾ cup shortening
1 cup sugar
1 egg
¼ cup light molasses
2 cups flour, sifted
2 tsp. baking soda
1 tsp. cinnamon
½ tsp. each cloves, ginger, nutmeg, allspice, salt

Cream together shortening and sugar, add egg and molasses; beat. Sift dry ingredients together and add to molasses mixture; mix well. Chill. Form into one-inch balls. Roll in granulated sugar. Place on a cookie sheet two inches apart. Bake at 375° for eight to ten minutes.

Yield: 4 to 5 dozen — Mrs. Neal P. Lavelle

Fudge

4½ cups sugar
1 – 14½ oz. can evaporated milk
2 T. butter
⅛ tsp. salt
8 oz. unsweetened chocolate, chopped
16 oz. sweet cooking chocolate, chopped
2 cups marshmallow creme
2 cups nuts, chopped

In a saucepan, combine sugar, milk, butter and salt. Bring to a boil and simmer six minutes. Remove from heat. Add chocolate and marshmallow and stir until thoroughly mixed. Add nuts. Spread into a buttered dish, cool, and cut.

Charles Pettibone

FUDGIE BROWNIES

2 oz. unsweetened chocolate
¼ cup butter or margarine
2 eggs, lightly beaten
1¼ cups sugar
½ cup flour, unsifted
¼ tsp. salt
½ tsp. vanilla
½ cup walnuts, chopped

Melt chocolate and butter together. Add rest of ingredients in order given and beat. Pour into a lightly greased eight-inch square pan. Bake at 300° for forty minutes.

Yield: 16 MRS. STEWART L. RICE

CHOCOLATE SQUARES

1⅛ cups butter
½ cup brown sugar
½ cup sugar
2 egg yolks
1 cup flour, sifted
1 cup rolled oats
1 – 12 oz. pkg. chocolate chips
1 cup nuts or coconut

Cream 1 cup butter and sugars until fluffy, beat in egg yolks. Add flour and oats and mix well. Place mixture in an ungreased 9″ x 13″ pan and bake at 350° for twenty minutes (will be pale). Remove from oven and cool. Melt chocolate chips and ⅛ cup butter in top of double boiler; spread while slightly warm on top of baked mixture and sprinkle with chopped nuts or coconut. Cut into small squares.

Yield: 48 MRS. FRANK E. JOSEPH, JR.

Spiced Mixed Nuts

¾ cup sugar
¾ tsp. salt
1 tsp. cinnamon
½ tsp. cloves
¼ tsp. allspice
¼ tsp nutmeg
1 egg white, lightly beaten
1 cup walnut halves
1 cup pecan halves
1 cup hazel nuts

Combine sugar, salt and spices; stir in egg white and 2½ T. water. Add nuts, half a cup at a time; stir with a fork until coated. Lift out, draining off excess syrup. Place, separated, on a greased cookie sheet. Bake at 275° for forty-five minutes or until golden and crusty. Store tightly covered.

Yield: 3 cups

Damaris D. Klaus

Index

A

B

C

D

E

F

G

H

I

J

L

M

N

O

P

Q

R

S

T

V

W

Bach for an Encore

Menu Classics

Book Three

Bach for an Encore

Menu Classics

"The wine of Love is music,
And the feast of Love is song:
And when Love sits down to the banquet,
Love sits long..."

Published By
THE JUNIOR COMMITTEE
of
THE CLEVELAND ORCHESTRA
Severance Hall
Cleveland, Ohio 44106

Bach for an Encore

First Printing - 20,000 copies - May 1983

TABLE OF CONTENTS

Pierce

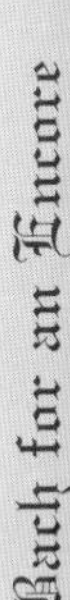

BACH FOR AN ENCORE – The third of the Bach Series Cookbooks, published for the benefit of The Cleveland Orchestra, is a unique offering of menu selections for entertaining on any scale from family to forty. Its appearance would not have been possible without the support of our hundreds of recipe contributors. Unfortunately, space did not permit us to include all of the fine recipes received. To standardize measurements and procedures, editorial adjustments have been made – we expect these will meet with the approval of the contributors.

Plan an adventure and let your mood find a menu to match. We know that your guests will enjoy your interpretation of these classic themes.

Bon Appetit!

Chairman: **Nancy L. Walsh**

Co-Editors: **Sara Hawk**
Linda Kresnye

Special thanks to the entire Cookbook Committee who gave untold hours of time and talent:

Brenda K. Ashley	*Publication Chairman*
Bonnie Femec	*Design Chairman*
Diane M. Gill	*Publication Chairman*
Carolyn Ross	*Testing Chairman*
Mary Anne Schmitz	*Data Processing Chairman*
Dianne Vogt	*Collection Chairman*

Christine Ambrose
Virginia Barbato
Connie A. Bukvic
Kathleen Griffin
Diane Hennessey
Katherine Mavec
Christine M. Ulrich
Rena Widzer

*All recipes submitted to **BACH FOR AN ENCORE** have been tested by our testers and reviewed and edited by the Committee.*

For your enjoyment, we have included wine suggestions where appropriate. We are most grateful to Pat O'Brien for sharing his experience in providing the selections.

Sonatas
Casual Occasions
Pierce

"SNOW MAIDEN"

*Stuffed Artichoke Bottoms

*Honey-Mustard Pork Roast

*Noodle-Rice Pilaf

Buttered Beets

*Walnut Raisin Spice Cake with

Cream Cheese Frosting

German Rhine Spatlese

STUFFED ARTICHOKE BOTTOMS

12 artichoke bottoms
½ lb. small shrimp
4 T. butter
½ lb. mushrooms, chopped
1 T. white wine
salt and pepper to taste
1 cup chicken stock
1 tsp. cornstarch
½ cup sour cream
dill for garnish

Melt butter over medium heat. Stir in chopped mushrooms, wine, salt and freshly ground pepper. Simmer 3 to 4 minutes covered. Heat the chicken stock. Mix cornstarch with sour cream, add it to the boiling chicken stock and cook for 1 minute. Arrange artichoke bottoms on four plates. Place the shrimp on the bottoms, then pour stock and mushroom mixtures over. Garnish with dill.

4 Servings — ANTAL DORATI

HONEY-MUSTARD PORK ROAST

5 to 6 lbs. center-cut pork roast
1 clove minced garlic
1 tsp. thyme
3 to 4 T. honey-mustard
1 T. flour
3 T. orange or lemon marmalade
salt and pepper to taste
¼ to ½ cup cider, apple juice or white wine

Mix garlic, thyme, honey-mustard, flour, marmalade, salt and pepper and spread on roast. Cook 25 minutes per pound at 325°. Approximately 30 to 35 minutes from start of cooking, add some of the cider or wine. Keep adding as it evaporates and cooks. Remove roast and let stand 15 minutes or so with a tent of foil placed loosely over it before slicing. Scrape pan drippings with a non-metallic spatula and use for gravy.

4 Servings PAT DE FABIO SHIMRAK

NOODLE-RICE PILAF

4 oz. fine noodles
1 cup rice
1 stick butter, melted
1 small can chicken bouillon
1 cup water
onion salt and white pepper to taste

Sauté uncooked noodles in butter. Watch carefully, stirring to golden brown. Add rice, bouillon, and water, cooking until tender. Season to taste.

5 Servings PAULA KAPPOS

WALNUT RAISIN SPICE CAKE WITH CREAM CHEESE FROSTING

1½ cups raisins
1½ cups walnuts
1½ tsp. baking soda
1½ cups boiling water
¾ cup butter
1½ cups sugar
2 whole eggs
2 egg yolks
2¼ cups sifted all-purpose flour
1½ tsp. lemon juice
¼ tsp. salt
1½ tsp. cinnamon
1½ tsp. vanilla

Grease and flour three 8-inch round cake pans. Finely chop raisins and walnuts, add soda and boiling water; cool 30 minutes. Sift flour, cinnamon, and salt; set aside. Beat butter until creamy. Slowly add sugar, beating until light and fluffy. Add eggs and egg yolks one at a time, beating after each addition. Add lemon juice and vanilla. Add flour mixture in fourths alternating with raisin-nut mixture in thirds. Bake at 350° for 25 to 30 minutes. After baking, cool for 5 minutes. Loosen edges and turn onto racks to cool. Frost with Cream Cheese Frosting.

CREAM CHEESE FROSTING

1 – 8 oz. cream cheese, softened
⅔ cup margarine
3 tsp. vanilla
1½ lbs. confectioners' sugar

Blend margarine and cream cheese. Add remaining ingredients and mix well.

12 to 16 Servings CHRISTINA THOBURN

"RITES OF SPRING"

*Asparagus Frittata
Baked Ham Slices
Brioche
*French Glacé Strawberry Pie
Macon Lugny

Asparagus Frittata

6 eggs
1 large onion, sliced
½ lb. asparagus, in 2-inch lengths
salt and pepper
¼ cup good olive oil or vegetable oil

Sauté onion and asparagus in oil 12 minutes. Mix eggs thoroughly with fork. Pour over vegetables. Move egg mixture from edge of pan allowing oil to seep through eggs. When eggs are three-fourths cooked, slide frittata out of pan onto dish. Invert pan over dish and return to heat, to finish cooking for 1 minute.

4 to 6 Servings — Pat de Fabio Shimrak

French Glacé Strawberry Pie

1 pre-baked cooled pie shell
3 oz. pkg. cream cheese
1 qt. strawberries
1 cup sugar
3 T. cornstarch

Spread cream cheese on shell. Wash, drain and hull berries. Cover shell with three-fourths of berries. Mash remaining berries until juice is extracted. If necessary, add water to make 1½ cups juice. Bring to boiling and gradually stir in sugar mixed with cornstarch. Cook over low heat, stirring constantly until thickened. Cool. Pour over berries in shell. Chill. Serve with whipped cream.

6 to 8 Servings — Nancy L. Walsh

AFTER THE CATCH DINNER

Catch of the Day

*Beer Batter

Cornsticks

Broccoli with Lemon

*Crisp Ginger Cookies with Sliced Peaches

or

*Sandwich Cookies

Rhone White or Macon Lugny

BEER BATTER FOR FISH, SHRIMP, FRUITS OR VEGETABLES

- 2 cups flour
- ½ tsp. salt
- 12 oz. beer
- 3 egg whites, beaten until soft peaks form
- 2 cups oil

Combine flour, salt and beer. Mix well (it will be firm). Stir in a small amount of beaten egg whites to lighten mixture, then fold in rest thoroughly. Heat oil in deep pot to 375°. Dip fish into batter and drop in oil. Fry until puffed and golden. Batter can be stored, refrigerated, 2 to 3 days.

GINNA HERRMANN

Sandwich Cookies

5 cups flour
1 cup butter
1 cup shortening
4 egg yolks
4 T. sour cream
1 cup + 2 T. sugar
2 tsp. baking powder
2 tsp. vanilla
1 – 18 oz. jar red raspberry preserves
confectioners' sugar

Mix all ingredients except for preserves. Roll dough on sugared board. Cut out cookies with small cutter. Using a thimble, cut center holes in half of the cookies. Bake on ungreased sheets at 375° for 10 to 20 minutes. Cool, spread bottom cookie with preserves. Top with cookie with hole. Dust with confectioners' sugar.

Yield: 12 dozen

Linda Kresnye

Crisp Ginger Cookies

4 cups sifted flour
½ cup sugar
½ tsp. baking soda
2½ to 3 tsp. ginger
1 tsp. cinnamon
2 cups butter
1¼ cups warm molasses

Sift flour, sugar, soda, ginger, and cinnamon. Cut in the butter until consistency of crumbs. Stir in warm molasses and mix quickly. Cover and chill. When stiff divide dough in half and shape into rolls 1½ inches in diameter. Wrap and refrigerate or freeze. Slice thin and bake at 350° for 10 minutes.

Yield: 4 to 6 dozen

Mrs. Harold Ensten

"PRIMAVERA CONCERTO"

*Budapest Canape

*Linguine Primavera Salad

or

*Ratatouille Pie

Crusty French Bread

*Frozen White Chocolate Mousse

Nuits St. George or Hermitage Blanc

BUDAPEST CANAPE

1 loaf bread
butter
anchovy butter
hard-cooked eggs
paprika
watercress

Cut bread into ⅓-inch slices. Shape into crescents, and sauté in butter until delicately browned. Spread with anchovy butter and set aside. Separate whites and yolks of eggs. Chop whites and season with paprika. Set aside. Force yolks through sieve. Sprinkle half of crescents with egg white and other half with yolk. Garnish with sprigs of watercress.

MRS. ZOLTAN GOMBOS

Linguine Primavera Salad

1 lb. linguine, al dente
1 cup broccoli florets, steamed 3 minutes
1 cup carrots, sliced, steamed 5 minutes
1 cup zucchini, sliced
1 cup mushrooms, sliced
¼ lb. ham, minced
½ of 16-oz. can small pitted black olives, drained
½ cup pecans
¼ cup Parmesan cheese, grated
¼ cup Romano cheese, freshly grated

Marinate linguine in half of vinaigrette salad dressing and refrigerate overnight. Add remaining ingredients using as much salad dressing as is necessary to coat all. Refrigerate several hours and toss right before serving. Garnish with extra cheese and nuts.

Vinaigrette Dressing

1½ cups olive oil
½ cup shallot vinegar or white wine vinegar
2 cloves garlic, pressed
1 cup green onions, sliced
¼ cup parsley, minced
2 T. fresh oregano, chopped or 2 tsp. dried
2 T. fresh basil, chopped
1 tsp. sea salt
freshly ground pepper

Combine dressing in screw-top jar. Congeals when refrigerated. Bring to room temperature before using.

8 Servings

Caryl Halle

Ratatouille Pie

1 lb. eggplant, peeled and cubed
2 zucchini, scrubbed and cubed
1 onion, chopped
4 tomatoes, peeled, seeded and chopped
¼ cup olive oil
½ tsp. basil
3 eggs
¼ cup Parmesan cheese
1 tsp parsley
½ tsp. oregano
¼ lb. mozzarella cheese

Sauté eggplant in oil. Add onion and unpeeled, cubed zucchini. Cook 10 minutes covered or until vegetables are soft. Add tomatoes. Cook about 15 more minutes. Let cool. Beat eggs. Add Parmesan cheese, basil, parsley, oregano and pepper. Add mixture to vegetables. Butter a 9-inch or 10-inch pie pan and pour in one-half of mixture. Sprinkle with Parmesan. Add remaining mixture, sprinkle with more Parmesan and mozzarella cheese. Bake at 400° 40 minutes or until set.

6 Servings

Katie Loretta

Frozen White Chocolate Mousse

- 8 oz. chocolate wafer cookies
- 3 T. sweet butter, melted
- ½ tsp. cinnamon
- ½ cup boiling water
- 12 oz. white chocolate, coarsely chopped
- 4 eggs, extra large, separated
- 3 cups whipping cream
- pinch of salt
- ½ tsp. cream of tartar
- ¾ cup sugar

Preheat oven to 375°. Separate 9-inch springform pan. Butter sides only. Reassemble and set aside. Pulverize cookies and cinnamon in food processor. Pour crumbs into a bowl and stir in butter. Pour two-thirds mixture into pan. Press crumbs against sides. Press remaining crumbs over bottom of pan. Bake at 375° 7 to 8 minutes. Remove from oven, cool and set aside. Over low heat melt chocolate with boiling water. Stir until smooth. Remove from heat and cool slightly. Whisk in egg yolks, one at a time. Cool mixture completely. Whip cream until it holds shape. Set aside. Beat egg whites until foamy. Add salt and cream of tartar. Beat until soft peaks form. Gradually add sugar and continue beating until stiff but not dry. Fold chocolate into egg whites. Then fold together whipped cream and chocolate mixture. Pour into crust. Freeze for 1 hour before covering. Cover and freeze at least 5 hours or more, or overnight. May be frozen up to 2 weeks. Serve with whipped cream, chocolate leaves or chocolate-covered strawberries.

8 to 10 Servings

Alyce Hobbs

SOUTH OF THE BORDER

*Tex-Mex Dip

*Tank Flank

*My Mom's Zucchini Casserole

Sesame Sticks

*Fruit Pizza

or

*Blueberry Pie

California Barbera or Gigondas

TEX-MEX DIP

3 medium ripe avocados
2 T. lemon juice
½ tsp. salt
¼ tsp. pepper
1 cup (8 oz.) sour cream
½ cup mayonnaise
1 package taco seasoning mix
2 cans Jalapeno Bean Dip
1 cup green onions, chopped
3 medium tomatoes, chopped (2 cups)
2 – 3½ oz. cans chopped black olives (drained)
1 – 8 oz. package shredded cheddar cheese
large tortilla chips

Peel, pit, mash avocados in medium bowl with lemon juice, salt and pepper. Combine sour cream, mayonnaise and taco seasoning. Spread bean dip on large platter. Top with avocado mixture, then sour cream-taco mixture. Sprinkle with green onions, tomatoes, olives. Cover with cheese. Refrigerate until serving. Serve with chips.

12 Servings

BARBARA WILSON

Tank Flank

2 to 2½ lbs. flank steak
⅔ cup soy sauce
⅔ cup chutney
⅔ cup oil
⅔ cup red wine
1 T. minced onion
2 cloves garlic, minced

SAUCE:
¾ cup mayonnaise
¼ cup horseradish

Pierce steak all over with fork. Mix soy sauce, chutney, oil, wine and garlic and marinate 12 to 24 hours. Grill or broil steak to desired doneness. Slice thinly against grain of meat. Mix mayonnaise and horseradish and serve on side.

4 to 6 Servings Sally DeRoulet

My Mom's Zucchini Casserole

4 cups zucchini, sliced
1 large onion, chopped
½ cup green pepper, chopped
1½ T. flour
1 T. brown sugar, packed
2 cups stewed tomatoes
grated cheese – swiss, cheddar or Parmesan
4 T. butter

Slice zucchini and place in a greased baking dish. Sauté onion and pepper in 4 T. butter until soft. Add flour, mix well. Add sugar and stewed tomatoes and cook over low heat until thickened, stirring often. Pour on top of zucchini and mix gently. Bake 45 to 60 minutes at 350°. Sprinkle cheese on top the last 15 minutes of baking.

6 Servings Helen Greenleaf

Fruit Pizza

½ cup melted butter
1 cup flour
2 T. sugar
1 – 8 oz. package cream cheese
⅓ cup sugar
1 tsp. vanilla
4 kinds of fruit, fresh or canned (drain the canned fruit well)
½ cup marmalade

Mix together melted butter, flour and sugar. Pat into a 10-inch pizza pan and bake at 375° for 10 to 15 minutes or until golden brown. Blend softened cream cheese with sugar and vanilla. Spread on cooled crust. Arrange fruit "artfully" on top. Suggested fruits are: fresh seeded grapes, kiwi, blueberries, plums, cherries, bananas, peaches, strawberries. Then top with glaze: heat ½ cup marmalade and bit of water. Cool. Then pour over fruit.

6 Servings — Nancy Gage

Blueberry Pie

1 10-inch unbaked pie crust
pastry for lattice top
3 pints fresh blueberries (clean, check for stems)
1½ cups sugar
⅓ cup flour
1 to 2 tsp. cinnamon
butter

Heat oven to 425°. Stir together sugar, flour and cinnamon. Add blueberries and mix. Pour into unbaked crust. Add dots of butter. Cover with lattice top. Bake at 425° for 45 to 50 minutes.

6 to 8 Servings — Fran Buckley

SCRUMPTIOUS BRUNCH

*The Great Puffy Pancake

Canadian Bacon Slices

Fresh Fruit with

*Currant and Cheese Dressing

*Orange Caramel Custard

Bernkastler Riesling Kabinett

The Great Puffy Pancake

½ cup flour
½ cup milk
2 eggs, slightly beaten
pinch nutmeg
4 T. butter
2 T. confectioners' sugar
juice of ½ lemon

Preheat oven to 425°. Mix flour, eggs, milk and nutmeg together, leaving batter a bit lumpy. Melt butter in large frying pan and add the batter. Bake 15 to 20 minutes until golden brown. Sprinkle with confectioners' sugar and return to oven briefly. Sprinkle with lemon juice. Cut into wedges. This can easily be doubled and put into 9 x 13-inch glass dish.

4 Servings — Dorothy Bergoine

Currant and Cheese Dressing

4 oz. cream cheese
1 T. lemon juice
2 oz. currant jelly
¼ cup cream

Mix all ingredients until smooth.

4 to 6 Servings — Charlotte Jackson

Orange Caramel Custard

¾ cup sugar
¼ cup water
pinch cream of tartar
1½ cups milk
½ cup heavy cream
3 eggs
2 egg yolks
⅓ cup sugar
¼ cup strained orange juice
1 T. orange liqueur
1 tsp. grated orange rind
thin strips of orange peel

In heavy skillet combine sugar, water and cream of tartar. Heat mixture over moderately low heat, stirring and washing down any sugar crystals clinging to the sides of pan with brush dipped in cold water, until sugar is dissolved. Cook mixture over moderate heat undisturbed until it turns a deep caramel. Pour caramel into four ¾-cup ramekins, coating the bottoms evenly. In saucepan, scald milk and heavy cream. In a bowl beat whole eggs, egg yolks and sugar until mixture is just combined. Add hot milk in a stream, stirring, then add strained orange juice and liqueur. Skim froth from the surface, stir in grated orange rind and pour mixture into ramekins. Set ramekins in baking pan, pour enough hot water to reach halfway up the sides of ramekins. Bake custards, covered with a baking sheet, in a preheated 325° oven for 25 to 30 minutes, or until they are almost set. Remove the custards from the baking pan, cool and chill covered, overnight. Release the edges of the custards from the ramekins with a knife, invert a dessert plate over each ramekin, and invert onto plates. Top the custards with very thin strips of orange peel which have been blanched in boiling water for 1 minute then well drained.

4 Servings

Paula Kappos

Lentil Soup

- A piece of smoked meat or a ham bone
- 1 package of lentils (rinsed and picked over)
- ½ cup diced celery
- 1 grated clove garlic (optional)
- 1 tsp. salt
- 2 quarts cold water
- 1 cup tomato juice
- 1 finely chopped onion
- 1 bay leaf
- ⅛ tsp. pepper
- 3 garlic sausages, sliced
- 1 T. bacon fat
- 1 T. flour
- vinegar (optional)

If using smoked meat, cook for one hour in water. Add lentils, celery, garlic, salt, water, tomato juice, onion, bay leaf and pepper. Cook slowly for 1½ hours. Chill. Remove meat and bone. Skim fat from the pan. Fry garlic sausage (knockers) lightly in bacon fat. Add to soup. Remove all but 1 T. fat from pan. Add flour and some of soup gradually. Mix with remaining soup. Season. A touch of vinegar may be added. Serve hot. If too thick, add water.

6 Servings — Mrs. Frank E. Joseph, Sr.

"POLONAISE"

*Quick and Easy Marinated Mushrooms

*Baked Chicken Mary Jane

*Swope Bread

*Old Dominion Pound Cake with Fresh Fruit

Chateauneuf Du Pape or California Zinfandel

Quick and Easy Marinated Mushrooms

⅔ cup vinegar
½ cup olive oil (be sure to use olive oil)
2 cloves garlic (optional)
1 tsp. sugar
1½ tsp. salt
1½ tsp. oregano
1 to 1½ tsp. pepper
2 T. water
1 medium Bermuda onion, sliced in rings
1 quart mushrooms, cleaned with larger ones halved lengthwise

Place onions and mushrooms in large plastic container with tight fitting top. Combine all other ingredients in blender; mix for a few seconds. Pour over mushrooms and onions. Store refrigerated up to two weeks. Invert every few days.

Barbara Silvers

Baked Chicken Mary Jane

- 1 cup sour cream
- 2 tsp. soy sauce
- ½ tsp. garlic salt
- 2 T. lemon juice
- 1 tsp. celery salt
- 1 tsp. paprika
- dash of pepper
- 1 small pkg. herb-seasoned stuffing crumbs
- 3 split chicken breasts, skinned and boned
- melted butter

Mix together sour cream, soy sauce, garlic salt, lemon juice, celery salt, paprika, and pepper. Dip chicken into mixture and then roll in the seasoned bread crumbs. Arrange pieces in a lightly greased baking dish. Drizzle them with melted butter and bake uncovered at 325° for 1 hour.

4 Servings

Ann Cicarella

Swope Bread

- 1 cup flour
- 2 cups whole wheat flour
- ½ cup sugar
- 1 tsp. salt
- 2 cups buttermilk
- 2 tsp. baking soda

Mix flours, sugar and salt together. Combine buttermilk and baking soda, add to flour. Mix thoroughly. Pour in greased 9 x 5-inch loaf pan. Bake at 350° for 1 hour 10 minutes.

Mrs. Robert Gardner

Old Dominion Pound Cake

8 or 10 eggs, separated
2¼ cups sifted all-purpose flour
¼ tsp. baking soda
1¼ cups granulated sugar
1½ cups butter, softened
2 T. fresh lemon juice
2¼ tsp. vanilla extract
⅛ tsp. salt
1 cup granulated sugar
1½ tsp. cream of tartar

Make day before serving. Let eggs stand at room temperature 1 hour before using. Meanwhile, butter well and flour a 10-inch bundt pan. Sift together flour, soda and 1¼ cups sugar. Preheat oven to 325°. In large bowl, with mixer at low speed, just barely blend butter and flour mixture, then add lemon juice and vanilla. Beat in egg yolks, one at a time, just until blended. Beat egg whites at high speed until frothy. Add salt; then gradually add 1 cup sugar mixed with cream of tartar. Beat well after each addition and continue beating until soft peaks form. Gently fold beaten egg whites into cake batter and turn into the prepared pan. Then, using a rubber spatula, gently cut through the cake batter one or two times. Bake at 325°, 1½ hours or until cake tester inserted in center comes out clean. (Do not peek at cake during first hour of baking.) Turn off oven heat; let cake remain in oven 15 minutes then remove to wire cake rack and cool 15 minutes more. Remove cake from pan, finish cooling on rack. Wrap in foil or store in cake box until served.

24 Servings — Mrs. James A. Wolf

"CLAIRE DE LUNE"

*Cold Cucumber Soup with Dill

*Fish en Papillot

*Tomatoes Stuffed with Vermicelli

*Oranges Filled with Fruits

*Chocolate Macaroons

California Chardonnay or Mersault

Cold Cucumber Soup with Dill

4 green onions with tops, sliced
4 T. unsalted butter
4 baking potatoes, peeled and sliced thinly
6 to 8 cups chicken stock skimmed of fat
2 T. dill weed
1½ cups milk
2 cups sour cream
2 medium cucumbers, peeled, sliced, and diced
chives
salt and pepper

Sauté onions in butter, add potatoes and stock. Bring to a boil, then simmer for 15 minutes. Cool and puree in blender. Add dill, milk and sour cream. Chill. Add cucumbers. Let flavors "marry" for a few hours or overnight. Serve with a sprinkling of chives, salt, and pepper.

8 Servings — Sara Cutting

Fish en Papillot

4 fresh filets (sole, halibut, snapper, etc.) same size, approximately ½ lb. each
½ cup mayonnaise or salad dressing
salt and pepper
2 tomatoes sliced thin
1 small onion, sliced very thin
1 green pepper, seeded and sliced thin
2 T. sherry or white wine (optional)

Spread each filet with mayonnaise or salad dressing. Salt and pepper to taste. Lay one fish filet on a double layer of foil (or single layer of heavy duty foil) twice the size of fish. Top with tomato slices, then onion slices, then green pepper slices. Sprinkle with wine if desired. Top with second filet, mayonnaise side down. Fold foil around the fish, leaving some room. The foil should be sealed tightly. Repeat with remaining 2 filets. Place on covered grill for 20 minutes. Open foil and serve (must be eaten immediately). Can also be done with any size filets. They should be paired by size. Cooking time must be adjusted.

4 Servings

Sally DeRoulet

Tomatoes Stuffed with Vermicelli

8 tomatoes

PESTO SAUCE:

- **½ cup fresh basil leaves, washed/dried**
- **1½ cloves garlic**
- **¼ cup grated Parmesan cheese**
- **¼ cup grated Romano cheese**
- **2 T. olive oil**

½ lb. vermicelli, cooked
2 oz. pine nuts
salt and pepper to taste
grated Parmesan cheese
fresh basil leaves for garnish

Hollow out tomatoes and remove seeds. Drain tomatoes upside down. Blend all Pesto Sauce ingredients in blender until smooth. (Makes about ½ cup sauce.) Place cooked vermicelli (hot or cold) in large bowl. Toss with Pesto Sauce and pine nuts. Season with salt, pepper, and grated Parmesan to taste. Fill tomatoes with pasta, top with basil leaves and serve. One-half pound vermicelli fills 8 tomatoes.

8 Servings — Brenda K. Ashley

Oranges Filled with Fruits

- 6 large navel oranges
- 4 stiffly beaten egg whites
- sugar
- 1 qt. strawberries or raspberries
- ⅓ cup orange juice
- ⅓ cup Grand Marnier
- 1 tsp. grated orange rind
- ¾ cup orange marmalade
- juice of 1 lemon
- ½ tsp. ground ginger
- pomegranate seeds or fresh currants

Cut oranges in half; remove pulp. Brush egg whites on the halves; roll in sugar. Place berries in the shells. Chill. Blend remaining ingredients except seeds. Chill. Pour over berries in shells just before serving. Decorate with seeds.

12 Servings — Mrs. R. Henry Norweb, Jr.

Chocolate Macaroons

- 2 oz. unsweetened chocolate
- 1 – 14 oz. can sweetened condensed milk
- 2 cups finely shredded coconut
- 1 cup chopped nuts
- 1 T. strong brewed coffee
- 1 tsp. almond extract
- ⅛ tsp. salt

Combine chocolate and milk. Cook over medium heat, whisking, until thick and glossy. Remove from heat, add other ingredients. Drop mixture by small teaspoonfuls on a greased baking sheet. Bake at 350° 10 minutes.

Yield: about 5 dozen — Mrs. R. Henry Norweb, Jr.

"EL SALON MEXICO"

Sangria

*Mexican Popover Casserole

Salad with Tarragon Salad Dressing

*Pineapple Walnut Cake

MEXICAN POPOVER CASSEROLE

1 lb. ground beef
2 – 8 oz. jars taco sauce
¼ cup chopped green pepper
¼ cup chopped onions
2 T. cornmeal
½ tsp. salt
½ tsp. pepper
1 tsp. parsley flakes
1 – 12 to 15 oz. can corn
2 cups shredded cheddar cheese
2 eggs
1 cup milk
1 cup flour
1 T. oil
½ tsp. salt
2 T. chopped green onions or black olives (optional)

Preheat oven to 425°. In large skillet, brown then drain ground beef. Stir in taco sauce, green pepper, onions, cornmeal, ½ tsp. salt, pepper and parsley. Heat to boiling and stir 1 minute. Pour into ungreased 9 x 13-inch pan. Sprinkle corn on top, then cheese over corn. Beat eggs, milk, oil, flour and ½ tsp. salt together, then pour over cheese. Sprinkle with onions or olives, if desired. Bake at 425° for 25 to 30 minutes until golden and puffy. Serve immediately.

6 to 8 Servings SALLY DEROULET

Pineapple Walnut Cake

2 eggs
2 cups cake flour
2 cups sugar
2 tsp. baking soda
1 tsp. vanilla
½ cup chopped walnuts
1 - 15½ oz. can crushed pineapple
and juice

Combine all ingredients in a large bowl. Mix with a spoon until well blended. Pour into an ungreased 9 x 13-inch pan. Bake at 350° for 35 to 40 minutes. Cool cake, then frost. Refrigerate before serving.

Frosting

8 oz. cream cheese, softened
½ cup butter
1½ cups powdered sugar
1 tsp. vanilla

Cream cream cheese and butter. Add powdered sugar and vanilla and mix 2 minutes until smooth.

18 to 24 Servings RUTH CRUSE

"COFFEE CANTATA"

Hot Spiced Tea

Coffee

*Pecan Rolls

*Strawberry Bread

*Pumpkin Muffins

Fresh Fruit

Pecan Rolls

1 cake yeast
1¼ cups milk
½ cup sugar
½ lb. butter
2 eggs
4½ cups flour
½ tsp. salt
chopped pecans, raisins
¼ cup light Karo syrup
½ cup brown sugar
4 T. butter

Crumble yeast in ¼ cup warm milk. Melt butter in 1 cup warm milk and cool. Add sugar and eggs. Add yeast mixture to flour and salt. Combine both mixtures and mix thoroughly. Knead, refrigerate a few hours or overnight. Let warm to room temperature, roll into rectangle, spread with melted butter and sprinkle with sugar, cinnamon, chopped pecans and raisins. Roll up as jelly roll, slice in 1 ½-inch slices. Heat syrup, brown sugar and butter. Pour into buttered muffin tins. Sprinkle with chopped pecans. Put rolls on top and let rise until doubled in bulk; then bake 30 minutes at 350°. Immediately turn on to wax paper, quickly scrape any sauce left in tin onto rolls.

Yield: 12 rolls

Sally Rosenfield

Strawberry Bread

1 – 10 oz. box frozen strawberries
1½ cups flour
1 cup sugar
1½ tsp. cinnamon
½ tsp. salt
½ tsp. baking soda
2 eggs, beaten
½ cup oil

Thaw berries and drain. Reserve liquid. Mix together flour, sugar, cinnamon, salt and soda. Beat eggs, oil and berries. Slowly add dry ingredients. Pour into greased and floured 9 x 5-inch loaf pan. Bake at 350° for 50 to 60 minutes. Strawberry butter: Mix reserved juice with one stick softened butter.

12 Servings — Marcie Avila

Pumpkin Muffins

1½ cups flour
2 tsp. baking powder
¾ tsp. salt
½ cup sugar
½ tsp. cinnamon
½ tsp. nutmeg
4 T. butter
½ cup raisins
1 egg
1½ cup cooked pumpkin
½ cup whole milk
1 to 2 T. sugar

Mix first 6 ingredients together. Cut in butter. Mix in raisins. In separate bowl, beat egg, then add pumpkin and milk. Add to butter mixture and mix only until blended. Fill greased muffin pans ⅔ full. Sprinkle ¼ tsp. sugar over each muffin. Bake at 400° for 20 to 25 minutes.

Yield: 12 muffins — Helen Greenleaf

COUNTRY DINNER

*Pork Chops with Parmesan Cheese and White Wine

New Potatoes

*Scalloped Carrots

*Thelma's Russian Tea Biscuits

California Zinfandel or Puligny Montrachet

PORK CHOPS WITH PARMESAN CHEESE AND WHITE WINE

6 pork chops, trimmed
salt and freshly ground pepper
6 T. butter or margarine, room temperature
½ cup bread crumbs
½ cup grated Parmesan cheese
2 T. finely chopped shallots
¼ cup dry white wine

Season chops with salt and pepper. Melt 2 T. of butter or margarine in skillet. Add chops and cook until golden brown on both sides. Transfer to platter and keep warm. Blend bread crumbs, cheese and remaining 4 T. butter or margarine. Divide mixture equally into 6 portions. Sprinkle shallots over bottom of skillet. Add wine and simmer for 1 minute, scraping particles from bottom of pan. Remove from heat. Arrange chops in shallow baking dish. Pat bread crumb mixture on each chop. Pour wine mixture around chops. Bake uncovered at 400° 10 minutes. Cover loosely with foil and continue baking 20 minutes.

6 Servings MARY ANNE SCHMITZ

Scalloped Carrots

2 lbs. sliced, cooked carrots
¼ cup butter
¼ cup minced onion
¼ cup flour
2 cups milk
¼ tsp. dry mustard
¼ tsp. celery salt
2 cups (8 oz.) shredded cheese
1 cup buttered bread crumbs

Melt butter. Sauté onion. Add flour. Add milk, stirring constantly. Add dry mustard, celery salt, and cheese. Stir. Add carrots. Place in buttered casserole. Top with buttered bread crumbs. Bake uncovered at 350° for 25 minutes.

8 to 12 Servings

Ruth Griffin

Thelma's Russian Tea Biscuits

4 cups flour
2 tsp. baking powder
1 stick butter
¾ cup sugar
½ cup oil
¼ cup orange juice
1 tsp. vanilla
3 eggs
8 oz. jar raspberry jam
½ cup yellow raisins
nuts
cinnamon mixed with sugar

Cream sugar and butter. Add flour, baking powder, oil, orange juice, vanilla and eggs. Roll between waxed paper to ¼-inch thick rectangle. Spread with jelly. Sprinkle with raisins, nuts, cinnamon sugar. Roll like jelly roll. Slice ¾-inch thick. Place on greased baking sheet. Brush with beaten egg. Sprinkle with sugar. Bake at 350° for 30 minutes.

Sally Rosenfield

AUTUMN COOKOUT

*Cider Sipper

*Hot Ryes

*Steve's Beach-Haven Chowder

BBQ Chicken

Corn on the Cob

*Cranberry Pudding Cake

or

*Pumpkin Mousse

California Zinfandel or Macon Lugny

CIDER SIPPER

½ gal. fresh apple cider, chilled
9 oz. vodka
Mix together and serve.

10 Servings

JENNY PERRY

HOT RYES

4 oz. grated Swiss cheese
½ cup cooked crumbled bacon
½ cup chopped ripe olives
¼ cup chopped onion
1 tsp. Worcestershire sauce
¼ tsp. salt
¼ cup mayonnaise
1 loaf cocktail rye bread or a box of rye crackers

Mix all ingredients. Spread on bread, bake on ungreased cookie sheet for 10 minutes at 350°.

CONNIE BUKVIC

Steve's Beach-Haven Chowder

¼ lb. salt pork, diced
1 cup finely chopped onion
3 cups cold water
4 cups potatoes, diced
2 doz. fresh clams or 2 – 8 oz. cans of chopped clams
2 cups heavy cream
⅛ tsp. thyme
salt and pepper to taste
2 T. butter
paprika

In a soup pot, fry pork for 3 minutes over high heat. Reduce heat, add onions and cook 5 minutes. Add water and potatoes. Bring to a boil, then simmer half covered for 15 minutes. Add clams, cream and spices. Bring to a boil. Reduce heat and simmer until served.

6 Servings

Nancy Gage

Cranberry Pudding Cake

2 cups flour
2 tsp. baking powder
½ tsp. salt
1 cup sugar
1 cup milk
3 T. melted butter
2 cups cranberries

Mix all ingredients. Pour into 8 x 8-inch greased pan. Bake 1 hour at 350°. Top with Sauce (p. 40).

Sauce

¼ lb. butter
1 cup sugar
¾ cup cream

Mix ingredients for sauce. Bring to a boil. Serve hot over individual pieces of warm or cool cake.

9 to 12 Servings Mrs. E. R. O'Day

Pumpkin Mousse

1 cup pumpkin
½ tsp. cinnamon
½ tsp. ginger
½ tsp. nutmeg
¼ tsp. ground cloves
1 – 1 oz. envelope unflavored gelatin
¼ cup rum
¼ cup water
4 eggs
⅔ cup sugar
1 cup heavy cream, whipped
sweetened whipped cream

Combine pumpkin and spices. Stir gelatin, water and rum over low heat until dissolved. Beat eggs until light; add sugar and continue beating 10 minutes. Combine pumpkin, gelatin and egg mixtures. Fold in whipped cream. Pour into soufflé dish or individual bowls. Refrigerate several hours. Serve with sweetened whipped cream.

8 Servings Lori Hanson

"BOLERO"

*Snappy Shrimp Parmesan

Green Salad

*Cantaloupe Sorbet

*Hungarian Loveknots

Chablis Grand Cru or California Pinot Blanc

SNAPPY SHRIMP PARMESAN

1 lb. raw, peeled, deveined shrimp, fresh or frozen
1 tsp. chopped fresh chives
½ clove garlic, minced
¼ cup butter
1 tsp. salt
1½ T. sherry
1 T. grated Parmesan cheese

Thaw shrimp if frozen. In 10-inch frying pan, sauté chives and garlic in butter until tender. Add shrimp and simmer 2 to 3 minutes or until largest shrimp is opaque in center when cut in half. Add sherry and sprinkle cheese over shrimp. Serve warm.

6 Servings

DIANE GILL

Cantaloupe Sorbet

4 cups peeled, sliced cantaloupe
2 cups fresh orange juice
2 tsp. fresh lemon juice
1 cup sugar
1 cup marsala
2 egg whites
fresh mint leaves

Puree melon in blender or food processor until smooth. Pour into bowl and stir in orange juice, lemon juice, sugar and marsala. Cover bowl and freeze until mushy. In another bowl, beat egg whites until stiff. Remove partially frozen cantaloupe mixture from freezer and whip smooth. Fold egg whites into melon mixture. Cover and refreeze until firm. Garnish with fresh mint leaves.

6 to 8 Servings Joyce Monachino

Hungarian Loveknots (Csöröge)

1 cup sour cream
4 egg yolks
2 cups sifted flour
1 T. rum (optional)
shortening for frying

Add flour to egg yolks, sour cream and rum to make a soft dough. Knead until smooth. Roll out very thin. Cut into diamond shapes, then make slit in the center, approximately 1½-inches long. Pull one end through center slit. Fry in deep hot fat until light brown. Drain on paper towel. Dust with powdered sugar when cool.

Irene M. Walsh

BLOSSOM PICNIC

Cold Barbequed Chicken
*Sugarless Barbeque Sauce
*Macaroni Salad
*Mint Brownies
Vouvray or California Chenin Blanc

Sugarless Barbeque Sauce

2 onions, sliced
¾ cup water
½ tsp. black pepper
1 tsp. paprika
2 T. Worcestershire sauce
1 tsp. chili powder
¾ cup catsup
2 T. vinegar
1 tsp. salt

Heat all together.

Mrs. Charles Husak

Macaroni Salad

1 lb. spiral macaroni
¼ cup milk
1 red onion, chopped
2 large tomatoes, chopped
2 small green peppers, chopped
½ cup sour cream
1½ cups mayonnaise
1 T. beef bouillon powder
2 tsp. red wine vinegar
1 tsp. dill

Cook macaroni and drain well, then toss with milk. Add onion, tomato and green pepper. Toss remaining ingredients with macaroni mixture. Refrigerate.

10 to 12 Servings

Linda Kresnye

Mint Brownies

1 cup butter
1½ cups sugar
4 eggs
2 tsp. vanilla
1 cup sifted flour
¾ cup cocoa
1 tsp. salt
1 tsp. baking powder
¾ cup coarsely chopped nuts
Mint Frosting and Glaze

Cream butter and sugar until light and fluffy. Beat in eggs, one at a time. Add vanilla. Sift flour, cocoa, salt and baking powder together. Blend into butter mixture. Stir in nuts. Spread in greased 9 x 13-inch pan. Bake at 350° for 20 to 30 minutes until edges are slightly firm and center still soft. Cool; frost with Mint Frosting then freeze 30 minutes. Then apply glaze and immediately cut into bars.

Mint Frosting

2 cups sifted confectioners' sugar
¼ cup softened butter
2 T. milk
1½ tsp. mint extract
few drops green food color

Combine ingredients, beating thoroughly.

Glaze

½ cup chocolate bits
1 T. butter
1½ T. water

Melt chocolate and butter. Add water, blend well.

Yield: 36 to 42 bars — Linda Kresnye

SUPER BOWL SUNDAY

*Zucchini Soup with Curry

*Handy-Dandy Sandwiches

Potato Sticks

*Orange-Buttermilk Cookies

ZUCCHINI SOUP WITH CURRY

¼ cup butter
4 medium zucchini, sliced
2 small onions, chopped
2 cloves garlic, pressed
½ to ¾ tsp. curry powder
1 cup cream or milk
2 – 13 oz. cans chicken broth
½ tsp. salt
sour cream, parsley, chives or green onion for garnish

In large skillet, melt butter. Add zucchini, onion, garlic and curry. Steam, covered, until tender, stirring occasionally. Put in blender and puree. Return to saucepan, or put in a casserole in which you can both cook and serve. Add cream or milk, and broth. Salt to taste. Heat and stir until well blended. Serve hot, or chill several hours or overnight. Garnish with sour cream and chives, parsley, or chopped green onions.

6 to 8 Servings

GINGER KUPER

Handy-Dandy Sandwiches

1½ lbs. sliced bacon
½ to ¾ cup chili sauce
4 to 6 T. sweet pickle relish
1 – 5 oz. jar dried beef, shredded
1 medium onion, minced
6 slices cheddar or American cheese
6 hard rolls or hamburger buns

Fry bacon until crisp; drain and crumble into a bowl. Add chili sauce, relish, shredded beef, and onion. Divide mixture onto 6 split rolls; sprinkle with cheese, then cover with tops. Wrap individually in foil. Bake at 300° for 20 to 30 minutes.

6 Servings Helen Greenleaf

Orange-Buttermilk Cookies

¾ cup butter
1 cup sugar
1 egg
2½ cups flour
½ tsp. salt
½ tsp. baking soda
½ cup buttermilk
3 T. orange juice
2 tsp. grated orange rind

Cream butter and sugar. Beat in egg. Sift together flour, salt and soda. Add dry ingredients alternately with buttermilk. Stir in juice and rind. Drop by teaspoonfuls onto an ungreased cookie sheet. Bake at 375° for 10 minutes. Cool.

Icing

1½ cups confectioners' sugar
3 T. orange juice
1 tsp. grated orange rind

Mix together. Spread on cooled cookies.

Barbara Leukart

Concertos
Festive Feasts
Pierce

MENU FOR ALL SEASONS

*Country Tomato Soup

*Veal Escallopes Marsala

Broad Noodles

*Green Salad with French Dressing

*Pecan Roll

Nebbiola D'Alba or Vouvray

Country Tomato Soup

½ cup butter or margarine
1 small clove garlic minced
1 cup chopped celery
1 cup chopped onion
½ cup chopped carrots
½ cup chopped zucchini
¼ cup flour
2 – 1 lb. 12 oz. cans whole tomatoes
2 T. brown sugar
1 tsp. marjoram
1 bay leaf
4 cups chicken broth
2 cups half & half
½ tsp. paprika
½ tsp. curry powder
¼ tsp. white pepper
salt to taste

Sauté garlic, celery, onion, carrots, zucchini in butter until tender. Stir in flour. Cook 2 minutes stirring constantly. Add tomatoes, brown sugar, basil, marjoram, bay leaf, chicken broth. Cover. Simmer 30 minutes. Discard bay leaf. Puree mixture in food processor or blender. Add half & half, paprika, curry powder, white pepper. Stir. Add salt. Garnish with sunflower seeds, if desired. Serve hot or cold.

Yield: 12 cups

Marcia Ball

VEAL ESCALLOPES MARSALA

1 lb. veal escallopes
flour well-seasoned with salt and pepper
6 T. butter
1 T. olive oil
⅔ cup Marsala

Cut veal in very thin slices and pound paper thin. Coat with flour. In large pan, heat butter and oil. Add veal and brown on both sides. Add Marsala and simmer, covered, for 10 minutes.

4 Servings — VIRGINIA WALTER

FRENCH DRESSING

1 cup olive oil
¾ cup sugar
¾ cup ketchup
2 cups cider vinegar
½ tsp. salt
½ small onion, minced

Mix above ingredients and blend well. Store in refrigerator. Shake well before using. Serve at room temperature.

Yield: 1 quart — ANITA SMITH

PECAN ROLL

4 eggs, separated
1 cup sifted confectioners' sugar
2 cups ground pecans
1 cup whipping cream
3 T. sugar
2 tsp. cocoa
½ tsp. vanilla

Preheat oven to 400°. Grease a 10 x 15-inch pan and line with waxed paper then grease paper. Beat egg yolks and sugar until thick and lemon-colored. Beat whites until stiff but not dry. Fold yolks and nuts into whites. Blend gently, but thoroughly. Spread evenly into pan. Place in oven and reduce heat to 350°. Bake 15 to 20 minutes until springy. Remove from pan right side up. Roll cake from short end without removing wax paper. Cool rolled up. Whip cream with sugar, cocoa and vanilla until soft peaks form. Unroll cake, remove wax paper, and spread with whipped cream. Reroll cake. Dust top with confectioners' sugar and refrigerate.

8 to 10 Servings

NANCY L. WALSH

"SEA SYMPHONY"

*Sole with Almonds

Rice

Honey Glazed Carrots

Salad

*Fluden

Pouilly Fuissé or White Graves

SOLE WITH ALMONDS

- **⅓ cup flour**
- **1¼ tsp. salt**
- **¼ tsp. freshly ground pepper**
- **1½ lbs. sole filets**
- **6 T. butter**
- **1 T. oil**
- **2 T. lemon juice**
- **½ cup sliced almonds**
- **2 T. butter**

Preheat oven to 225°. Sauté almonds in 2 T. butter until golden. Remove from pan and set aside. Combine flour, salt and pepper. Coat each filet. In a large skillet, heat 3 T. butter and oil. Pan fry filets over medium heat until golden, about 1 to 2 minutes on each side. Do not crowd in pan. Transfer to ovenproof platter and place in oven. Fry remaining filets, adding more butter as needed. When done, turn heat to high, add lemon juice to pan and cook for a few seconds. Pour lemon butter over fish and garnish with almonds.

4 Servings — CHERYL LEWIS

FLUDEN
(LAYERED APPLE RAISIN CAKE)

3 eggs
¾ cup sugar
¾ cup melted shortening
3 cups of flour (more if needed)
juice of 1 orange
juice of ½ lemon
pinch of salt
1 tsp. vanilla
2 heaping tsp. of baking powder
½ tsp. baking soda
chopped nuts
cinnamon sugar
coconut
plum jelly
sliced apples
raisins

Beat eggs with sugar. Add lemon and orange juice; then shortening, vanilla and salt. Mix slightly and set aside. Combine baking powder, soda and flour. Add flour mixture to egg mixture and knead into dough. (Add more flour if dough is sticky.) Refrigerate for 30 minutes then divide dough into 4 pieces. Roll out 1 piece and place in a greased and floured 9 x 13-inch baking pan. Spread plum jelly over dough. Arrange apple slices on top, then sprinkle with raisins, coconut, cinnamon sugar, and chopped nuts. Continue rolling out dough and layering in same manner. End with dough on top. Sprinkle with cinnamon sugar and nuts. Bake at 400° for 10 minutes. Then lower oven to 350° and bake about 50 minutes longer or until golden brown on top and done in center. Cut into small squares while warm.

12 Servings DEBORAH WEISS

"THE GOLDEN COCKEREL"

*Baked Artichoke Appetizer

*Chicken Sauté Marengo

Rice

*Mom's Nut Torte

Cote Rotie or Petite Syrah

BAKED ARTICHOKE APPETIZER

1 can artichokes, drained
1 cup mayonnaise
1 cup grated mozzarella cheese
1 cup grated Parmesan cheese

Mix ingredients. Spoon into 1-quart baking dish. Bake at 350° for 30 minutes. Serve hot with crackers.

THE COMMITTEE

Chicken Sauté Marengo

4 chicken joints
¼ cup butter
6 small peeled onions
2 tsp. paprika
3 T. tomato pureé
10 oz. beer
1 bay leaf
5 oz. light cream
seasoning to taste

Brown chicken in butter. Add onions and cook until onions soften. Season and add paprika. Stir in tomato pureé and beer. Add bay leaf. Cover and simmer until chicken is tender (about 45 minutes). Remove bay leaf. Skim fat and stir in cream. Simmer until heated through.

4 Servings

Mrs. Jean Hodgekins

Mom's Nut Torte

12 eggs separated
1½ cups sugar
1½ cups ground walnuts
4 whole graham crackers, ground
grated rind of ½ lemon
1 tsp. rum or whiskey
1 tsp. vanilla
1 tsp. cinnamon
1 tsp. lemon juice
1 recipe Custard Frosting

Beat egg yolks and sugar until lemony. Fold in vanilla, rum, cinnamon, lemon rind, and juice. Fold in nuts and graham cracker mixture. Gently fold in egg whites beaten stiff but not dry. Pour into three greased and floured 9-inch layer pans. Bake at 375° for 10 minutes, reduce heat to 325° for 15 minutes. Frost when cool.

Custard Frosting

1 egg
½ cup sugar
2 heaping T. flour
1 cup milk
1 T. instant coffee (optional)
1 tsp. vanilla
1 cup butter

Cream eggs and sugar. Add flour and milk and beat until smooth. Add coffee. Cook over low heat, stirring constantly until comes to a boil. Remove from heat. Add vanilla. Refrigerate until cold. Beat butter into cold custard about 10 to 15 minutes.

12 to 16 Servings

Linda Kresnye

"LA MER"

*Shrimp O'Hara

Rice

Sautéd Zucchini with Tomatoes

*Minetry's Miracle

Muscadet or California Chardonnay

SHRIMP O'HARA

4 T. butter
½ cup celery, chopped
½ cup green pepper, finely chopped
1½ lb. raw shrimp
½ tsp. curry
½ tsp. dill weed
2 cups (or less to taste) sour cream
salt to taste

Peel and devein raw shrimp. Cut shrimp lengthwise if desired. Sauté celery and green pepper in butter until soft. Add shrimp and sauté until cooked. Sprinkle salt, dill weed and curry over shrimp and vegetables. Add 2 cups sour cream (or less) and stir until heated through.

6 Servings RUTH GRIFFIN

MINETRY'S MIRACLE

1 lb. sweet butter
2 cups sugar
1 dozen eggs, separated
1 lb. Amaretti (Italian macaroons)
1 cup Bourbon
4 – 1 oz. squares unsweetened chocolate (melted and cooled)
1 tsp. vanilla
1 cup chopped pecans
2 dozen ladyfingers
1½ cups heavy cream, whipped for decoration

Cream butter and sugar together until light and fluffy. Beat yolks until light then beat into creamed mixture. Soak macaroons in Bourbon (macaroons should be fresh from bakery – not prepackaged "hard" cookie type). Beat melted chocolate into butter mixture. Add vanilla and pecans. Beat whites until stiff but not dry. Fold into chocolate mixture. Line a 10-inch springform pan (on bottom and sides) with split ladyfingers. Alternate layers of macaroons and chocolate in pan. Chill overnight. Remove sides and decorate if desired with whipped cream.

16 to 20 Servings BRENDA K. ASHLEY

"ROMAN CARNIVAL OVERTURE"

*Italian Sausage Hunter's Style

*Neapolitan Salad

Pasta

Toasted Garlic Bread

*J. B.'s Lemon Souffle

Barbera or Chianti Classico

Italian Sausage Hunter's Style

- 4 lbs. fresh sausage, cut in 6-inch pieces (sweet or hot, or mixture)
- 8 T. oil
- 4 cloves garlic, chopped
- 2 onions, sliced
- 4 green peppers, sliced
- 16 large mushrooms, quartered
- 4 oz. brandy
- 8 oz. red wine
- 4 T. tomato paste
- 2 cups stock, chicken or beef
- 4 bay leaves
- pinch of basil
- salt and pepper

Place the sausage in a pot with the oil. Cover and cook over medium heat for 5 minutes. Occasionally uncover to turn the sausage, or shake the pot to prevent sticking. Add the garlic, onion, green pepper and mushrooms, and sauté for another 5 minutes. Add the remaining ingredients and simmer, partially covered, for about 10 minutes stirring occasionally.

8 Servings JENNIFER LANGSTON

NEAPOLITAN SALAD

2 large cauliflower florets
1 tsp. salt
½ tsp. pepper
4 T. wine vinegar
10 T. olive oil
2 T. capers
2 tsp. minced parsley
2 doz. pitted, chopped black olives
sweet red pimento

Cook florets in boiling water for 7 minutes. Drain, chill. Mix remaining ingredients. Combine with florets. Garnish with red pimento.

8 Servings GINNA HERMANN

J. B.'S LEMON SOUFFLE

1 – 1 oz. envelope unflavored gelatin
½ cup cold water
⅛ tsp. salt
4 egg yolks
1 – 6 oz. can lemonade (frozen)
grated rind of one lemon
4 egg whites
½ cup sugar
½ pint whipping cream, whipped

Soften gelatin in cold water in saucepan. Add salt, egg yolks, beat thoroughly. Cook, stirring constantly until gelatin dissolves. Beat in lemonade and rind. Chill, stirring, until mixture mounds when dropped from a spoon. Beat egg whites, gradually adding sugar until stiff peaks form. Fold into gelatin mixture. Fold in whipping cream. Turn into 1-quart soufflé dish or into individual dessert dishes. Chill until firm.

6 to 8 Servings JOYCE BRAUN

PATIO LUNCH

*Banana-Orange Slush

*Eggs Madras

*Raisin Bran Muffins

*Cold Raspberry Souffle

Grey Reisling

BANANA-ORANGE SLUSH

1 cup sugar
2 cups boiling water
1 – 6 oz. can orange juice concentrate, undiluted
1 – 15¼ oz. can crushed pineapple, undrained
3 bananas, peeled and sliced
2½ T. lemon juice
1 – 10 oz. jars maraschino cherries, drained
mint sprigs for garnish (optional)

Combine all ingredients in bowl. Mix well. Cover. Refrigerate for 24 hours stirring occasionally. Freeze overnight or until firm. Remove from freezer 15 to 20 minutes before serving to allow fruit to "slush." Makes a delicious addition to brunch, lunch or dinner. Can be kept frozen for a month or more.

Yield: 2 qts. or 10 to 12 Servings MRS. L. A. BURNS

Eggs Madras

6 hard cooked eggs
½ cup chutney, chopped
salt
½ cup mayonnaise
1 to 2 T. curry powder
1 tsp. soy sauce
milk or cream

Slice eggs in half lengthwise. Mash yolks and mix with chutney. Fill whites with yolk mixture. Combine mayonnaise, curry powder, soy sauce. Add milk or cream to desired consistency. Spoon this sauce over the eggs. Serve on bed of lettuce for first course, or with thick curry sauce as a finger appetizer (messy).

4 Servings — Mrs. Robert Neary

Raisin Bran Muffins

1 – 15 oz. box Raisin Bran cereal
2½ cups sugar
5 cups flour
5 tsp. soda
2 tsp. salt
1 cup melted shortening or oil
4 beaten eggs
1 qt. buttermilk

Mix cereal, sugar, flour, soda, and salt. Add remaining ingredients and mix well (by hand). Pour into greased muffin tins. May store in refrigerator up to 5 or 6 weeks. Bake at 375° for 20 minutes.

Yield: 5-1/2 dozen — Lois McCormick

COLD RASPBERRY SOUFFLE

1 – 10 oz. pkg. frozen raspberries
1 – 1 oz. envelope gelatin
4 eggs, separated
½ cup sugar
pinch of salt
¼ cup sugar
1 cup heavy cream, whipped to hold peak

Oil a 1-quart soufflé dish. Use a 6-inch piece of wax paper and make a 3- to 4-inch collar around the dish. Thaw the raspberries and drain well. Sprinkle the gelatin over ¼ cup raspberry juice to soften. Puree raspberries and remaining juice. Set aside. In a double boiler, beat egg yolks slightly and gradually beat in ½ cup sugar and pinch of salt. Cook mixture over simmering water, stirring constantly until thickened (may take 5 to 7 minutes). Remove and stir in gelatin until dissolved. Let mixture stand until cool but not set. Beat egg whites until they hold a shape and gradually beat in ¼ cup sugar to make a shiny meringue. Beat heavy cream, until thick, not stiff. Fold egg whites into berry mixture. Fold whipped cream into berry puree. Combine both mixtures. Pour into prepared dish and chill 2 to 3 hours then remove collar.

4 to 6 Servings SUSAN LEVINE

Variation:

1 lb. fresh raspberries
¼ cup cold water

Reserve 8 raspberries for decoration. Puree and sieve the remainder. Follow above directions using water to soften gelatin. Decorate when set with raspberries and pistachio nuts.

THE COMMITTEE

HEARTY FARE

*Company Pork Chops

*Squash Casserole

Buttered Peas

Tossed Green Salad

Rolls

*French Silk Pie

California Johannisberg Reisling

COMPANY PORK CHOPS

6 to 8 pork chops
2 to 4 slices pineapple cut in half
1 thin slice lemon per chop
1 slice onion (thin) per chop
1 T. brown sugar per chop
1 T. chili sauce per chop

Place chops in baking dish. On each chop place ingredients above in stated order. Cover and bake at 350° for 30 minutes. Uncover, bake 30 to 45 minutes until browned, basting frequently.

6 to 8 Servings MRS. JOHN LADD DEAN

Squash Casserole

4 large yellow squash
½ stick butter
3 eggs
2 T. sugar
¼ cup all-purpose flour
1 T. baking powder
salt and pepper to taste

Cook squash. Scoop out pulp, mash. Add butter and remaining ingredients. Pour into greased casserole. Bake in 325° oven for 1 hour.

6 to 8 Servings — Mrs. Boris Chusid

French Silk Pie

CRUST:
- 3 egg whites
- ¼ tsp. cream of tartar
- ⅛ tsp. salt
- ¾ cup sugar
- ½ cup ground pecans

FILLING:
- ½ cup butter
- ¾ cup sugar
- 1 square unsweetened chocolate, melted
- 1 tsp. vanilla
- 2 eggs

Crust: beat egg whites until frothy. Add salt and cream of tartar. When soft peaks form, slowly add sugar. Beat until very stiff. Fold in pecans. Place in well-greased 9-inch glass pie pan. Bake at 275° 1 hour or until dry. Filling: cream together butter and sugar. Add cooled chocolate and vanilla. Add eggs, one at a time, beating 5 minutes after each addition. Pour filling into crust and chill at least 1 hour. Serve with additional whipped cream.

6 to 8 Servings — Dianne Vogt

LIGHT 'N EASY

*Chicken and Watercress Sandwiches

*Crab in a Pocket

Assorted Relishes

*Emily's Southern Pound Cake

Vouvray or California Chenin Blanc

CHICKEN AND WATERCRESS SANDWICHES

1 loaf homemade white bread
1 stick butter, softened
1 T. curry powder
watercress
mayonnaise
chicken breast, cooked, skinned and sliced thin

Freeze loaf of bread for 2 hours. Cut off crusts and slice into ¼-inch slices. Mix softened butter and curry powder. Spread one side of each slice with curry butter. Top with watercress sprigs. Spread sprigs lightly with mayonnaise. Arrange sliced chicken breast over them. Spread chicken lightly with mayonnaise. Top with watercress sprigs, then top with bread, buttered side down. Stack sandwiches, wrap in a dampened tea towel and chill. Cut sandwiches into 1½-inch thick slices.

12 Servings BARBARA BOHLMAN

Crab in a Pocket

1½ lb. crabmeat
1 ¼ cups mayonnaise
3 green onions, chopped
1 T. seasoning salt
1½ tsp. lemon juice
2 tomatoes, chopped
8 to 10 oz. shredded mozzarella or provolone cheese
6 small-size pita breads, cut in half

Combine all ingredients, fill all 12 pockets with filling. Lay on baking sheet and bake at 350° until pita bread is lightly crisped (15 to 20 minutes). Makes 12 half sandwiches.

Shirley Schoenberger

Emily's Southern Pound Cake

½ lb. butter, softened
3 cups sugar
3 cups flour
6 eggs at room temperature
1 T. vanilla
1 T. almond flavoring
chopped almonds (optional)
½ pint heavy cream

Cream butter and sugar. Beat in eggs one at a time. Add flavorings and almonds. Alternately add cream and flour. Butter and flour loaf pan. Bake for 1 hour and 15 minutes at 325°. Start with cold oven.

12 Servings

Denise Crenshaw

"EVENING SONGS"

Shrimp Cocktail

*Chicken in White Wine

Rice Pilaf

*Mandarin Cocoa Torte

Graves Sec or Piesporter Goldtropfchen

CHICKEN IN WHITE WINE

2 whole chicken breasts
salt
nutmeg
2 T. butter
2 T. onion, minced
¼ lb. mushrooms, sliced
⅔ cup dry white wine
1 tsp. cornstarch
2 tsp. additional wine

Bone, skin, halve breasts. Sprinkle with salt and nutmeg. Brown in butter. Add onion, mushrooms and wine. Bring to a boil. Cover, reduce heat, simmer 15 minutes. Remove chicken to warm platter. Bring pan juices to a boil, stirring until reduced slightly. Mix cornstarch with 2 teaspoons of wine, stir into juices until thickened. Spoon sauce over chicken.

4 Servings MARCIA BALL

Mandarin Cocoa Torte

CHEESE CUSTARD:

- 8 oz. cream cheese
- ½ cup sugar
- 3 eggs

COCOA:

- ½ cup butter
- 1 cup sugar
- ⅓ cup cocoa
- 1 tsp. vanilla
- 2 eggs
- ½ cup flour
- ½ cup chopped nuts

GLAZE:

- 2 T. cornstarch
- 1½ T. sugar
- 1 cup orange juice
- 1 small can mandarin oranges

Beat cream cheese until smooth. Gradually add ½ cup sugar and continue beating at medium speed 2 minutes. Add 3 room-temperature eggs, 1 at a time. Beat 5 minutes until light and fluffy. Cream butter and 1 cup sugar. Add cocoa and vanilla. Cream 3 minutes. Add 2 eggs, 1 at a time, beat 1 minute. Remove from mixer. Add flour, chopped nuts, and stir until mixed. Grease bottom only of two 8-inch cake pans. Put wax paper on bottom then turn greased side up. Divide cocoa mix evenly between pans. Pour cheese evenly on top of cocoa in each pan. Bake 30 minutes at 350°. Let stand 10 minutes. For the glaze, mix cornstarch and sugar. Gradually stir in juice. Bring to boil over medium heat, stirring constantly. Simmer 2 to 3 minutes. Remove one cake from pan. Remove paper. Turn cheese side up on serving plate. Spread glaze over layer. Put other layer on top. Spread glaze over top and sides. Decorate with oranges. Let stand 30 minutes at room temperature, then refrigerate until served.

10 to 12 Servings — Nancy L. Walsh

"LE MIDI"

*Sallie's Pasta Potpourri

*Herb Bread

*Pears in Wine

*Chocolate Chews

Frascati

SALLIE'S PASTA POTPOURRI

12 oz. bulk Italian sausage
1 cup sliced fresh mushrooms
2 tsp. dried basil, crushed
½ tsp. salt
¼ tsp. garlic powder
2 eggs
1/4 cup milk
½ cup grated Parmesan cheese
8 oz. spaghetti noodles
¼ cup butter
12 cherry tomatoes, halved

In a 10-inch skillet brown sausage; add mushrooms. Cook until mushrooms are tender; drain. Stir in basil, salt and garlic powder; keep warm. In mixing bowl, beat eggs slightly; stir in milk and cheese. Set aside. Meanwhile, in large saucepan cook spaghetti according to package directions; drain. Return to saucepan, add butter, stirring until melted and well combined. Add meat mixture and egg mixture; blend well. Stir in tomatoes. Turn into serving dish. Serve immediately.

4 to 6 Servings VICKIE FRANKENBURG

Herb Bread

2 cups warm water (105 – 115°)
2 pkg. active dry yeast
2 T. sugar
2 tsp. salt
2 T. soft butter
½ cup + 1 T. Parmesan cheese
1½ T. dried oregano leaves
4½ cups sifted all-purpose flour

Sprinkle yeast over water in large bowl. Let stand for a few minutes; stir to dissolve. Add sugar, salt, butter, ½ cup cheese, oregano, 3 cups flour. Beat on low speed until blended. At medium speed beat until smooth, 2 minutes. Scrape bowl and beaters with wooden spoon. Gradually beat in remainder of flour. Cover bowl with waxed paper and towel. Let rise in warm place free from drafts for 45 minutes or until lightly bubbly and more than double. Preheat oven to 375°. Lightly grease 1½ or 2-quart casserole, or 2 loaf pans. With wooden spoon stir down batter. Beat vigorously ½ minute or 25 strokes. Turn into greased casserole or pans. Sprinkle evenly with Parmesan cheese. Bake 55 minutes, until brown. Turn out onto wire rack.

Sally Syme

PEARS IN WINE

2½ lbs. fresh pears
2 cups dry white wine
½ cup sugar
1 lemon
1 - 2 inch length cinnamon, or ¼ tsp. ground
1 tsp. vanilla extract
¼ orange marmalade
¼ cup apricot preserves

Peel and core the pears and cut them into eighths. Place in a saucepan and add wine and sugar. Peel the lemon and cut the peel into fine julienne strips (make sure you have no pith). Add the peel to saucepan. Bring to a boil and simmer 5 to 10 minutes or until pears are tender. Transfer pears and lemon to serving dish. Bring liquid to a boil again and add remaining ingredients. Bring to a boil again and cook 10 minutes. Pour sauce over pears. Chill before serving.

6 to 8 Servings NANCY L. WALSH

CHOCOLATE CHEWS

½ cup vegetable oil
4 squares unsweetened chocolate, melted and cooled
2 cups sugar
4 eggs
2 tsp. vanilla
2 cups flour
2 tsp. baking powder
½ tsp. salt
confectioners' sugar

Mix oil, chocolate and sugar. Blend in eggs one at a time. Add vanilla. Stir flour, baking powder, and salt into oil mixture. Chill 2 to 3 hours, or overnight. Roll about one teaspoon of dough into ball, then roll in powdered sugar. Place on greased cookie sheet 2 inches apart. Bake 10 to 12 minutes at 350°. Nuts and dates can be added to dough if desired.

Yield: 3 to 4 dozen DIANE GILL

"LES NUITS D'ETE"

*Crab Rice Squares

Grilled Steaks

*"Pasta House" Salad

Browned Potatoes

*Lemon Meringue Pie

Cahors or California Chardonnay

CRAB RICE SQUARES

3 cups long-grain rice, cooked
2 cups milk
1 cup grated cheddar cheese
1 – 6 oz. can crabmeat, drained
3 eggs, beaten
¼ cup minced parsley
¼ cup minced onion
¼ cup minced pimiento
1 tsp. Worcestershire sauce
Curry Shrimp sauce

Preheat over to 325°. Grease a 9 x 13-inch baking dish. Combine first 9 ingredients and blend thoroughly. Pour into dish. Bake 45 minutes until set. Cut into squares. Spoon sauce over each serving.

CURRY SHRIMP SAUCE

1 can cream of shrimp soup
½ cup sour cream
1 tsp. lemon juice
½ tsp. curry powder

Combine all ingredients in top of double boiler set over simmering water and cook, stirring constantly, until heated.

12 Servings DIANE GARDNER

"Pasta House" Salad

1 head iceberg lettuce
⅓ head romaine lettuce
1 – 4 oz. jar pimiento
1 – 8 oz. jar artichoke hearts, drained
1 large red onion, sliced
½ cup Parmesan cheese
salt and pepper, to taste
⅓ cup red wine vinegar
½ cup olive oil

Combine first 7 ingredients. Combine vinegar and oil and shake well. Pour over lettuce mixture. Toss and marinate in refrigerator 1 hour.

6 Servings — Ruth Cruse

Lemon Meringue Pie

1 9-inch pie shell, baked
1½ cups boiling water, divided
1¼ cups sugar
5 T. cornstarch
2 eggs, separated
⅛ tsp. salt
2 large lemons, juice, grated rind
2 tsp. sugar
½ tsp. cream of tartar

Boil 1¼ cups water and sugar together until sugar dissolves. Add cornstarch moistened with ¼ cup of water. Cook three minutes until clear. Remove from heat. Add egg yolks, salt, lemon juice, rind. Cook for two minutes. Cool slightly. Turn into pie shell. Beat egg whites with sugar and cream of tartar until shiny. Spread over pie filling. Brown under broiler for a few minutes.

8 Servings — Irene M. Walsh

SPRING DINNER

*Chilled Strawberry Soup

*Lamb Wassail

Parslied New Potatoes

*Baked Celery

*Grandma Sharkey's Cheesecake

Gigondas or California Merlot

CHILLED STRAWBERRY SOUP

1½ cups water
¾ cup dry rosé wine
½ cup sugar
2 T. fresh lemon juice
1 – 2-inch cinnamon stick
1 qt. strawberries (pureed)
½ cup whipping cream
¼ cup sour cream

Combine water, wine, sugar, lemon juice, and cinnamon. Boil uncovered 15 minutes. Add strawberry puree and boil 10 minutes more, stirring occasionally. Discard cinnamon and chill. Whip cream. Combine with sour cream. Fold into strawberry mixture. Serve chilled. Garnish with mint leaves and a dollop of sour cream.

6 Servings — MEREDITH BASS

Lamb Wassail

1 frozen leg of New Zealand spring lamb (5 or 6 lbs. defrosted)
1 cup Burgundy or dry red wine
¼ cup water
1 clove minced garlic
2 T. grated onion
zest of one lemon, cut in thin strips
½ tsp. salt
½ tsp. cinnamon
¼ tsp. nutmeg

Bone and trim excess fat from lamb with sharp knife. Cut slits in meat. Combine all seasonings. Pour over meat and marinate 1½ to 2 days. Turn occasionally. Drain lamb, reserve marinade. Place lamb, fat side up, on rack in appropriate pan; brush with reserved marinade. Roast at 325° for about 1 hour and 45 minutes or until meat thermometer reads 140°. Allow to rest 10 minutes before slicing.

6 to 8 Servings Diane Gill

Baked Celery

4 cups celery, sliced diagonally
1 – 3 oz. can sliced water chestnuts
1 can cream of mushroom soup
¼ cup diced pimiento
¼ cup soft bread crumbs, buttered
¼ cup sliced almonds

Cook celery in salted water 8 minutes; drain. Mix remaining ingredients (except crumbs) with celery. Place in casserole. Sprinkle on buttered crumbs. Bake at 350° for 35 minutes.

6 to 8 Servings Mrs. Alfred J. Hart

Grandma Sharkey's Cheesecake

- 2 – 8 oz. pkg. cream cheese
- 1 lb. small curd cottage cheese (well drained)
- 1½ cups sugar
- 4 eggs
- 1 stick (¼ lb.) butter
- 1 T. lemon juice
- ⅓ cup cornstarch
- 1 pint sour cream
- ¾ cup graham cracker crumbs

Cream the cream cheese. Add cottage cheese. Beat well. Add sugar. Beat in eggs one at a time. Add cornstarch, lemon juice and butter. Add sour cream last. Grease a 10-inch spring-form pan. Sprinkle with graham cracker crumbs. Pour cheese mixture over crumbs. Bake at 325° for 1 hour until cake comes away from sides of pan. Allow cake to cool in oven after it is turned off.

12 Servings — Kathy Rockman

"ROYAL FIREWORKS MUSIC"

*Oriental Salmon Barbeque

*Rice Salad

*Chocolate Chocolate Chip Cake

California Pinot Noir or

California Sauvignon Blanc

ORIENTAL SALMON BARBEQUE

1½ lbs. salmon steaks or filets
½ cup sweet wine or sherry
2 tsp. honey
2 tsp. prepared horseradish
¼ cup soy sauce
½ tsp pepper
4 scallions, coarsely chopped
2 T. sesame or peanut oil

Combine wine, honey, horseradish, soy sauce, pepper and scallions. Place in shallow dish, add salmon and marinate, refrigerated, for 2 to 3 hours turning once. Coat grill with oil; have coals grey-hot. Place fish on grill. Add 2 T. oil to marinade. Brush fish with marinade as it cooks, approximately 7 minutes on first side and 5 minutes on second side, or until fish flakes.

4 Servings

MARTHA AARONS
The Cleveland Orchestra

Rice Salad

2½ cups long-grain white rice
3 tomatoes, cored
1 – 10 oz. pkg. frozen peas
2 stalks celery
2 yellow squash
2 green peppers
1 red pepper
5 carrots
½ cup white wine vinegar
1 tsp. Dijon mustard
salt and pepper to taste
1½ cups oil

Bring a large pan of water with a slice of lemon to boil. Add 1 tsp. salt and rice. Stir until rice returns to boil. Let rice bubble steadily, stirring occasionally, for 12 minutes exactly. Drain, set aside. Peel, seed and core tomatoes. Cut in strips. Put in a bowl. Pour boiling water over peas, let set for 1 minute. Drain, rinse with cold water. Add to tomatoes. Halve celery stalks lengthwise, cut thin slices on an extreme diagonal. Add to other vegetables. Cut a thick lengthwise slice from each side of squash. Discard remaining column of seeds. Halve the strips lengthwise, then slice very thinly on extreme diagonal. Add to other vegetables. Core and seed green and red peppers. Cut in ½-inch dice. Add to other vegetables. Trim and peel carrots and cut into ½-inch dice. Put carrots into a saucepan, bring to a boil, simmer 2 minutes, drain and rinse with cold water. Add to other vegetables. Refrigerate vegetables until just before serving. Prepare dressing by whisking vinegar, mustard, salt and pepper together. Add oil, a little at a time, whisking constantly. Pile the rice into a bowl, add dressing, correct seasonings, refrigerate. Stir in vegetables just before serving.

10 Servings — Sheryl Julian

Chocolate Chocolate Chip Cake

⅓ cup shortening
1 cup sugar
½ tsp. vanilla
2 – 2 oz. squares unsweetened chocolate, melted and cooled
1 egg
1¼ cups sifted all-purpose flour
½ tsp. soda
½ tsp. salt
¾ cup water
1½ cup semisweet chocolate pieces
1 cup chopped walnuts (optional)

Cream shortening and sugar until light and fluffy. Blend in vanilla and cooled chocolate. Add egg, beating well. Sift together flour, soda, and salt. Add to creamed mixture alternately with ¾ cup water beginning and ending with dry ingredients. Fold in 1 cup chocolate pieces and chopped walnuts. Spread batter in greased and lightly floured 9 x 9-inch pan. Sprinkle with remaining chocolate pieces. Bake at 350° for 45 minutes or until cake tests done. Dust with confectioners' sugar when cooled.

8 Servings

Katie Loretta

"SORCERER'S APPRENTICE"

*Veal Blanket

Buttered Noodles

Tossed Salad

*Apple Tart

Chateau Leoville Las Cases

California Cabernet

VEAL BLANKET

1 onion chopped
½ lb. veal stew in chunks
¼ tsp. basil
freshly ground pepper
¼ cup white wine
½ cup chicken broth
½ lb. mushrooms, halved and sautéed
1 – 10 oz. package frozen artichoke hearts
2 tsp. cornstarch

Brown onion in 10-inch frying pan using 2 tsp. cooking oil. Remove onion from pan. Brown veal on all sides using high heat. Add oil if necessary. Add onion, wine, basil and pepper. Cover and bake at 260° for 1 to 2 hours until tender. Add chicken broth only as needed to moisten pan. When meat is tender, add remaining broth and enough water to make one cup. Stir in cornstarch and thicken over low heat. Add sautéed mushrooms and defrosted artichokes and heat through.

3 to 4 Servings DOTTIE SCHNELL

Apple Tart

1½ cups flour
1 cup ground almonds
¼ cup sugar
1 egg, beaten
½ cup butter
3 cups pared, cored and sliced apples
1 T. lemon juice
2 T. flour
¼ tsp. ground cinnamon
¾ cup orange marmalade, divided
2 T. butter
¼ tsp. almond extract

Prepare pastry: combine flour, almonds and sugar. Cut in butter until mixture resembles coarse crumbs. Stir in egg. Mix first with fork, then with fingers until dough holds together. Reserve ½ cup dough for lattice; press remainder into bottom and sides of 9-inch fluted flan pan. Refrigerate until ready to fill. Prepare filling: toss apples with lemon juice. Combine apples with 2 T. flour, cinnamon and ½ cup orange marmalade. Place in pastry-lined pan; dot with butter. Roll remaining pastry in a 9-inch round; cut into ¾-inch strips. Weave a lattice over apples; trim edges even with pan. Bake at 325° for 40 minutes or until apples are tender. Cool 15 minutes. Melt remaining ¼ cup marmalade; stir in almond extract. Spoon over filling between lattice strips.

8 Servings VICKIE FRANKENBURG

Symphonies
Glorious Galas
Pierce

"SYMPHONIE FANTASTIQUE"

*Scaloppine Cleviden

*Fettucine

Tomatoes Provencal

Pear Sorbet

*Easy Chocolate Truffles

Brunello Di Montalcino or Corvo

SCALOPPINE CLEVIDEN

10 thin slices veal (scaloppine), about 1½ lbs.
salt and freshly ground pepper to taste
flour for dredging
1 egg
2 cups seasoned bread crumbs
3 T. olive oil
3 T. butter
juice of ½ lemon
6 thin, seeded lemon slices
fresh parsley for garnish

Pound veal until very thin. Trim veal of fat and cut into 2 x 4-inch slices. Sprinkle with salt and pepper and dredge lightly in flour. Beat egg, dip veal in egg, then in bread crumbs. Heat 1½ T. oil and 1½ T. butter in a skillet and cook the veal, 3 or 4 pieces at a time, until golden brown on both sides. Remove veal and place on paper towels. Add remaining oil and butter and continue cooking the rest of the veal. Add more oil and butter if needed. Place veal in baking dish, cover and bake in 350° oven for 15 minutes. Uncover and cook for 5 minutes. Squeeze juice of ½ lemon over meat. Garnish with lemon slices and parsley.

4 Servings DONNA CATLIOTA

FETTUCINE

¼ cup margarine
4 eggs
¼ cup heavy cream
8 oz. bacon, cooked
1 lb. fettucine
1 cup Parmesan cheese
pepper to taste
¼ cup chopped parsley

Two-and-one-half hours before serving time, take out eggs, cream and margarine and allow them to come to room temperature. Cook fettucine in boiling salted water for about 15 minutes. Meanwhile beat together eggs and cream just until blended. Heat oven-proof serving dish in 250° oven. Drain fettucine thoroughly, but DO NOT RINSE. Turn pasta into heated dish. Toss pasta with margarine. Pour egg mixture over pasta and toss until pasta is well coated. (Heat from pasta cooks eggs and thickens sauce.) Add bacon, cheese, pepper and parsley; toss to mix. Serve immediately.

6 Servings MARY ANN GREINER

EASY CHOCOLATE TRUFFLES

8 oz. unsweetened chocolate, grated
2 sticks sweet butter
¾ lb. confectioners' sugar
1 T. Grand Marnier
4 oz. sweetened chocolate, grated

Put unsweetened chocolate, butter, confectioners' sugar and Grand Marnier into food processor. Blend until smooth. Take 1 teaspoon of chocolate mixture and roll into a tiny ball in the palm of your hand. Roll the truffle in the sweet, grated chocolate. Put truffles on lined serving plate or into candy cups.

Yield: 40 to 50 SUSAN LEVINE

"THE CREATION"

*Baked Sole with Raspberry Sauce

*Richard Nelson's Spoonbread Souffle

*Auntie's Favorite Nut Cake

California Chardonnay

Baked Sole with Raspberry Sauce

- 6 – 6 oz. filets of sole (or salmon or halibut)
- ½ cup white wine
- ¼ cup clarified butter
- salt to taste
- white pepper to taste
- 2 sliced lemons
- 1 cup red wine vinegar
- 2 T. red raspberry puree
- 2 T. sugar
- 1 cup cream
- dash salt
- ½ tsp. lemon juice
- 1 tsp. chopped shallots
- ½ cup butter

Brush baking dish with clarified butter. Skin filets, season, and place skinned side down in dish. Sprinkle with white wine and lay lemon slices on top of fish. Cover with foil and bake at 350° for 20 minutes or until fish flakes easily. Prepare sauce: bring vinegar, puree, sugar, cream, salt, lemon juice and shallots to boil. Reduce heat and simmer until liquid is reduced to about ⅔ cup or until mixture is syrupy. Remove from heat and whisk in 2 T. butter at a time. (Hold at room temperature.) Transfer fish to serving platter. Pour sauce around fish and serve.

6 Servings BONNIE FEMEC

Richard Nelson's Spoonbread Souffle

2 cups cold milk
½ cup white cornmeal
½ cup butter
1 – 6 or 7 oz. roll garlic pasteurized processed cheese
4 eggs, separated
1 tsp. baking powder
1 tsp. sugar
½ tsp. salt

Mix cold milk and cornmeal in a 2-quart saucepan. Cook over medium heat, stirring occasionally, until consistency of thick cream sauce. (Be careful not to burn.) Remove from heat. Stir in butter until melted. Add cheese. Stir until smooth. Cool. Add well-beaten egg yolks, baking powder, sugar and salt. Beat egg whites until stiff but not dry. Fold into cornmeal mixture. Pour into well-buttered 2-quart soufflé dish. Bake at 350° for 45 to 50 minutes, until top is puffed and golden.

6 Servings Mrs. William J. Williams

Auntie's Favorite Nut Cake

BOTTOM LAYER:

1 cup + 2 T. flour
15 T. butter
1 to 2 T. sour cream
¼ cup sugar
2 egg yolks

FILLING:

6 oz. apricot jam

TOP LAYER:

7 T. sugar
3 eggs
2 egg white
1 cup walnuts ground very fine
2 T. lemon juice
rind of ½ lemon
powdered sugar

Lightly butter a 9 x 13-inch pan. Cut butter into flour with pastry blender until well blended. Add sour cream, sugar and egg yolks. Mix until blended. Spread in pan. Spread jam over dough. In mixer combine sugar, eggs, egg whites and mix for 5 minutes. Add nuts, lemon juice and rind. Pour filling over jam. Bake at 350° for 35 to 40 minutes. Cool slightly. Cut in 1½-inch squares. Sprinkle with powdered sugar.

Yield: 40 squares CYNTHIA CARR

HOLIDAY DINNER

*Roast Duck

Wild Rice

Parkerhouse Rolls

Creamed Peas

*Cranberry Conserve

*Ranch Pudding with Whipped Cream

Fleurie or German Rhinekabinet

ROAST DUCK

5½ lbs. duck, quartered
juice of one lemon
2 tsp. salt
1 tsp. juniper berries (crushed)
pinch crumbled sage
1 T. butter
1 medium onion, chopped
6 ribs celery (including tops)
1½ cups heated sherry
6 oz. fresh mushrooms

Trim excess fat from duck and prick skin to allow fat to drain while roasting. Rinse and dry. Place duck in large bowl. Pour lemon juice over pieces, turning once. Let stand 30 minutes. Remove from bowl. Rub pieces with salt, juniper berries and sage. Place skin side up on rack. Dot with butter. Roast at 450° for 20 minutes. Turn and cook 10 minutes more. Drain off all fat and turn over. Reduce heat to 350°. Add onion and celery to pan. Roast 2 more hours, basting every half hour. Cover pan for last hour of cooking. Add mushrooms 30 minutes before serving.

4 Servings NANCY L. WALSH

Cranberry Conserve

1 lb. fresh cranberries
2 cups sugar
¾ cup chopped walnuts
1 – 12 oz. jar orange marmalade
2 T. lemon juice

Mix cranberries, sugar and walnuts in large pan and cover with foil. Center in 350° oven and bake for 30 minutes. Remove and stir well. Return to oven for 30 minutes more. Remove and add marmalade and lemon juice. Stir well and chill. Will keep refrigerated up to 2 months.

Yield: 4 cups — Joan Gretter

Ranch Pudding with Whipped Cream

1 cup dark brown sugar
¾ cup light corn syrup
4 eggs
¼ cup whiskey, rum, or brandy
¼ cup butter or margarine
1 tsp. vanilla
½ tsp. salt
1 cup chopped walnuts or pecans
1 cup raisins
½ cup walnut or pecan halves
whipped cream

Butter a 9 x 9-inch baking dish. Sprinkle 1 cup nuts and raisins evenly on bottom. Combine brown sugar, corn syrup, eggs, whiskey, melted butter, vanilla and salt in bowl and blend well. Pour over nuts and raisins. Arrange nut halves on top. Bake at 400° for 10 minutes. Reduce temperature to 325° and bake 25 minutes more. Serve warm with whipped cream.

6 Servings — Meredith Bass

"MOLL ROE"

*Gaelic Steak

Mashed Potatoes with Minced Parsley

*Vegetable Crunch Salad

*Double Chocolate Threat

French Bordeaux Rouge

California Cabernet Sauvignon

GAELIC STEAK

beef filets (one per person)
2 T. butter or margarine
1 onion, sliced
½ lb. fresh mushrooms, sliced
½ cup Irish Whiskey
½ cup heavy cream
salt and pepper

Melt butter or margarine in frying pan. Brown beef filets on both sides; remove from pan and set aside. In same pan, cook onion and mushrooms. When cooked, remove from pan and set aside. Add Irish Whiskey; stir in pan, picking up accumulated juices; add heavy cream. Return filets, onion and mushrooms to pan; add salt and pepper. When filets are cooked to degree you like, serve.

4 Servings VINCENT DOWLING

Vegetable Crunch Salad

2 cups broccoli florets
2 cups cauliflower florets
1 cup sliced celery
1 cup cherry tomatoes (whole)
1 cup sliced zucchini
¾ cup sliced green onion
½ cup pitted olives, sliced
½ cup sliced carrots
1 cup (8 oz.) Italian Dressing (oil-free dressing can be used)
Bacon bits (optional)
Shredded cheddar cheese (optional)

In large bowl, combine all ingredients except bacon and cheese. Cover well and marinate in refrigerator 4 hours or overnight. Stir occasionally. Just before serving toss with bacon and cheese.

8 Servings SANDY ABOOKIRE

Double Chocolate Threat

⅓ cup butter
2 squares unsweetened chocolate
1 cup sugar
2 eggs, well beaten
⅔ cup flour
½ tsp. baking powder
¼ tsp. salt
1 tsp. vanilla
1 cup whipping cream, for garnish

Melt butter and chocolate in top of double boiler over hot water. Remove from heat; add sugar and eggs, mix well. Sift together flour, baking powder and salt. Stir in chocolate. Add vanilla. Pour into greased and floured 8 or 9 inch square pans. Bake at 350° for 20 minutes. Cool. Remove brownie from pan and cut into strips wide enough to fit the sides of a 2-quart spring form pan. Cut strip in half to make 2 thinner layers. Line the bottom and sides of pan with brownie layers. Spoon prepared filling into brownie-lined pan, wrap well and chill overnight. To serve, loosen from sides of pan with knife, then dip into hot water. Unmold onto serving plate. Whip cream until stiff and cover top and sides of cake.

Filling

1½ lbs. semisweet chocolate
½ cup strong coffee
3 eggs, separated
½ cup coffee liqueur
½ cup whipping cream

Melt chocolate with coffee in top of double boiler over hot water. Remove from heat. Beat yolks well. Stir into chocolate. Add liqueur. Cool. Beat egg whites until stiff but not dry. Whip cream until stiff. Fold whites and cream into chocolate mixture.

12 Servings — Lynne Alfred

"OISEAUX EXOTIQUES"

*Tom's Pheasants

Wild Rice

Green Salad Vinaigrette

*Chocolate Decadence

Le Corton or Puligny-Montrachet

TOM'S PHEASANTS

2 pheasants
½ cup flour
½ cup olive oil
½ cup butter
1 clove garlic, split
¼ tsp. basil
2 shallots, minced fine
1 cup button mushrooms
1 large tomato, skinned and sliced
1 cup dry white wine
1 cup red wine
1 cup sour cream
salt and pepper

Quarter pheasants. Pour flour, salt and pepper in a paper bag and shake until mixed. Drop in pheasants, one piece at a time, shake to coat and set aside. In a large skillet heat oil and butter. Add garlic, remove when well browned. Add pheasants and brown well; remove and drain. Put 4 T. of olive oil-butter from pan into an earthenware casserole. Arrange pheasant sections in casserole. Sprinkle with basil, add shallots, mushrooms, tomato, salt and pepper. Pour wine over all. Cover and bake at 325° for 1½ hours. Remove cover and continue baking 20 minutes more. Add sour cream, cover and bake 5 minutes.

4 Servings

THOMAS GRETTER

Chocolate Decadence

1¼ lb. dark sweet chocolate
½ cup plus 2 T. (1¼ sticks) unsalted butter
5 eggs
1 T. sugar
1 T. flour
1¼ cups whipping cream
2 T. powdered sugar
2 T. orange liqueur
1 - 10 oz. package frozen raspberries, thawed

Prepare one day in advance. Preheat oven to 425°. Melt 1 lb. chocolate with butter in double boiler; set aside. In large metal bowl over boiling water, beat sugar and eggs with wire wisk until sugar dissolves and mixture is warm. With electric mixer, immediately beat mixture until triple in volume (5 to 10 minutes). Fold flour and chocolate mixture into egg mixture. Pour into 8-inch round cake pan lined with parchment paper. Bake exactly 15 minutes, allow to cool. Place in freezer for at least 24 hours. When ready to serve, remove cake from pan and peel off paper. Place on serving plate. Whip cream with powdered sugar and orange liqueur until peaks form. Top cake with whipped cream mixture, reserving some for piping through pastry bag to make rosette decorations around top. With potato peeler, form curls from remaining chocolate and pile curls in center of whipped cream topping. Puree raspberries in blender and sieve out seeds. Allow cake to sit at room temperature for 30 minutes before serving. Serve with raspberry puree.

12 Servings

Evie Dobrin
Dobie's Corner

"EINE KLEIN NACHTMUSIK"

*Cream of Broccoli Soup

*Pork and Sauerkraut

Baked Potatoes

Hearty Rye Bread

*Chocolate Almond Cheesecake

Gewurztraminer or Gigondas

Cream of Broccoli Soup

1 bunch broccoli
4 T. butter
6 T. flour
5 cups chicken stock
salt
freshly ground pepper
½ cup heavy cream
½ cup milk
¼ tsp. nutmeg
dash cayenne (optional)

Reserve enough broccoli florets for garnish. Cut remaining broccoli into 2-inch pieces. Place all but garnish into saucepan, add water to cover. Salt to taste. Cook about 5 minutes or until tender crisp. Cook garnish in separate pan. Immediately refresh the garnish, set aside. Drain the other broccoli and refresh. In large saucepan, melt butter. Add flour, whisking until flour bubbles up. Add chicken stock; stir until it comes to a boil and is thick and smooth. Add broccoli, not garnish, simmer uncovered about 30 minutes. Puree in processor or blender. Return to saucepan, bring to boil. Add salt and pepper to taste. Add cream, milk, nutmeg, pinch of cayenne and cooked garnish. Heat. Serve immediately.

6 to 8 Servings — Kathy Fleegler

Pork and Sauerkraut

4 to 6 lbs. loin pork roast
2 – 16 oz. cans Bavarian-style sauerkraut
2 apples, cubed
1 large onion, sliced
4 T. brown sugar
1½ tsp. salt

Drain sauerkraut and put sauerkraut directly into shallow 10 x 12-inch roasting pan. Mix apples, onion, brown sugar and salt. Pour on top of sauerkraut. Salt meat and place on bed of sauerkraut. Roast at 350°, 45 minutes per pound of meat. As meat juices seep into sauerkraut, move it around and from under meat so all sauerkraut gets flavor of meat and browns equally.

6 Servings Lydia Herforth

Chocolate Almond Cheesecake

CRUMB CRUST:

- 1½ cups chocolate wafer crumbs
- 1 cup blanched almonds, chopped
- ⅓ cup sugar
- 6 T. butter, softened

FILLING:

- 1½ lbs. cream cheese, softened
- 1 cup sugar
- 4 eggs
- ⅓ cup heavy cream
- ¼ cup Amaretto or other almond-flavored liqueur
- 1 tsp. vanilla

TOPPING:

- 2 cups sour cream
- 1 T. sugar
- 1 tsp. vanilla
- slivered toasted almonds for garnish

Combine first 4 ingredients and press onto the bottom and sides of a buttered 9½-inch spring-form pan. Cream the cream cheese and sugar. Beat in eggs one at a time. Add heavy cream, liqueur, vanilla and beat until light. Pour into shell and bake at 375° for 40 minutes. Cool on rack for 5 minutes. Combine topping ingredients, spread evenly over cake and bake for 5 more minutes. Transfer cake to a rack. Let it cool completely. Chill, lightly covered, overnight. Remove sides of pan and press almonds around the top edge.

8 Servings

BARBARA BOHLMAN

STRICTLY FOR COCKTAILS

*Marinated Shrimp

*Hot Cream Cheese Crab

*Chinese Barbequed Ribs

*Sauerkraut Balls

Assorted Crackers

*Mushroom Tartlets

*Herb Curry Dip

Assorted Vegetables

*Strawberry Meringue Tarts

*Chocolate Brandy Cheesecake

MARINATED SHRIMP APPETIZER

1 lb. fresh shrimp, shelled and deveined
celery tops
¼ cup pickling spice
2 cups sliced red onions
7 bay leaves
1½ cups salad oil
¾ cup white vinegar
3 T. capers and juice
2½ tsp. celery seed
½ tsp. salt
6 or 7 drops tabasco sauce

Bring water to boil, add pickling spices and celery tops and cook 5 minutes. Add cold, raw shrimp and simmer 3-5 minutes until cooked. Drain. In glass bowl, alternate shrimp, onions, and bay leaves. Mix together remaining ingredients and pour over shrimp mixture. Refrigerate at least 24 hours. Drain and serve with cocktail picks.

4 to 5 Servings

MRS. JOHN J. DWYER

Hot Cream Cheese Crab

1 – 8 oz. pkg. cream cheese
1 – 3 oz. pkg. cream cheese
1 cup or more crab
3 T. chopped green onions and tops
1½ T. milk
1 tsp. horseradish
cracked pepper
sliced almonds

Cream together all ingredients except almonds. Put in shallow pie pan and bake at 375° for 15 minutes or until bubbly. Garnish with sliced almonds. Serve hot or cold.

12 to 15 Servings — Carole Kay

Chinese Barbequed Ribs

2½ to 3 lbs. baby-back pork ribs
⅔ cup brown sugar
6 T. crystallized ginger
¼ cup wine vinegar
1¼ cups water
⅔ cup soy sauce
2 cloves crushed garlic
2 T. cornstarch mixed with ¼ cup water

Arrange ribs on roasting rack with ¼ cup water on bottom of pan. Bake covered 350° for 1 hour 15 minutes. Combine remaining ingredients except cornstarch. Boil 1 minute, then thicken with cornstarch. Dip ribs in sauce and bake uncovered at 350° for 45 minutes.

8 to 10 Servings — Ruth Ann Berger

Sauerkraut Balls

1 medium onion, minced
2 T. butter or margarine
1 cup finely minced ham
1 cup finely minced corned beef
½ tsp. garlic salt
1 T. prepared mustard
3 T. fresh parsley, minced
¼ tsp. black pepper
2 cups sauerkraut, drained and chopped
⅔ cup flour, divided
½ cup beef stock
2 eggs, well beaten
½ cup fine bread crumbs
½ cup cold mashed potatoes

Sauté onion in butter until tender. Add ham, corned beef and cook, stirring often, for 5 minutes. Add garlic salt, mustard, parsley, pepper and sauerkraut. Mix. Add ½ cup flour and beef stock. Mix well. Cook for 10 minutes, stirring often. Spread mixture out on a platter to cool. When cool shape into 1-inch balls. Refrigerate for 1 hour. Roll each ball into remaining flour. Then, dip ball into beaten eggs and roll into bread crumbs. Deep fry until golden brown. Drain on paper towels.

Yield: 5 dozen

Mrs. Robert Weaver

Mushroom Tartlets

1 stick butter
1 cup flour
1 – 3 oz. pkg. cream cheese
2 T. butter
½ lb. finely chopped mushrooms
2 T. finely chopped scallions
½ tsp. salt
½ tsp. pepper
1 T. flour
½ cup heavy cream

Prepare dough: in food processor, mix butter, flour and cream cheese until it forms a ball. Take walnut-size piece of dough and press into tart pan. Prepare filling: melt butter and sauté finely chopped mushrooms, scallions, salt and pepper. Cook over medium heat until vegetables are soft. Sprinkle with flour and cook 1 minute. Add cream, cooking until thick. Put teaspoonful of mixture in each tart. Bake at 450° for 10 minutes.

Yield: 24 to 30 small tarts DIANNE VOGT

Herb Curry Dip

1 cup mayonnaise
½ cup sour cream
1 tsp. tarragon
¼ tsp. salt
⅛ tsp. curry powder
1 T. snipped parsley
1 T. grated onion
1½ tsp. lemon juice
½ tsp. Worcestershire
2 T. capers, drained

Blend all ingredients and chill well.

Yield: 2 cups DIANNE VOGT

Strawberry Meringue Tarts

3 egg whites at room temperature
½ tsp. almond extract
½ tsp. cream of tartar
dash of salt
1 cup sugar
1 cup sour cream
whole strawberries

Combine egg whites, almond extract, cream of tartar and salt; beat until frothy. Gradually add sugar, 1 T. at a time, beating until glossy and stiff peaks form. Do not underbeat. Drop meringue by tablespoonfuls onto cookie sheet that has been covered with heavy brown paper. Using back of small spoon, make a small depression in top of each meringue. Bake at 250° about 30 minutes. Turn oven off and leave meringues in oven with door closed for 1 hour. Cool meringues away from drafts. Meringues may be stored in air-tight container. When ready to serve, place one tablespoon sour cream in each meringue; top each with a whole strawberry.

Yield: 25 to 40

Margaret Simon

Chocolate Brandy Cheesecake

- 1 – 8 oz. pkg. chocolate wafers
- 6 T. unsalted butter
- 3 – 8 oz. pkgs. cream cheese
- 1¼ cups sugar
- 5 – 1 oz. squares unsweetened baking chocolate
- 1 – 8 oz. carton sour cream
- ⅓ cup brandy
- 3 large eggs

Have eggs, cream cheese, and sour cream at room temperature when you start. Preheat oven to 350°. Melt butter, and pulverize the wafers in a blender or food processor. Toss wafers with melted butter, mixing thoroughly; then sprinkle over bottom of a 10-inch spring-form pan and press down firmly. Melt chocolate in the top of a double boiler over barely simmering water. Thoroughly cream the cream cheese with the sugars, scraping the bowl constantly. Beat in eggs one at a time; then the sour cream. Scrape the bowl once more. Mix in the melted chocolate and brandy. Pour into pan and place in oven. Immediately turn oven down to 275° and bake for 1 hour 15 minutes or until center is set and edges are puffy. Garnish with chocolate shavings when cool. Store in refrigerator. Serve at room temperature.

12 Servings — Mark Kaplan

CELEBRATION DINNER

Champagne Punch

*Deviled Crab

Belgian Endive
with Vinaigrette Dressing

*Beef Wellington

Green Beans Almondine

Assorted Rolls

*Normandy Chocolate Mousse

Pommard or Clos Vugeot

DEVILED CRAB

¾ cup milk
1 tsp. dry mustard
¼ tsp. paprika
½ tsp. salt
⅛ tsp. pepper
¾ cup bread crumbs
2 dashes tabasco sauce
3 hard-cooked eggs, diced
⅓ cup melted butter
½ tsp. Worcestershire sauce
2 T. mayonnaise
1½ cups flaked crab meat
3 T. sherry
Parmesan cheese

Mix all ingredients except Parmesan cheese. Put into shells and cover with extra buttered bread crumbs. Sprinkle with Parmesan cheese. Bake 20 minutes at 375°. Fills 8 shells.

8 Servings MARY NEWBOLD

Beef Wellington

1 filet of beef
¼ cup shortening
1 lb. mushrooms, finely chopped
1 T. chopped shallots
1 T. chopped onion
1 T. butter
½ tsp. salt
dash fresh ground pepper
1 T. chopped parsley
1 T. chopped chives
¼ cup heavy cream

RICH PASTRY:
2½ cups flour
1 tsp. salt
1 egg yolk plus milk to equal ½ cup
1 cup butter
1 egg white

Place filet and shortening in shallow pan. Roast in preheated 450° oven for 25 minutes. Cool. Sauté shallots and onion in butter for about 1 minute. Stir in mushrooms and cook over low heat until liquid has disappeared and mushrooms are dark. Remove from heat. Season with salt, pepper, parsley and chives. Add cream and cool. To prepare pastry, cut butter into flour. Add salt, egg yolk, and milk. Roll pastry large enough to cover filet. Lift filet from pan and put a thick coating of mushroom mixture over entire surface. Wrap in pastry, brush with egg white, and bake in preheated 450° oven for 15 to 20 minutes or until golden brown. Meat will be rare. (Note: can be frozen before second baking. Remove from freezer 3 hours before brushing with egg white.)

8 Servings

Rena Widzer

Normandy Chocolate Mousse

1 lb. dark sweet German chocolate
2 oz. bitter chocolate
7 T. strong coffee
2 T. kirsch or rum
5 eggs, separated
4 T. sweet butter
1 cup heavy cream
2 dozen lady fingers

Put sweet and bitter chocolate and coffee in a heavy pan over low heat. Stir until the chocolate is dissolved, then add the kirsch or rum. Remove from heat. Add the egg yolks, one at a time, then add the butter bit by bit. Beat the cream over a bowl of ice until thick. Add slowly to the chocolate. Fold in the stiffly beaten egg whites. Lightly butter a 9-inch spring-form pan and line with split lady fingers. Fill with the mousse and chill overnight. Unmold before serving. Decorate with whipped cream and shredded chocolate if desired.

8 Servings — Cheryl Lewis

"SONG OF THANKSGIVING"

*Cream of Chestnut Soup

Candied Cranberries

*Stuffed Cornish Game Hens

*Butternut Squash Casserole

Rolls

*Pumpkin Pie

California Sauvignon Blanc or Julienas

CREAM OF CHESTNUT SOUP

¼ cup butter
1 medium onion, chopped
3 ribs celery, chopped
2 cups chicken broth
1 – 1 lb. jar peeled chestnuts, unsweetened
2 T. softened butter
1 T. flour
1 cup light cream
salt or white pepper to taste

Melt butter in saucepan; add chopped onion and celery and cook until soft, but not brown. Puree mixture. Add the chestnuts and one cup of chicken broth and puree until smooth. Blend in remaining chicken broth. Return mixture to saucepan and bring to a boil. Knead 2 T. butter and the flour together until blended. Using a whisk, add a little at a time to hot soup mixture to thicken it. Season to taste with salt and pepper. Add cream and bring to a boil. If too thick, add more cream.

4 Servings

MRS. BEN M. HAUSERMAN

Stuffed Cornish Game Hens

4 – 1 lb. Cornish Game Hens, fresh or thawed if frozen
2 small boxes wild rice mix
2 cups sliced mushrooms
6 stalks celery sliced
4 T. butter
1 to 1½ sticks butter

Rinse and drain hens. Sprinkle insides with salt and pepper and set aside. Cook wild rice according to instructions using slightly less water. (Can substitute white wine for half of water.) Set aside. Sauté mushrooms and celery in 4 T. butter for 2 to 3 minutes. Combine rice, mushrooms and celery. Stuff hens with mixture. Melt butter and brush on outside of hens. Bake at 400° for 10 minutes, then reduce heat to 350° and continue baking an additional 40 to 50 minutes, basting with butter every 10 minutes or so.

4 Servings — Suzanne Maxwell

Butternut Squash Casserole

2 cups fresh butternut squash, peeled and cut into chunks
1 cup apples, peeled, cored and cut into chunks
3 T. melted butter
3 T. brown sugar
1 tsp. nutmeg
¼ cup chopped pecans

Arrange squash and apples in layers in a 1½ quart casserole. Combine butter, brown sugar, nutmeg and pecans. Drizzle over all. Bake at 350° for 1 hour.

4 Servings — Suzanne R. Blaser

Pumpkin Pie

1½ cups canned pumpkin
⅔ cup brown sugar
1 tsp. cinnamon
½ tsp. ginger
½ tsp. salt
2 eggs, slightly beaten
1½ cups milk
½ cup heavy cream
¼ tsp. cloves
allspice
1 9-inch unbaked pie shell

Mix all ingredients, except allspice together. Pour into unbaked pie shell. Sprinkle top with allspice. Bake at 450° for 10 minutes; reduce heat to 350° and continue baking 30 to 40 minutes longer.

8 Servings

Tony Loehnert

TREE TRIMMING PARTY

*Wassail

Eggnog

Salted Mixed Nuts

*See's Fudge

*Bourbon Balls

*Fruitcake Cookies

*Bavarian Cream Trifle

*Christmas Pudding

WASSAIL

2 quarts apple cider or juice
½ cup brown sugar
1 tsp. whole allspice
1 tsp. whole cloves
3-in. stick cinnamon
1 cup brandy (optional)
orange slices

Mix cider and sugar. Place spices in percolator basket or tie in cheesecloth. Perk or simmer 30 to 35 minutes. Remove spices. Add brandy and garnish with orange slices.

10 Servings LINDA KRESNYE

SEE'S FUDGE

½ lb. butter or margarine
3 packages (6 oz.) chocolate chips
2 cups nuts
1 T. vanilla
4½ cups granulated sugar
1 tall can evaporated milk

In a large mixing bowl, mix the butter, chocolate chips, nuts and vanilla. In a large kettle, over low heat, stir the sugar and milk together until the sugar is dissolved. Increase heat slightly to bring to a rolling boil. Cook exactly 7½ minutes after reaching a rolling boil. Pour over contents of bowl. Stir until thoroughly mixed. Pour into a 13 x 9-inch pan. Let set and cut.

Yield: 4 pounds — MARY L. MOORE

BOURBON BALLS

2¼ cups finely crushed vanilla wafers
1 cup powdered sugar
2 T. cocoa
1 cup ground walnuts
3 T. light corn syrup
½ cup bourbon
½ to 1 cup powdered sugar (to roll balls in)

Mix wafers, 1 cup sugar, cocoa and nuts together. Add syrup and bourbon and mix. Roll in powdered sugar.

Yield: 3 1/2 dozen — JENNY PERRY

Fruitcake Cookies

1½ cups golden raisins
¼ cup diced citron
½ lb. chopped candied cherries
¼ cup rum
1 stick sweet butter
½ cup firmly packed brown sugar
2 eggs
1½ cups unsifted all-purpose flour
1 tsp. baking soda
2 tsp. ground cinnamon
½ tsp. ground cloves
½ tsp. ground nutmeg
⅛ tsp. salt
¼ lb. chopped pecans

Put raisins, citron and cherries in a bowl. Pour on rum or flavoring and let stand for at least one hour. Cream the butter. Add sugar and eggs and beat until fluffy. Sift flour with baking soda, spices and salt. Add to the butter mixture and blend well. Add nuts and the rum-soaked fruit. Cover and refrigerate overnight. Form batter into balls the size of walnuts. Bake on greased cookie sheets at 325° for 10 to 12 minutes. Flavor improves on keeping.

Yield: 7 dozen

Patricia Korb

Bavarian Cream Trifle

1 cup plus 2 T. white wine
3 envelopes unflavored gelatin
9 eggs, separated
1½ cups sugar
4½ cups milk
3 cups heavy cream
angel food or pound cake, sliced in slivers ½″ thick
fresh or frozen unsweetened berries and peaches
sliced banana
red raspberry jelly

Pour wine into bowl and sprinkle with gelatin. Set five minutes. Heat slightly and stir until dissolved. Cool. Whisk egg yolks. Add sugar gradually and beat until thick. Beat in gelatin mixture. Stir in milk and transfer to heavy pan. Cook over high heat, stirring constantly until mixture coats back of metal spoon. (Do not overcook or mixture will curdle.) Mixture will be thin. Set over ice and whisk until cool. Beat egg whites until peaks form. Whip cream. Fold into egg yolk mixture. Spread cake slices with jelly and arrange on bottom and sides of trifle bowl. Spoon in portion of cream mixture. Add portion of fruits. Repeat cream, cake and fruits as desired ending with cream. Garnish with whipped cream or fruit slices. (Prepare one day in advance.)

16 Servings HELEN REED

CHRISTMAS PUDDING

15 oz. raisins (dark)
15 oz. sultanas or light raisins
10 oz. currants
2 cups dark brown sugar
8 oz. mixed peel
8 oz. glacé cherries
grated rind of lemon
3 cups soft breadcrumbs
1 cup flour
4 oz. chopped almonds
2 cups finely chopped suet
1 tsp. salt
¼ tsp. nutmeg
6 eggs
½ pint brandy or rum

Mix dry ingredients in large bowl. Beat eggs and add with brandy or rum. STIR WELL. Put in 2 one-quart oven-proof bowls and cover with wax paper or foil and tie firmly leaving loops with which to lower pudding into saucepan of simmering water about one inch deep. Cook in simmering water for 3 to 4 hours. Be careful not to let the pan boil dry. This pudding keeps indefinitely in refrigerator and improves with age. Serve hot with Brandy Hard Sauce.

16 Servings JEAN HOLDEN

ALSATIAN NEW YEAR'S DAY SUPPER

*Smoked Trout Paté

*Choucroute Garni

Boiled Potatoes

*Amaretto Chocolate Mousse

German Rhine Wine or Torres Coronas

SMOKED TROUT PATÉ

- 2 whole smoked trout
- ¾ cup unsalted butter, at room temperature
- freshly ground black pepper, to taste
- 2 heaping tsp. drained green peppercorns
- 8 slices white bread, crusts removed
- 5 sprigs parsley (for garnish)

Pull skin from trout, removing spines and vertebrae. Separate the flesh from the bones and pick through the flesh to remove any small bones missed. Slice butter and work it with the smoked fish in a food processor or a little at a time in a blender until smooth. Pile into a bowl. Beat in the black pepper, green peppercorns, and pack the mixture into a 3-cup crock or divide it among 6 small ramekins. Smooth the tops and cover with plastic wrap. Refrigerate. Toast the bread and cut into triangles. Pile toasts around the molds and decorate the center(s) with parsley. Serve at once. (Also good served with melba toast.)

6 Servings SHERYL JULIAN

Choucroute Garni

2 T. oil
2 medium onions, sliced
1 clove garlic, minced
1 tart apple, pared and diced
1 carrot, sliced thin or grated
1 cup dry white wine or beer
1 bay leaf
8 juniper berries
10 peppercorns
2 cloves
parsley sprigs
2 – 16 oz. cans sauerkraut
1 lb. Canadian bacon, or ham, or smoked pork chops
4 knockwurst or other sausage

In a heavy pot or large skillet, cook the onions, garlic, apple, and carrot in oil until onion browns slightly. Add wine and herbs. Let simmer. Rinse sauerkraut until desired sourness is reached and press dry. Stir sauerkraut into pot, adding meats and cook until well heated, about 20 to 25 minutes.

4 Servings — Meredith Bass

Amaretto Chocolate Mousse

6 oz. pkg. semi-sweet chocolate
24 whole blanched almonds
½ cup Amaretto
2 envelopes unflavored gelatin
¼ cup water
4 egg yolks
⅓ cup sugar
2 cups milk
4 egg whites, beaten stiff
1 pt. whipping cream (not ultra-pasteurized)
2 pkgs. split lady fingers

Melt chocolate pieces over hot water. Dip bottom of each almond in melted chocolate and place on waxed paper. Chill almonds until chocolate is firm. To remaining melted chocolate, add Amaretto and stir well. Set aside. In saucepan, combine gelatin and water. Let gelatin soften. Then stir in egg yolks, sugar, and milk. Heat gently and stir until mixture thickens slightly and coats metal spoon. Stir in Amaretto-chocolate mixture. Chill until mixture mounds when spooned. Fold in beaten egg whites. Whip cream. Set aside 1 cup of whipped cream for trim (refrigerate). Fold in remaining whipped cream. Chill again until mixture mounds when spooned. Line bottom and sides of ungreased 9-inch spring-form pan with split lady fingers. Trim lady fingers so they don't extend above pan. Sprinkle with more Amaretto. Spoon partly-set chocolate mixture into lady finger "crust". Chill about 2 hours until firm. At serving time or an hour before, pipe 24 rosettes (using the reserved whipped cream) around edge of mousse. Press a chocolate-trimmed almond into center of each rosette so the chocolate part shows. Remove sides from spring-form pan and place dessert on serving plate.

10 Servings CHERYL LEWIS

"A MIDSUMMER NIGHT'S DREAM"

*Paté Coquillette

*Spinach Stuffed Artichokes

*Filet a la Moutarde

Croissants

*Pears a l'Orange

Chambolle-Musigny or Savigny-Les-Beaune

PATÉ COQUILLETTE

½ lb. unsalted butter
¾ cup onions, chopped
1 small tart apple, peeled, cored and sliced
1 lb. chicken livers, cleaned, trimmed
1½ tsp. salt
freshly ground white pepper
¼ cup cognac
2 to 4 T. heavy cream
¼ lb. clarified butter

In heavy skillet, melt 3 T. butter. Add onions, cook until tender. Add apple, and cook 3 to 4 minutes longer. Transfer to blender or food processor. Add 3 T. butter to skillet and add chicken livers. Cook until brown (3 to 4 minutes). Season livers with salt and pepper, add cognac. Cook until cognac evaporates. Remove livers to chopping board and mince. Cool to room temperature. Add livers to apple mixture and add 2 T. cream. Blend until smooth. Cream 10 T. butter in bowl and add liver paste. Mix well. Pack mixture in small terrine and chill for 30 minutes or until very cold. Pour clarified butter on top, covering surface completely. Cover terrine with plastic wrap and chill 24 hours before serving. May be garnished with truffles.

8 Servings KATHY COQUILLETTE

Spinach Stuffed Artichokes

1 lb. fresh spinach or 1 – 10 oz. pkg. frozen spinach
4 T. butter
salt to taste
dash nutmeg
pepper to taste
12 cooked artichoke bottoms (canned)
1½ cups thick Bechamel Sauce
6 T. grated Parmesan

Blanch spinach, drain and chop. Sauté spinach in butter and add seasoning. Heap on artichoke bottoms. Top each with 2 T. Bechamel Sauce. Sprinkle with grated cheese. Brown in broiler.

Bechamel Sauce

½ stick butter
1 cup flour
4 cups milk, heated
1 carrot, sliced
½ onion, stuck with cloves
Bouquet garni

Melt butter and stir in flour until smooth. Cook over low heat a few minutes and add milk. Stir until thickened. Add carrot, onion, and bouquet garni. Simmer 10 minutes and strain.

6 Servings

Katherine Mavec

Filet a la Moutarde

6 filet mignon steaks
3 T. butter
12 T. cream
6 T. cognac
3 T. Dijon mustard

Cook steaks in butter in a hot skillet to desired doneness. Remove steaks and keep warm. Rinse skillet with cognac; add cream, quickly stirring until sauce is reduced by half. Blend in mustard; pour over steaks.

6 Servings — Cynthia Bailey

Pears a l'Orange

6 ripe pears (preferably Bosc)
1 cup orange juice
grated peel of one orange
¼ cup Cointreau
juice of one lemon
3 to 4 T. honey
whipping cream

Cut the pears in half and core. Do not peel. Place pears cut side down in a shallow, buttered, oven-proof dish. Mix together the orange juice, grated rind, Cointreau, lemon juice and the honey. Pour over pears. Bake at 300° for 20 minutes or until pears are tender. Baste often. Refrigerate pears in syrup until serving time. Serve very cold, with whipped cream (1 or 2 T.) and garnish with fresh mint if available.

6 Servings — Diane Gill

String Quartets
Family Fare
Pierce

"THE SEASONS"

*Veal Meatballs

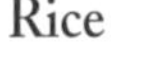

Rice

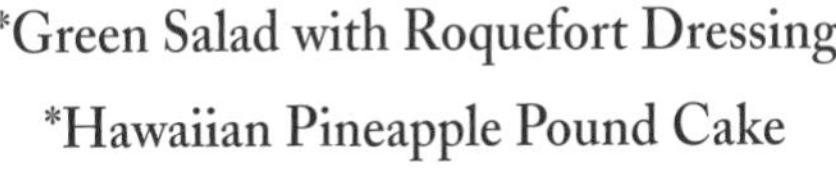

*Green Salad with Roquefort Dressing

*Hawaiian Pineapple Pound Cake

Schloss Volrades Spatlese

VEAL MEATBALLS

1 lb. ground veal
1 egg
¼ cup bread crumbs
1 small onion, grated
salt and pepper to taste

SAUCE:
1 large ripe tomato (2 medium)
1 medium onion, cut into eighths
1 – 8 oz. can tomato sauce
salt and pepper to taste

Combine sauce ingredients in medium saucepan. Heat over low flame. Meanwhile, in a bowl mix veal, egg, onion and bread crumbs together. Shape into walnut size meatballs (about 12 to 14). Place meatballs in sauce, cover and cook 45 minutes.

4 Servings

SUSAN FLOWERMAN
The Cleveland Orchestra

ROQUEFORT DRESSING

½ lb. roquefort or blue cheese
1 cup "real" mayonnaise
1 cup sour cream

Crumble cheese with fork. Add mayonnaise and mix. Fold sour cream into mixture slowly. Do not beat.

DIANNE VOGT

HAWAIIAN PINEAPPLE POUND CAKE

1 – 20 oz. can crushed pineapple
¾ cup shortening
¾ cup butter or margarine
2½ cups sugar
5 large eggs
3 cups all-purpose flour
1 tsp. baking powder
¼ cup buttermilk
1 tsp. vanilla
1 T. rum, optional
glaze

Drain pineapple well; save syrup for glaze. Cream shortening, butter and sugar until light and fluffy. Add eggs, one at a time, beating well after each addition. Mix flour and baking powder. Set aside. Combine buttermilk, vanilla and rum. Add flour mixture to cake batter alternately with buttermilk mixture. Stir in crushed pineapple. Pour into a well-greased and floured large bundt pan or tube pan and bake at 325° for 70 minutes or until cake tests done. Remove from oven and spoon half the glaze over cake. Let stand 10 to 15 minutes and then turn onto a serving plate. Spoon on remaining glaze. Cool before cutting.

GLAZE

¼ cup pineapple syrup
¼ cup butter or margarine
¾ cup powdered sugar
2 T. rum

Combine syrup, butter and sugar in a small sauce pan. Heat and stir until butter is dissolved and sugar is melted. Remove from heat and add rum.

REGINA DAILY

MOM'S NIGHT OUT

*Pork and Apple Casserole

Buttered Noodles

*Fudge Upside Down Cake

Gewurztraminer or Seyval Blanc

PORK AND APPLE CASSEROLE

2 lbs. fresh pork shoulder, cut into 2-inch cubes
¼ cup flour
1½ tsp. salt
½ tsp. pepper
½ tsp. paprika
3 T. oil
1 large onion, sliced thin
1 bay leaf, crumbled
1 tsp. sage
1 clove garlic, chopped
1½ cups fresh cider, or
1¼ cups cider, ¼ cup Calvados
4 carrots, sliced
2 tart apples, peeled, cored, sliced
1 cup celery, diagonally sliced
1 small turnip, in 2 x ½-inch sticks
chicken broth

Coat pork in flour mixed with 1 tsp. salt, ¼ tsp. pepper and paprika. Brown in heavy casserole. Remove and cook onion until golden. Return meat and add bay leaf, sage, garlic and cider. Bring to a boil, cover and bake to 350° for one hour. Add carrots, apples, celery, turnips, ½ tsp. salt and ¼ tsp. pepper. Bring to a boil on top of stove and add chicken broth to barely cover vegetables. Cover and bake 30 minutes longer until vegetables are tender. Uncover last 10 minutes to thicken, if desired.

4 to 6 Servings BARBARA LEUKART

Fudge Upside Down Cake

1 T. shortening
¾ cup sugar
½ cup milk
1 tsp. vanilla
1 cup flour
1 tsp. baking powder
½ tsp. salt
1½ T. cocoa
¼ cup cocoa
½ cup white sugar
½ cup brown sugar
½ cup chopped nuts
1½ cups boiling water

Cream ¾ cup sugar and shortening. Add milk and vanilla. Sift flour, baking powder, salt and 1½ T. cocoa into mixture. Pour into a greased 8 x 8-inch cake pan. Prepare topping by combining ¼ cup cocoa, ½ cup white sugar and brown sugar. Spread nuts over batter, then cover with cocoa-sugar mixture. Pour boiling water over topping and batter. Bake at 350° for 35 minutes. Cut into squares. Serve with whipped cream if desired.

8 to 10 Servings

Marcia Ball

"COSI FAN TUTTE"

*Five-Minute Crabmeat Spread

*Chestnut Chicken Casserole

*Four Minute Veggies

*Double Chocolate Pie

St. Veran

Five-Minute Crabmeat Spread

1 pt. sour cream
6 oz. crabmeat (canned or frozen), drained
3 T. horseradish
1 pkg. Italian Dressing

Mix all ingredients. Serve with party rye.

Dorothy Bergoine

Chestnut Chicken Casserole

2 cups cooked chicken
1 cup chopped celery
1 cup cooked rice
1 can cream of mushroom soup
1 small onion, chopped
¾ cup mayonnaise
1 can sliced water chestnuts
½ cup toasted slivered almonds

TOPPING #1:
1 cup crushed cornflakes
½ stick melted butter

TOPPING #2:
1 small bag potato chips, crushed
½ cup shredded cheddar cheese

Mix ingredients; place in ungreased baking dish. Top with either topping. Bake at 350° for 45 minutes.

4 to 6 Servings MIMI CALFEE

Four Minute Veggies

Leftover cooked or canned vegetables
Walnut or pecan pieces
Crumbled blue cheese

Lightly grease a shallow pan or dish. Arrange vegetables in pan. Sprinkle with nuts, then blue cheese (sparingly). Broil three to five minutes.

BARBARA HAAS

Double Chocolate Pie

- 1 to 1½ cups fine chocolate wafer crumbs
- ¼ lb. melted butter
- 6 oz. semisweet chocolate
- 3 eggs
- 1½ tsp. rum
- 1 cup heavy whipping cream

Mix together chocolate wafer crumbs and butter. Press into greased 9-inch pie pan. Melt chocolate. Cool slightly. Beat in 1 egg, 2 egg yolks, and rum. Beat whipping cream to soft peaks and fold into chocolate. Beat egg whites until stiff. Fold into chocolate. Fill pie shell and refrigerate 4 to 6 hours.

8 Servings — Katie Loretta

FALL LUNCH

*Ham-Cheese Chowder

*Tomato Salad

*Black Banana Bread

or

*Pecan Muffins

HAM-CHEESE CHOWDER

½ cup coarsely shredded carrot
¼ cup chopped onion
¼ cup butter or margarine
3 T. flour
4 cups milk
1½ cups diced cooked ham
½ tsp. celery seed
½ tsp. Worcestershire sauce
1 cup sharp processed American or cheddar cheese, cubed
snipped chives

In large saucepan cook carrot and onion in butter until tender but not brown. Blend in flour; add milk. Cook and stir until thickened and bubbly. Stir in diced ham, celery seed, and Worcestershire sauce. Heat through. Add cheese, stirring until melted. Garnish with snipped chives.

4 Servings ELAINE MAIMONE

TOMATO SALAD

1 large can tomatoes
2 T. vinegar
2 tsp. sugar
1 T. butter
dash salt
1⅓ small pkg. lemon gelatin
1 onion, chopped
1 green pepper, chopped
1 cup celery, chopped

TOPPING:
½ cup sour cream
½ cup mayonnaise
1 onion, chopped
1 cucumber, diced

Cook tomatoes, vinegar, sugar, salt, and butter 5 minutes. Add lemon gelatin and cool. Fold in onions, pepper and celery. Mold.

12 Servings MARY W. HARRELL

Black Banana Bread

- 2 over-ripe bananas
- 1 cup sugar
- 1 tsp. baking soda
- ⅛ tsp. salt
- 2 cups flour
- 2 eggs
- ¼ cup buttermilk or 2 oz. milk with 1 T. vinegar
- 2 oz. vegetable oil

Blend bananas, sugar, soda and salt. Add flour and eggs in turn, blending well. Add oil and buttermilk. Mix well. Bake at 300° for 1 hour. Makes 1 large loaf or 2 small ones.

12 Servings RITA BUCHANAN

Pecan Muffins

- ½ cup butter
- 1¼ cups firmly packed brown sugar
- 2 eggs
- 1 tsp. baking soda
- 1 cup buttermilk
- 1 tsp. vanilla
- ½ tsp. salt
- 1¾ cups flour
- ¾ cup chopped pecans

Cream butter with sugar until fluffy. Add eggs one at a time. Dissolve baking soda in buttermilk; mix in vanilla and salt. Add alternately with flour. Mix in pecans. Line muffin tins and fill ¾ full with batter. Bake at 375° for 15 to 20 minutes.

Yield: 1 dozen NANCY L. WALSH

AFTER SCHOOL SNACKS

*Grandma's Gum Drop Cookies

*Bird Seed

*Whole Wheat Peanut Butter Cookies

*Butter Cookies

Fresh Fruit

GRANDMA'S GUM DROP COOKIES

2¼ cups brown sugar
3 eggs
1 T. water
2 cups flour
1 tsp. baking powder
¼ tsp. salt
1½ cups small gum drops (not black)
½ cup nuts
(at Christmas, use red and green gumdrops)

Mix sugar, eggs and water well; add flour, baking powder, salt; mix well, then add gum drops and nuts. Spread on jelly-roll pan. Bake at 350° until light brown (20 minutes). Dust with powdered sugar.

KAREN SHANAHAN

BIRD SEED

Peanuts
Raisins
M & M's or
Semi-Sweet Morsels

Mix together equal portions of above in bowl.

THE COMMITTEE

Whole Wheat Peanut Butter Cookies

½ cup butter or margarine
½ cup peanut butter
½ cup sugar
½ cup brown sugar
1 egg
½ tsp. vanilla
1¼ cups whole wheat flour
½ tsp. baking powder
¾ tsp. baking soda
¼ tsp. salt

Cream margarine, peanut butter and sugars. Add egg and vanilla. Add flour, baking powder, baking soda and salt. Chill. Shape into balls and flatten with a fork. Bake on a greased cookie sheet 8 to 12 minutes at 375°. (Note: if "sugar conscious," the total sugar can be reduced to ⅓ to ½ cup, very successfully.)

Yield: 4 dozen Marcia Ball

Butter Cookies

¾ lb. butter
1½ cups sugar
2 tsp. vanilla
2 whole eggs (large or extra-large, not jumbo)
3½ cups flour
2½ tsp. baking powder

Cream butter with wooden spoon. Add sugar, vanilla and eggs. Mix flour and baking powder together. Add flour mixture to butter mixture. Use cookie press to shape. Bake on ungreased cookie sheet at 325° to 350° for 12 minutes.

Yield: 5 dozen Ursula Hlavacek

FAMILY DINNER

*Braised Short Ribs of Beef

*Potato Casserole

Buttered Green Beans

*Honey Glazed Carrots

*Open Pear Crunch Pie

Beaujolais or California Zinfandel

BRAISED SHORT RIBS OF BEEF

2 lbs. boneless short ribs of beef, well trimmed
½ cup flour
2 to 3 T. oil
1 medium onion, chopped
1 carrot, diced
1 stalk celery, diced
1 clove garlic, chopped fine
salt and pepper to taste
2 beef bouillon cubes
½ cup boiling water
½ cup Cabernet Sauvignon wine

Dredge meat with flour. Season. Brown on all sides in oil in Dutch oven. Add vegetables. Dissolve bouillon cubes in water. Add bouillon and wine to vegetables and meat. Cover and bake at 300° for 2 to 3 hours, or until meat is very tender. If there is too much liquid, uncover during last 30 to 60 minutes of cooking time. Turn meat once to keep top from drying out.

3 to 4 Servings JENNY PERRY

Potato Casserole

6 medium potatoes
¼ cup butter
1 can cream of mushroom soup
1½ cups cheddar cheese, grated
1 pint sour cream
⅓ cup chopped onion
1 cup corn flake crumbs
3 T. melted butter
salt to taste

Cook potatoes until tender, about 25 minutes. Cool, peel and grate. In large saucepan, heat butter with soup. Blend in cheese, add salt to taste, sour cream and onions. Stir in potatoes. Place in 2½-quart buttered casserole. Mix corn flake crumbs and melted butter. Place on top of casserole. Bake at 350° for 45 minutes.

6 Servings — Mary Anne Greiner

Honey Glazed Carrots

6 medium carrots
1 cup water
½ tsp. salt
2 T. butter
½ tsp. dried mint leaves
2 T. brown sugar
1 T. honey
dash of salt

Clean and slice carrots. Cook with salt in boiling water until tender, about 20 to 25 minutes. Drain. Melt butter and stir with mint leaves. Add carrots, sugar, honey and salt and cook until well-glazed, turning constantly.

4 Servings — Paula Kappos

Open Pear Crunch Pie

1 basic-pastry pie shell
¼ cup apricot jam
1 T. water
5 pears
½ cup sugar
3 T. lemon juice
1 T. grated lemon rind
½ cup brown sugar
1 tsp. cinnamon
½ tsp. nutmeg
¼ tsp. ginger
⅓ cup butter
½ cup flour
2 T. toasted sesame seeds (optional)

Preheat oven to 425°. Bake pie shell for 8 to 10 minutes. Lower heat to 400°. Heat jam and water until of spreadable consistency and brush over pie shell. Peel, core and slice pears. Mix with sugar, lemon peel, and juice. Arrange in pie shell. Combine brown sugar, flour, butter, spices and sesame seeds, mixing with fingertips until the consistency of coarse meal. Spread over pears. Bake for 45 minutes until pears are tender. Serve with softly whipped cream.

6 to 8 Servings — Katherine Mavec

FRIDAY NIGHT SUPPER

*Bob's Favorite Chopped Sirloin
Buttered Spinach
Mashed Potatoes
*Cherry Ice Cream Dessert
California Pinot Noir or Monthelie

BOB'S FAVORITE CHOPPED SIRLOIN

1 lb. ground sirloin
1 egg
1 sprig parsley, chopped
salt, pepper, garlic salt to taste
2 oz. butter
3 oz. Burgundy wine
6 large mushrooms, sliced
1 green pepper, sliced
1 – 8 oz. can tomato puree
grated Parmesan cheese

Mix together ground sirloin, egg, chopped parsley and seasonings. Shape into 2 large patties and sauté in butter until browned on both sides. Pour in wine and allow patties to cook in wine for 5 minutes, turning a few times. Add mushrooms and green pepper. When these are par-cooked, add tomato puree then simmer 15 to 20 minutes. Remove from pan, place in casserole, sprinkle with Parmesan cheese and brown under broiler. Serve immediately.

2 Servings EUNICE PODIS WEISKOPF

Cherry Ice Cream Dessert

1 cup flour
1 cup sugar
1 tsp. baking soda
dash salt
1 egg
1 – 16 oz. can tart, pitted cherries, drained (reserve juice for sauce)
1 tsp. butter or margarine
¼ cup brown sugar
¼ cup nuts, chopped

Mix flour, sugar, soda and salt. Make hole in center; add cherries and egg. Mix well. Melt 1 tsp. butter in an 8 x 8-inch pan then add mixture. Sprinkle with brown sugar and nuts. Bake at 325° for 45 minutes. Cut in squares and cool. Top each square with vanilla ice cream and warm sauce just before serving.

Sauce

1 cup cherry juice
1 cup sugar
½ tsp. almond extract
1 tsp. butter or margarine
1 T. flour

Combine all ingredients and cook, stirring until thickened.

6 Servings — Sharon Freimuth

“BEATRICE AND BENEDICT”

Hot Cocoa

*Breakfast Egg Casserole

*Raisin Bran Bread

*Peach Clafouti

Breakfast Egg Casserole

12 eggs, beaten
2 cans cheddar cheese soup
4 tsp. dry mustard
8 slices fresh bread, shredded
2 lbs. sausage, browned and drained
melted butter

Combine eggs and soup. Add mustard. Add shredded bread and combine well. Spread in greased 9 x 13-inch pan. Sprinkle sausage, then melted butter on top. Chill overnight. Bake at 350° for 30 minutes.

12 Servings

Paula Kappos

Raisin Bran Bread

1 cup whole wheat flour
1¼ cups all-purpose flour
2¼ tsp. baking powder
1 tsp. salt
½ cup shortening
¾ cup granulated sugar
2 eggs
1 cup 100% Bran or All Bran cereal
¾ cup raisins
½ cup milk

Sift together first 4 ingredients. Beat shortening and sugar until creamy. Add eggs and beat until light and fluffy. Stir in cereal and raisins. Alternately add milk and flour mixture. Turn into greased 5 x 9-inch loaf pan. Bake in a preheated 350° oven approximately 1 hour. Cool in pan 10 minutes then remove to rack to cool completely.

12 Servings SARA HAWK

PEACH CLAFOUTI

3 T. sugar
4½ cups sliced, peeled peaches
1½ cups milk
1½ cups cream
5 eggs
6 T. flour
pinch of salt
4 T. sugar
1½ tsp. vanilla
confectioners' sugar

Sprinkle a well-buttered, 2-quart, shallow, oval baking dish with 3 T. sugar. Evenly distribute sliced peaches over sugared baking dish. In mixer or blender combine milk, cream, eggs, flour, and pinch of salt. Mix briefly about 2 minutes. Add 4 T. sugar and vanilla and blend very briefly. Pour mixture over fruit. Bake in preheated 375° oven for 45 to 50 minutes until puffed and golden. Sprinkle with sifted confectioners' sugar and serve warm.

12 Servings SUSAN LEVINE

"RODEO"

*Bobbie's Corn-Pumpkin Chowder

Hamburgers 'n Hot Dogs

*Hot Dog Relish

Tossed Salad

*Best French Vanilla Ice Cream

Hot Fudge Sauce

BOBBIE'S CORN-PUMPKIN CHOWDER

2 large yellow onions, thinly sliced
2 T. butter
1½ tsp. flour
1 can condensed chicken broth, undiluted
1 lb. can pumpkin
1 – 17 oz. can cream-style corn
3 cups milk
1 cup light cream
1 tsp. salt
⅛ tsp. pepper
¼ tsp. ginger
¼ tsp. nutmeg
¼ tsp. coriander
2 tsp. parsley

In a 6-quart dutch oven, sauté onions in butter about 10 minutes. Remove from heat and stir in flour, then add broth. Simmer, covered for 10 minutes. Remove and puree in food processor. Return to pan and add pumpkin, corn, milk, cream and seasonings. Simmer slowly 20 to 25 minutes covered.

10 Servings DORI HAAS

HOT DOG RELISH

3 lbs. green tomatoes
4 red apples
3 sweet red peppers
4 onions
1½ T. coarse salt
1½ tsp. pepper
1½ tsp. cinnamon
¾ tsp. ground cloves
2½ cups sugar
2 cups cider vinegar

Stem and quarter tomatoes, apples, peppers and onions. Put through food chopper using coarse blade. Combine remaining ingredients and bring to a boil in large kettle. Add chopped vegetables and simmer uncovered about 30 minutes or until thick, stirring occasionally. Ladle into hot sterile jars and seal immediately.

Makes about 7 pints — GINNA HERMANN

BEST FRENCH VANILLA ICE CREAM

6 egg yolks
1½ cups sugar
¼ tsp. salt
4 tsp. vanilla
4 cups heavy cream
2 cups half-and-half cream
4 T. unsalted butter, melted

Beat egg yolks until thickened. Add sugar, salt and vanilla. Mix heavy cream with half-and-half. Add to egg mixture. Stir in butter. Chill well. Freeze in ice cream freezer using crushed ice.

8 to 10 Servings — MRS. S. TIMOTHY KILTY

"THE BEGGAR'S OPERA"

*Cream of Vegetable Soup

*Ham Loaf

*Pineapple Casserole

*Fluffy White Cake with

*Seven Minute Icing

German Rhine Spatlese

CREAM OF VEGETABLE SOUP

2 T. butter
1 clove garlic, chopped
1 medium onion, sliced
¼ head cauliflower
2 carrots, sliced
2 stalks celery, sliced
6 asparagus stalks, cut into 1-inch pieces
1 leek, chopped
1 large potato, peeled and chopped
1 cup spinach, chopped
salt and pepper
4 cups chicken or veal stock
Tabasco
1 cup heavy cream
1 T. chopped parsley
1 T. grated Parmesan

In large soup pot, melt butter and sauté onion and garlic for several minutes. Prepare vegetables. Add all but spinach to pot and cook 5 minutes. Add stock and simmer 20 minutes. Add spinach and simmer 10 minutes more. Mix cream and flour with a little soup broth until smooth. Pour slowly into the soup, stirring constantly. Simmer until slightly thickened. Garnish with parsley and cheese.

6 to 8 Servings JENNIFER LANGSTON

Ham Loaf

- 1 lb. ground ham
- 1 lb. ground pork
- 1 egg, beaten
- ¾ cup milk
- 1 cup crushed graham crackers
- ¾ cup brown sugar
- 1½ tsp. ground mustard
- ½ can tomato soup
- ¼ cup vinegar (any kind)

Mix meat, egg, milk and crushed graham crackers together. Shape into a loaf and place in baking dish. Mix brown sugar and dry mustard; add tomato soup and vinegar. Mix and heat. Pour sauce over loaf and bake at 350° for 1 hour. Baste once if needed.

8 to 10 Servings — Mrs. Paul E. Westlake

Pineapple Casserole

- ¼ lb. butter, melted
- ½ cup sugar
- 1 T. flour
- salt
- 2 beaten eggs
- 1 – 20 oz. can crushed pineapple and juice
- 5 slices broken bread

Mix all ingredients except the bread. Then add the bread. Bake in a 1-quart casserole at 325° for 45 minutes or until golden brown.

6 to 8 Servings — Sara Hawk

Fluffy White Cake

2⅓ cups all-purpose flour
2 cups sugar
4 tsp. baking powder
1 tsp. salt
1½ cups milk
⅔ cup shortening
5 egg whites, unbeaten
1 tsp. almond flavoring

Combine and blend in large mixer bowl flour, sugar, salt and baking powder. Add milk and shortening. Beat two minutes at medium speed. Add egg whites and flavoring. Beat two minutes more. Pour into two greased and floured 9-inch layer pans or a 9 x 13-inch pan. Bake at 375° 30 to 35 minutes in layers; 35 to 40 minutes in 9 x 13-inch pan. When cool, frost with Seven Minute Icing.

Seven Minute Icing

2 egg whites
1½ cups sugar
½ cup water
1 T. white corn syrup
½ tsp. salt
1 tsp. vanilla

In double boiler, combine all ingredients except vanilla. With electric mixer at high speed, beat 1 minute; then place over rapidly boiling water and beat until mixer forms peaks when beater is raised (can take longer than 7 minutes). Remove from boiling water and transfer into large mixer bowl. Add vanilla and continue beating until thick enough to spread.

10 to 12 Servings — Diane Vogt

BOUNTIFUL BRUNCH

*Chili Egg Puff

Fresh Fruit Salad with

*Halle's Dressing

*Bran Muffins

*"Midnight Special" Poppyseed Cake

CHILI EGG PUFF

10 eggs
½ cup unsifted flour
1 tsp. baking powder
½ tsp. salt
1 – 16 oz. carton of small-curd creamed cottage cheese
1 lb. Jack cheese, shredded
½ cup butter, melted
2 – 4 oz. cans diced green chiles

In a large bowl, beat eggs until light and lemon colored. Add flour, baking powder, salt, cottage cheese, Jack cheese and melted butter. Blend until smooth. Stir in chiles. Pour mixture into a well-buttered 9 x 13-inch baking dish. Bake at 350° for 35 minutes or until top is browned. (May be made night before and refrigerated until ready to bake.)

10 to 12 Servings JANICE THOMPSON

Halle's Tea Room Fluffy Fruit Dressing

1 cup unsweetened pineapple juice
½ cup lemon juice
3 eggs, beaten
1 cup granulated sugar
2 cups whipping cream

Mix fruit juices. Add eggs and sugar. Cook in double boiler until thickened. Cool. Whip cream and fold into cooked mixture.

Jane Brooke

Bran Muffins

2 cups bran buds
2 cups oatmeal
2 cups shredded wheat
4 eggs
3 cups sugar
1 tsp. salt
1 cup vegetable oil
4 cups buttermilk
5 tsp. baking soda
5 cups flour
2 cups nuts, raisins, or dates (optional)
2 cups boiling water (see directions)

Mix cereals together. Beat eggs, sugar, salt and oil together. Then add to cereal. Combine soda with flour and add to cereal mixture alternately with buttermilk. Add nuts, raisins or dates. (If you do not want to bake right away, pour 2 cups boiling water over batter, cover and store in refrigerator up to 2 weeks. If stored, stir mixture before spooning in tins.) Bake at 400° for 20 minutes.

Yield: 5 dozen

Inez Donofrio

"MIDNIGHT SPECIAL" POPPY SEED CAKE

1 cup poppy seed
1½ cups milk
⅓ cup honey
¼ cup water
1 cup softened butter or margarine
1½ cups sugar
4 egg yolks
1 cup sour cream
1 tsp. vanilla
2½ cups sifted flour
1 tsp. baking soda
½ tsp. salt
4 stiffly beaten egg whites

Soak poppy seeds in milk overnight. Next day, drain off excess milk. In a 1-quart saucepan cook poppy seeds with honey and water 3 minutes. Cool. Cream butter and sugar until soft and fluffy. Add cooled poppy seed mixture. Add egg yolks one at a time beating well after each addition. Blend in sour cream and vanilla. Sift together flour, soda and salt. Gradually add to poppy seed mixture, beating well after each addition. Carefully fold in stiffly beaten egg whites. Pour batter into lightly greased and floured 10-inch tube pan. Bake in preheated 350° oven 1 hour 15 minutes or until tester comes out clean. Cool in pan at least 5 minutes. Remove and cool on a wire rack. Sprinkle with powdered sugar.

12 to 16 Servings

IRVING NATHANSON
The Cleveland Orchestra

"BIRD QUARTET"

*Parmesan Oven-Fried Chicken

*Pasta with Broccoli

Italian Rolls

*Apricot Coconut Balls or

*Cheesecake Dreams

Pinot Grigio or Sassella

PARMESAN OVEN-FRIED CHICKEN

2½ to 3 lbs. chicken, cut up
¾ cup fine bread crumbs
¼ cup grated Parmesan
¼ cup chopped, blanched almonds
½ cup unsalted butter
2 T. parsley, minced
1 tsp. salt
¾ tsp. garlic powder
¼ tsp. thyme
⅛ tsp. pepper

Preheat oven to 375°. Combine crumbs, cheese and almonds in a pie pan and set aside. Blend softened butter, parsley and seasonings and spread over chicken. Roll pieces in crumb mixture coating well. Place chicken, skin side up, in ungreased 9 x 13-inch pan. Bake uncovered, without turning, at 375° for 55 to 65 minutes or until golden brown.

4 Servings KATHY COQUILLETTE

Pasta with Broccoli

1 bunch broccoli
4 T. olive oil
4 T. butter
2 T. coarsely chopped garlic
hot pepper flakes (optional) or freshly ground black pepper to taste
1 to 1½ cups water
½ lb. linguine or spaghettini broken into 2-inch lengths
1 tomato, chopped

Cut broccoli into florets and quarter stalks. Peel stems off, then cut into 2-inch lengths. Heat oil and butter in large skillet. Add garlic and pepper. When oil is hot add broccoli, one cup of water, and uncooked pasta. Mix well. Add tomatoes. Cover and cook over medium heat about 10 minutes. Mix often, adding more water if necessary, so pasta does not stick.

4 Servings JENNIFER LANGSTON

Apricot Coconut Balls

1½ cups dried apricots ground in small pieces
2 cups shredded coconut
⅔ cup sweetened condensed milk
confectioners' sugar

Combine apricots and coconut. Add milk and blend. Shape into small balls and roll in sugar. Let stand till firm.

KAREN SHANAHAN

Cheesecake Dreams

- ⅓ cup firmly packed light-brown sugar
- 1 cup all-purpose flour
- ½ cup chopped walnuts
- ⅓ cup melted margarine
- 1 - 8 oz. pkg. cream cheese, softened
- ¼ cup sugar
- 1 egg
- 2 T. milk
- 1 T. lemon juice
- 1 tsp. vanilla

Preheat oven to 350°. Grease an 8 x 8-inch baking pan. In small bowl, mix first three ingredients. Stir in melted margarine until well blended. Set aside ⅓ cup crumbs and pat rest in pan. Bake 12 to 15 minutes. In small bowl, at medium speed, beat cream cheese and sugar until smooth. Beat in remaining ingredients. Pour over baked crust. Sprinkle on remaining crumbs. Bake 25 minutes more until set. Cool on rack. Cut into 2-inch squares, then cut diagonally in half.

Yield: 32 — Tory Willoughby

"RIGOLETTO"

*Special Company Spaghetti

Garlic Bread

*Lemonade Jello

Spumoni

*Biscotti

Chianti Classico or Gattinara

Special Company Spaghetti

3 garlic cloves, minced
1 onion, chopped
¼ cup olive oil
3 large tomatoes, peeled and chopped
1 – 8 oz. can tomato sauce
1 tsp. salt
1 tsp. sugar
pinch of pepper
½ tsp. Italian seasoning
20 raw shrimp, peeled and deveined
1 – 7 oz. can minced clams
½ to 1 lb. spaghetti, cooked

Sauté garlic and onion in oil for about 5 minutes. Add tomato, tomato sauce and seasonings. Cook and simmer for one hour. Add shrimp and simmer uncovered 5 minutes. Add clams and simmer an additional 5 minutes. Pour sauce over spaghetti and serve immediately.

4 Servings

Shirley Schoenberger

Lemonade Jello

1 – 6 oz. box of lemon gelatin
2 cups boiling water
1 – 12 oz. can of frozen lemonade
9 oz. frozen "whipped" topping

Dissolve gelatin in boiling water. Add lemonade and stir. Whisk in whipped topping. Pour into 6-cup mold and refrigerate overnight. To serve, unmold on a platter and garnish with fresh fruit, cherry tomatoes or olives. (This separates; top is clear and bottom is creamy.)

16 Servings Carolyn Ross

Biscotti (Anise Toast)

1¼ cups sugar
1½ sticks of butter or margarine
3 eggs
¼ cup milk
3 T. crushed anise seed
3½ cups unsifted flour
3 tsp. baking powder

Cream butter and sugar, add eggs, milk and crushed anise seed. Slowly add flour and baking powder. Make two long strips of dough on a cookie sheet. Bake at 375° for 30 minutes. Remove and allow to cool slightly. Cut strips in 1-inch pieces. Return slices to cookie sheet and bake at 425° for about 10 minutes or until brown.

Mrs. J. A. Williams, Jr.

"SUMMERTIME"

*Flank Steak

Skewered Tomatoes, Mushrooms and Onions

Breadsticks

*Six Threes Ice Cream

*Iowa Brownies

California Cabernet or Côtes du Rhône

FLANK STEAK

1 cup salad oil
½ cup soy sauce
¼ cup honey
½ tsp. garlic powder
½ tsp. ginger (optional)
1 T. minced, dried onion
1½ lbs. flank steak

Combine ingredients. Pour over flank steak and marinate overnight. Broil or grill steak. Baste with the marinade while cooking. To serve, slice on the angle.

4 Servings CAROLYN ROSS

Six Threes Ice Cream

3 bananas, mashed
juice of 3 oranges
juice of 3 lemons
3 cups sugar
3 cups whipping cream
3 cups milk

Mix all ingredients together, stir. Pour into an electric ice cream freezer and freeze.

Yield: 1 gallon MARY L. MOORE

Iowa Brownies

1 stick margarine
1 cup sugar
1 – 1 lb. can Hershey's syrup
4 eggs
1 cup flour
1 cup chopped nuts

Combine all ingredients together. Pour into 9 x 13-inch pan. Bake at 350° for 30 minutes. These will look gooey when you take them out of the oven. Pour icing over baked brownies.

Icing

1 stick margarine
1½ cups sugar
⅓ cup evaporated milk
½ cup chocolate chips

Boil all ingredients except chocolate chips for 1 minute, then add chocolate chips.

KAREN SHANAHAN

"LE PAUVRE MATELOT"

*"Hello Mom" Casserole

*Cranberry Jello Salad

*Lazy Daisy Cake

Côtes du Rhône

"HELLO MOM" CASSEROLE

1 – 5 oz. pkg. egg noodles
3 T. butter
3 T. flour
1½ cups milk
salt and pepper to taste
1 medium can tuna or crabmeat
1 pkg. or jar pimento cheese
3 hard-cooked eggs
12 ripe olives
1 small can mushrooms
1 green pepper, chopped fine
buttered crumbs

Cook noodles in boiling water until tender. Drain. Make white sauce of butter, flour, milk, salt, and pepper. Combine all ingredients. Pour into buttered baking dish, top with buttered crumbs and bake at 350° for 45 minutes.

6 to 8 Servings

DEDE BAKER

Cranberry Jello Salad

1 – 6 oz. pkg. raspberry jello
1 cup hot water
1 can jellied cranberry sauce
1 cup sour cream
2 cups nuts, chopped

Dissolve jello in hot water and cool. Beat sour cream and cranberry sauce until well blended; then add nuts. Combine mixture with jello and refrigerate.

11 to 12 Servings MARY L. MOORE

Lazy Daisy Cake

2 eggs
1 cup flour
1 cup sugar
1 tsp. baking powder
½ tsp. salt
1 tsp. vanilla
½ cup milk
4 T. unsalted butter

Beat eggs well, add flour, sugar, baking powder, salt, vanilla. Bring milk to a boil, melt butter in milk. Add to first mixture. Pour into greased 9 x 9-inch cake pan. Bake at 350° for 25 minutes.

Frosting

3 T. melted butter
5 T. brown sugar
½ cup coconut
2 T. milk

Make frosting by combining melted butter, brown sugar, coconut and milk. Spread on cake. Broil in oven until light brown.

KATHY COQUILLETTE

"MIRACULOUS MANDARIN"

*Oriental Chicken Stir-Fry or

*Oriental Pork Platter

Rice

*Chinese Chews

*Almond Cookies

St. Veran or California Pinot Noir

ORIENTAL CHICKEN STIR-FRY

¼ cup oil
3 whole broiler-fryer chicken breasts, boned, skinned and cut into 1-inch chunks
3 cups broccoli florets
1 medium red pepper, cut into 1-inch squares
½ lb. mushrooms, sliced
3 T. thinly sliced scallions
1 cup chicken broth
3 T. dry sherry
1 T. cornstarch
1 T. soy sauce
½ tsp. liquid hot pepper sauce
⅓ cup cashew nuts

In large skillet, preferably an iron one, or a wok, heat oil. Add chicken and cook over moderate heat for 5 minutes, stirring frequently, until chicken is white. Remove from wok. Place broccoli, red pepper, mushrooms and scallions in wok. Cook 3 minutes, stirring frequently. In a small bowl, mix chicken broth, sherry, cornstarch, soy sauce and liquid hot pepper. Return chicken to wok along with chicken broth mixture. Cook, stirring constantly, 5 minutes until sauce thickens slightly. Sprinkle with cashew nuts.

6 Servings

REGINA DAILY

Oriental Pork Platter

12 slices thin cooked pork
¼ cup soy sauce
½ cup sherry
3 T. vegetable oil
2 medium onions, sliced
2 medium green peppers, diced
2 yellow squash, sliced
½ lb. fresh mushrooms, sliced
1½ cups water
1 tsp. instant chicken broth
2 tsp. salt
1 – 8 oz. can water chestnuts, sliced
2 T. cornstarch
¼ cup cold water

Marinate pork in soy sauce and sherry for several hours. Heat oil in frying pan. Brown pork, remove and keep warm in some heated marinade. Sauté onion; add green pepper and squash and sauté for 2 minutes. Add mushrooms, marinade, chicken broth, water chestnuts, salt and water and heat until vegetables are crisp-tender. Mix cornstarch with ¼ cup water and add to skillet. Heat until thickened.

4 to 6 Servings KATHLEEN GRIFFIN

Chinese Chews

2 cups flour
1 cup butter
1 cup brown sugar
1½ cups brown sugar
2 T. flour
¼ tsp. salt
1 cup chopped pecans
2 eggs
1 tsp. vanilla
½ tsp. baking powder

Mix first 3 ingredients to crumbs and press into shallow 9 x 9-inch pan. Bake at 300° for 10 minutes. Beat together all remaining ingredients and spread over crust. Bake again at 300° for 40 minutes or until light brown. Inside should be fairly moist when removed from oven. Cool and cut into squares.

Yield: 2 dozen DIANE GILL

Almond Cookies

4 oz. soft almond paste
4 oz. unsalted butter, softened
½ c. sugar
¼ tsp. salt
½ tsp. baking powder
¾ c. flour
¼ tsp. almond extract
1 egg white

Mix together sugar and almond paste. Add softened butter, 2 T. at a time, beating well after each addition. Beat in egg white. Add almond extract. Sift dry ingredients and add. Drop by teaspoonfuls onto greased cookie sheet. Bake at 375° for 10 to 12 minutes.

Yield: 3 dozen VIRGINIA BARBATO

"LE BOEUF SUR LE TOIT"

*Deviled Flank Steak

Steak Fries

*Broccoli-Onion Deluxe

*Chocolate Cherry Cake

Beaujolais or Côtes du Rhône

DEVILED FLANK STEAK

1½ to 2 lbs. flank steak
1 garlic clove
1 tsp. salt
1 tsp. rosemary
½ tsp. ginger
½ cup prepared mustard
2 T. soy sauce

Preheat oven to broil. Score meat on both sides. Mash garlic, salt, spices with spoon back to make paste. Stir in mustard and soy sauce. Spread ½ mixture on one side of steak. Broil on this side for 5 minutes. Turn and spread mixture on other side. Broil 5 minutes. Cut against grain into thin slices. Serve hot or cold.

4 to 6 Servings ELIZABETH B. NUECHTERLEIN

Broccoli-Onion Deluxe

1 lb. broccoli (or 1 – 10 oz. pkg. frozen cut broccoli)
2 cups frozen whole small pearl onions
4 T. butter or margarine
2 T. flour
¼ tsp. salt
dash pepper
1 cup milk
1 – 3 oz. pkg. cream cheese
2 oz. cheddar cheese, grated
1 cup soft bread crumbs

Cut broccoli into 1-inch pieces. Cook in boiling, salted water. (Cook frozen broccoli by package directions.) Drain. Cook onions in boiling salted water. Drain. In saucepan, melt 2 T. butter. Blend in flour, salt and pepper. Add milk. Cook, stirring until thick and bubbly. Reduce heat and stir in cream cheese until smooth. Place vegetables in 1½-quart casserole. Pour sauce over, mix lightly. Top with cheddar cheese. Melt 2 T. butter and toss with bread crumbs. Cover and bake at 350° for 30 minutes. Remove lid. Sprinkle crumbs over top. Bake 15 to 30 minutes more until heated through.

6 Servings — Meredith Bass

Chocolate Cherry Cake

1 box devil's food cake mix
1 – 21 oz. can cherry pie filling
2 large eggs, beaten
1 tsp. almond extract

Preheat oven to 350°. Combine all cake ingredients and stir until well mixed. Pour into greased and floured 9 x 13-inch pan and bake 25 to 30 minutes or until toothpick inserted in center comes out dry. Frost while warm.

Frosting

1 cup sugar
5 T. butter
⅓ cup milk
1 cup chocolate chips

Combine sugar, butter and milk in saucepan. Bring to boil for 1 minute. Remove from heat and stir in chocolate chips. Stir until smooth and slightly thick. Pour over warm cake.

Carolyn Ross

Index

A

B

C

D

E

F

G

H

I

J

L

M

N

O

P

Q

R

S

T

V

W

Z

BACH'S TRIO COOKBOOK
c/o Junior Committee of The Cleveland Orchestra
11001 Euclid Avenue
Cleveland, Ohio 44106-1796

Make checks payable to:
MUSICAL ARTS ASSOCIATION

Please send me:

PRINTED BOOK:

_____ copies of **Bach's Trio** @ **$29.95** $ _______

Plus **$9.95** postage and handling per book $ _______

For Ohio delivery please add **7%** sales tax per book $ _______

or:

CDs:

_____ copies of **Bach's Trio** @ **$12.95** $ _______

Plus **$4.95** postage and handling per CD $ _______

For Ohio delivery please add **7%** sales tax per CD $ _______

TOTAL ENCLOSED $ _______

Name ______________________________

Street ______________________________

City ____________________ State __________ Zip _______

All proceeds from the sale of this cookbook are for the benefit of The Cleveland Orchestra.

- -

BACH'S TRIO COOKBOOK
c/o Junior Committee of The Cleveland Orchestra
11001 Euclid Avenue
Cleveland, Ohio 44106-1796

Make checks payable to:
MUSICAL ARTS ASSOCIATION

Please send me:

PRINTED BOOK:

_____ copies of **Bach's Trio** @ **$29.95** $ _______

Plus **$9.95** postage and handling per book $ _______

For Ohio delivery please add **7%** sales tax per book $ _______

or:

CDs:

_____ copies of **Bach's Trio** @ **$12.95** $ _______

Plus **$4.95** postage and handling per CD $ _______

For Ohio delivery please add **7%** sales tax per CD $ _______

TOTAL ENCLOSED $ _______

Name ______________________________

Street ______________________________

City ____________________ State __________ Zip _______

All proceeds from the sale of this cookbook are for the benefit of The Cleveland Orchestra.

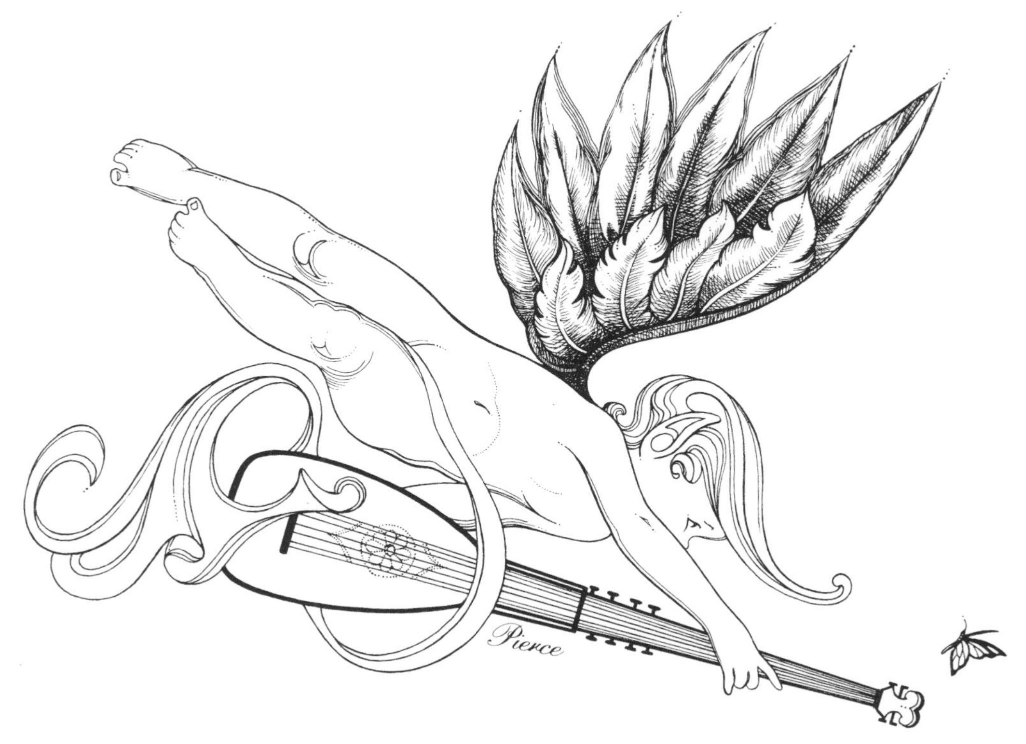

Bach for an Encore

Notes

NOTES

Notes